G000040027

CORFE CASTLE Encyclopaedia

Covering the Purbeck parishes of
Church Knowle, Corfe Castle,
Kimmeridge, Langton Matravers and
Worth Matravers

RODNEY LEGG

Dorset Publishing Company
National School North Street Wincanton Somerset BA9 9AT

To Charles Nunneley
who has Corfe Castle in his care

Printing credits
Typeset and layout by Julie Green. Set in Caxton 10 on 12 1/2 point. Printed by F W B Printing at Bennetts Mead, Southgate Road, Wincanton, Somerset BA9 9EB. Telephone 01-963-33755.

Publishing details
Published by Dorset Publishing Company at Wincanton Press, National School, North Street, Wincanton, Somerset BA9 9AT. Telephone 01-963-32583.

Distribution
Trade distribution and library sales by Halsgrove from Lower Moor Way, Tiverton, Devon EX16 6SS. Telephone 01-884-243-242.

Updatings
Information for further editions will be welcomed by the author, Rodney Legg, at Wincanton Press, National School, North Street, Wincanton, Somerset BA9 9AT.

International standard book number
ISBN 0 948699 73 6

Other Purbeck titles by Rodney Legg

Brownsea: Dorset's fantasy island

Exploring the Heartland of Purbeck

Guide to Purbeck Coast and Shipwreck

The Fight for Tyneham [editor]

Lawrence of Arabia in Dorset

Lawrence in Dorset

Lulworth and Tyneham Revisited

Lulworth Encyclopaedia

Lulworth Pictorial

Old Swanage

Purbeck's Heath: claypits, nature and the oilfield

Purbeck Coastal Walks

Purbeck Island [two editions]

Purbeck – The Country Magazine [editor]

Purbeck Walks [three editions]

Swanage Encyclopaedic Guide

Tyneham: Dorset's ghost village

Tyneham Ghost Village

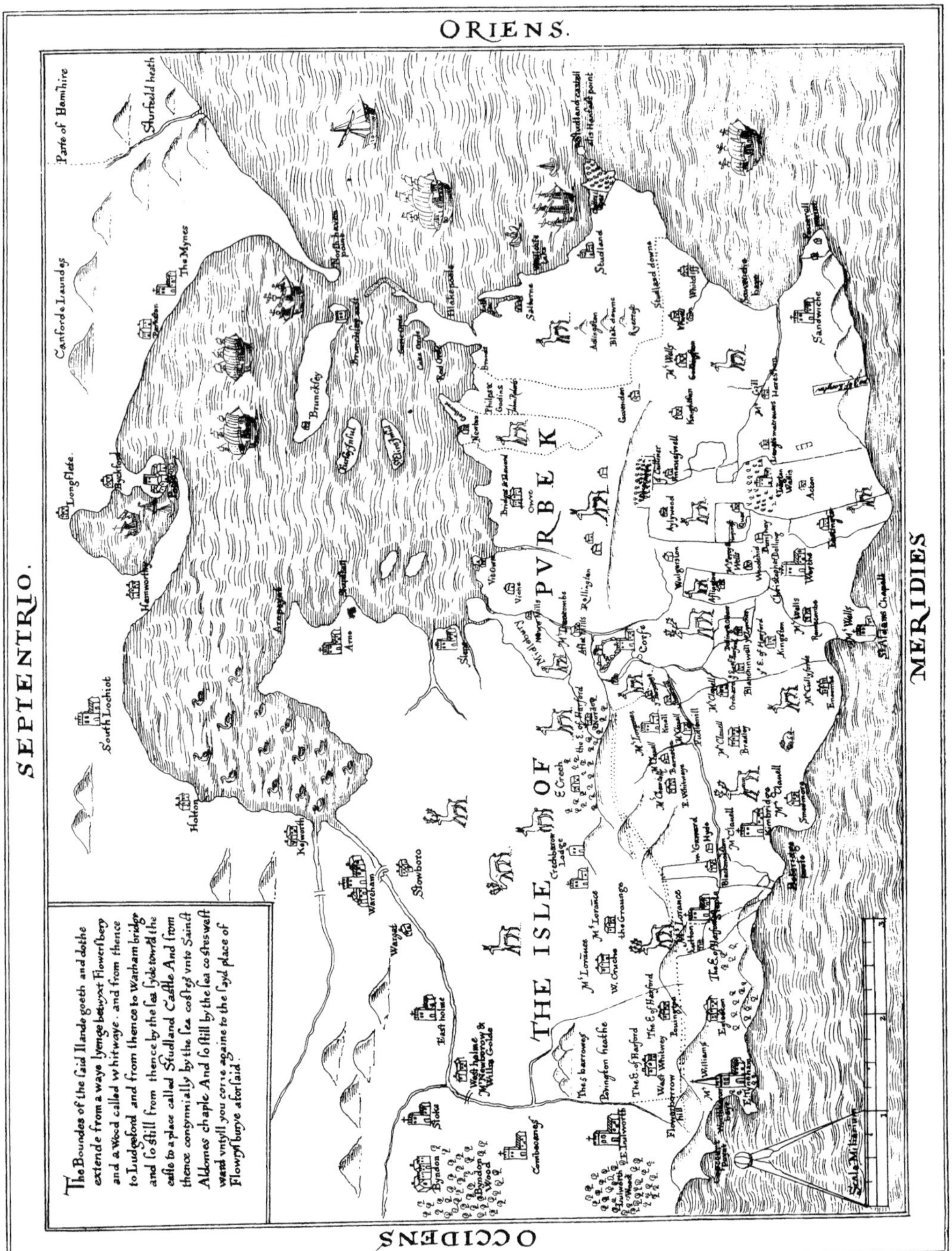

Photo-lithographic Facsimile of a Map of the Isle of Purbeck drawn by Ralph Treswell about 1585.6. Preserved at Kingston Lacy.

Elizabethan map: Ralph Treswell surveyed the Corfe Castle Estate for the Bankes family, in 1585.

A

Acton – the cul-de-sac quarrying hamlet west of Langton Matravers (SY 990 785), surrounded by National Trust land, acquired as part of the Bankes Estate [1982].

It is a clustered, nuclear, settlement that is unusual in lacking any kind of communal or business building, such as a church, public house, school, or shop. Furthermore the lack of any "Old" names furnish an absence of evidence that there ever were such premises, at least in recent times. Beyond that is another matter as its recorded history stretches back to a Domesday Book entry [1086].

Acton's buildings date from the 17th through to the 20th centuries. They are No. 83 and No. 85; 1 to 3 Acton Cottages; 1 to 3 Alma Cottages (a Crimean War battle-name); Blacklands (southern offshoot towards the Priest's Way); 1 and 2 Brighton Villas; East View; Enzeli; 1 and 2 Farm Cottages; Fernlea (lofty 1896-dated Victoriana); Harris's Cottage; 1 to 6 Highland Cottages (typical long and squat stone-roofed range of traditional Purbeck cottages); Hillcroft; 1 to 3 Jubilee Terrace; Lane End Cottage (beside the narrow street); Marblers; Marblers Bungalow; 1 and 2 Myrtle Cottages; Quarry Cottage (beside a stone stile and alley); Sea View; 1 to 3 The Square; Stone House; Victoria Cottage; West Cottage; West View Bungalow; and West View House.
(Placenames / National Trust / Langton Matravers)

Acton Quarries – a cluster of 14 small-scale workings on National Trust land west of Langton Matravers. These produce relatively small dimension building stone. One of the operators specialises in gravestones and other high quality monumental work. Each quarry functions under a licence in which stone is dug in quarter-acre "Mineral Area" blocks, subject to land restoration before the replacement area is released, plus a similar sized "Service Area" on which cut stone is stored and worked.

Acton hamlet: typical Purbeck stone cottage in the heart of the quarrylands.

These quarries provide a cross-section of varying geological exposures:

Purbeck Marble – Roman and mediaeval monumental work (no longer dug).

Burr Stone – Saxon building stone (no longer dug).

Rag Stone – Modern rough lump-stone for garden rockeries and landscaping.

Grub – Formerly left in place to hold all of the above as the roof for underground workings (no longer dug).

Roach – Historic and modern building stone.

Thornback – Ditto.

Wetson – Ditto.

Freestone – Ditto.

Downsvein – Historic provider of roof tiles [1650-1900], via mine shafts (no longer dug, because it lies too deep for modern open pit extraction).
(Placenames / Industrial archaeology / Langton Matravers)

Aeolian Sky – 6,540-ton freighter outward bound from London [21 October 1979], via Rotterdam, for Dar-es-Salaam, East Africa. In the English Channel she was in collision with the 1,000-ton German coaster *Anna Knuppel* [morning of 3 November 1979].

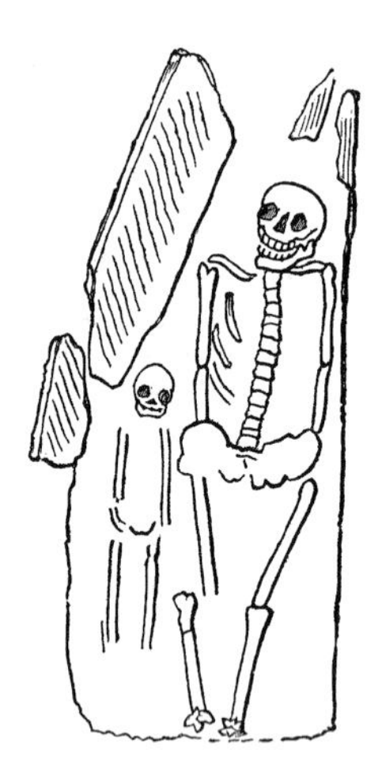

Afflington Barrow: a Victorian excavation revealed an original Bronze Age cremation covered by an inverted urn, and much later Romano-British inhumations with skeletons lying in stone cists.

The initial plan was to tow the *Aeolian Sky* into the Solent but her bows were alarmingly low in the water and it was thought safer to take her to the anchorage off the eastern breakwater of Portland Harbour.

She never reached Portland. The ship continued to take in water and the crew were rescued by lifeboat [early hours of 4 November 1979]. By 04.00 hours that morning, a Sunday, she had gone down in 100 feet of water, about 5.5 miles south-west of St Alban's Head. A Trinity House vessel reported that deck cargo was floating off. Drums of insecticide and other toxic chemicals are stowed on the decks as it is reckoned safer to have dangerous cargoes in a position where they can wash away, rather than packed in the holds of a vessel. More containers floated free from the wreck during the December gales and some 600 were picked up in the Solent.

Some containers which had been thought to have come from the *Aeolian Sky* were later found to have been unreported losses from the *Tozeur* – it was one of several cases in which full emergency procedures went into action to collect a few harmless cans.
(Shipwrecks / Worth Matravers)

Afflington – though now having dwindled to a farmstead, this former marble-producing hamlet east of Kingston (SY 970 801) was still a community of 50 people in 1800. The height of its mediaeval prosperity was marked by the grant of a market and fair, from Henry III [1270].
(Placenames / Corfe Castle)

Ailwood Down – the southern slopes of Nine Barrow Down, east of Corfe Castle (SY 994 814). Registered common land, owned by the National Trust; having been inherited with the Bankes Estate [1982].

This picturesque chalk downland was listed by the Nature Conservancy Council, as a site of special scientific interest – paradoxically for its interesting level of non-interest. The turf

Burial mound: the Bronze Age Afflington Barrow.

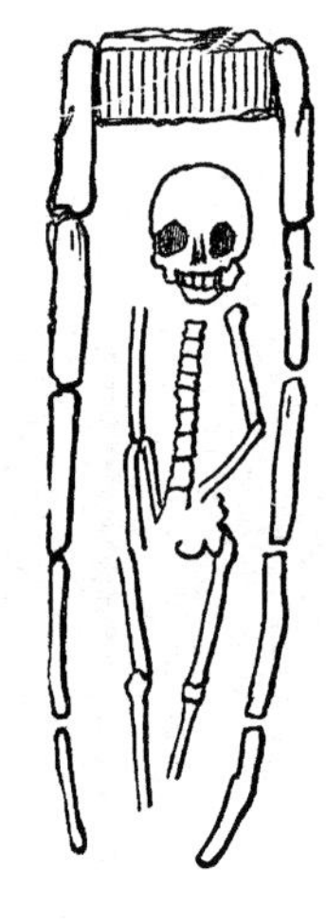

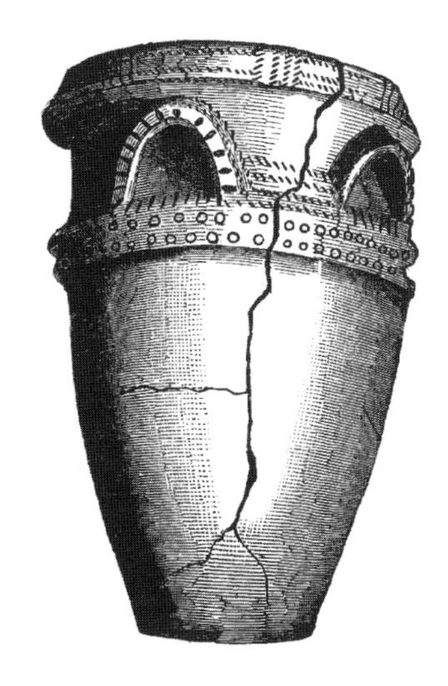

was found to contain only a poor flora; it has been impoverished by the intensely dry and exposed conditions of a steep south-facing escarpment.

This contrasts with the floral riches of the cooler northern flank of nearby Ballard Down, also now in Trust ownership.

(Placenames / National Trust / Corfe Castle)

Air crashes (Church Knowle parish) – a Messerschmitt Bf.110 crashed into Creech Barrow Hill during a day of Battle of Britain dog-fights [25 August 1940]. The crew parachuted into captivity.

It is also possible that the volcano-shaped mass of Creech Barrow Hill, swelling out of the Purbeck heaths, also claimed Short Stirling R9306 of 90 Squadron [16 February 1943]. The bomber flew into the ground in Dorset but conflicting locations have been given. Blandford has been recorded but Creech Barrow would seem much more likely.

(Aviation / Church Knowle)

Air crashes (Corfe Castle parish) – Fairey Swordfish K5985, on a flight along the Channel coast from Gosport, hit trees at Kingston, on the hill to the south of Corfe Castle [18 March 1938].

Messerschmitt Bf.110C (3U+JT) belonging to the 9th Staffel of Zerstorergeschwader 26 made a forced-landing near Corfe Castle after being engaged by the RAF whilst taking part in the German attack on the Westland Aircraft

Omega sign: now protects much of Dorset's best landscape, with this section of ridgeway being in the heart of the Purbeck Hills.

Company at Yeovil [16.00 hours, 7 October 1940]. Gefreiter Bernhardt Demmig, the pilot, survived and was taken prisoner of war but his Bordfunker, Obergefreiter Josef Bachmann, was killed.

They were shot down by Squadron Leader Michael Robinson, in a Spitfire, who had just taken command of 609 Squadron at RAF Warmwell [4 October 1940]. Flying Officer Richard Brooker joined in the kill, in a Hurricane of 56 Squadron from RAF Boscombe Down.

Hurricane P3984 of 238 Squadron from the newly opened RAF Chilbolton, Hampshire, crashed into the roadside quarry immediately north of Castle Hill [10 October 1940]. Pilot Officer Bob Doe parachuted to safety, on Brownsea Island, after breaking through cloud at 16,000 feet into the sights of Messerschmitt Bf.109s. Both locations are now owned by the National Trust.

Spitfire R7142 of 140 Squadron broke up when trying to pull out of a dive and plunged into heathland at Rempstone [16 December 1941].

Hurricane Z3349, a Mark II fighter of 245 Squadron, force-landed on Furzey Island – in the salt-marshes of Poole Harbour [29 March 1942]. Another Hurricane was lost in the waters off neighbouring Green Island [March 1943]. Its pilot was picked up by the Air-Sea Rescue Launch *Commodore*.

Eight crewmen died and four were rescued after a military Catalina flying-boat of 210 Squadron, returning from a training flight to Poole Harbour and its base at RAF Hamworthy, ploughed into the salt-marshes surrounding Round Island [04.25 hours, 24 August 1943]. It had gone a mile off course on descending into thick fog.

Two Liberator bombers crashed in the parish of Corfe Castle during the final year of the Second World War. One is said to have flown into a steep hillside above Encombe House, in dense fog [date unknown], and the second fell on Furzey Island in Poole Harbour [July 1944] with the loss of all its American crew.
(Aviation / Corfe Castle)

Air crashes (Kimmeridge parish) – Messerschmitt Bf.110 (L1+FZ) crashed in flames at Swalland Farm, a mile south-east of the village on the Luftwaffe's routed Adlertag (Eagle Day) attack [13 August 1940]. It belonged to Lehrgeschwader 1, a specialist unit formed to test new aircraft of all types, and innovative tactics, under operational conditions.

Another Bf.110 (3U+DS), belonging to Zerostorergeschwader 26, the Geschwader named Horst Wessel after the Nazi writer of a militant anti-Semitic song which became a national anthem, crash-landed near Gaulter Gap [27 September 1940]. It had three "kill" bars, denoting victories over RAF aircraft. Crewman Fritz Schupp and Karl Nechwatal were taken prisoner. Their fighter-bomber, which had been taking part in an abortive raid on the Parnall Aircraft Company at Yate, near Chipping Sodbury, was claimed by Spitfires from RAF Warmwell.

Three out of ten North American P-51 Mustang Mark XV fighter-bombers of 2 Squadron Royal Air Force, based at RAF Sawbridge, Hertfordshire, flew into Smedmore Hill when a mission went wrong in poor visibility [26 May 1943]. They had taken off from Thruxton, Hampshire, at 16.50 hours on Ranger Operation Asphalt. This cross-Channel offensive action was to have been against rail movements in the Rennes-Laval area.

They flew south-west in line abreast formation until reaching a wall of fog between Kimmeridge and St Alban's Head. The order to climb was given by Flight-lieutenant G. Kenning, at 17.35 hours.

Seven of the aircraft were able to clear Smedmore Hill but other three-code letters U, Y, and W – crashed into the northern slope. Their three pilots were killed – Flying Officer N. J. Miller, Pilot Officer J. B. McLeod, and Flying Officer D. Hirst.
(Aviation / Kimmeridge)

Air crashes (Langton Matravers parish) – a Spitfire of 152 Squadron from RAF Warmwell successfully crash-landed at Spyway Farm after a Battle of Britain dog-fight [8 August 1940]. It was flown by Pilot Officer Walter Beaumont. The location has since been acquired by the National Trust [1992].

The world's largest hot-air balloon, *Gerard Heineken*, attempting a long-distance endurance record, fell foul of power cables at Coles Farm, Langton Matravers, after travelling just half-way across Purbeck [evening of 25 July 1979]. No one was hurt and, in a way, they were probably spared a greater disaster – insufficient height would almost certainly have seen them dumped on the cliffs or into the English Channel.
(Aviation / National Trust / Langton Matravers)

Air crashes (Worth Matravers parish) – Miles Magister P6362 of 32 Maintenance Unit of the Royal Air Force dived into the top of the Purbeck cliffs half a mile south-west of the Telecommunications Research Establishment, in a field on the north side of Emmetts Hill [14 September 1940].

A Messerschmitt Bf.109 belonging to Lehrgeschwader 2, a unit testing improvised aircraft under operational conditions, came down following engine failure on a weather reconnaissance flight [30 November 1940]. Unteroffizier Paul Wacker belly-landed at Woodyhyde Farm. The tail section of his machine survives, having been used to repair the captured test-flown Bf.109 that is now in the Royal Air Force Museum, at Hendon.

Wellington X9677 of 218 Squadron from RAF Marham, Norfolk, crashed into the sea off St Alban's Head whilst on a bombing mission to Bordeaux [10-11 October 1941]. Three members of the crew were picked up by lifeboat but the other three drowned.

Hit by anti-aircraft fire from an escort vessel, Luftwaffe ace Oberleutnant Werner Machold,

Going upstairs: external steps, into Almshouses in East Street, Corfe Castle.

Staffelkapitan of Jagdeschwader 2 Richthofen, turned his Messerschmitt Bf.109E landwards and successfully crash-landed among the stone workings at Worth Matravers [6 June 1941]. He was taken into captivity and ditto his fighter, for inspection by the Royal Aircraft Establishment, Farnborough, on account of its improved Zusatz-gear mechanism which fed nitrous oxide to boost the engine power.
(Aviation / Worth Matravers)

AI (Air Interception) radar – developed by wartime scientists at the Telecommunication Research Establishment, at Worth Matravers and Langton Matravers [1940]. It was fitted in the perspex nose-cones of Bristol Beaufighter night-fighters and first proven operationally from RAF Middle Wallop [1941].
(Aviation / Langton Matravers and Worth Matravers)

The Almshouses – ancient and modern, on the east side of East Street at Corfe Castle, with the older part having a flight of exterior stone steps to the two apartments upstairs, plus a plaque: "Jubilee House, circa 1677, Restored 1977." There were four flats on the ground floor. Originally endowed by Sir Edmund Uvedale in 1621. Now known as Corfe Castle Charities Almshouses.
(Placenames / Corfe Castle)

Anchoress's Cell – a monumental slab of Purbeck marble, incised with a cross, is mounted on the wall in the porch of the parish church at Worth Matravers. It was hit by the plough in 1957, at the top of the southern side of Pier Bottom, north of St Aldhelm's Chapel (SY 963 759). Beneath was a grave with a female skeleton.

Adjoining were stone foundations and the rubble of what was presumed to be the cell of an anchoress. The stone is dated to between 1250-75.
(Mediaeval archaeology / Worth Matravers)

Arfleet Mills – formerly on the Corfe River, half a mile north of Corfe Castle (SY 962 828), but demolished [1925] when its surroundings and site were consumed by the expanding Norden ball clay workings. A branch mineral line came southwards at this point and then crossed the B3351 at a level crossing, to serve pits in the first of the two fields towards Rollington Farm.

As for Arfleet Mills, they are of some interest as an historical footnote. It existed as a placename from 1286 ("Alflode") with the version that Ralph Treswell gives in 1586 ("Afflett") and almost identically by Edward Boswell in 1765 ("Affleet"), repeated by Isaac Taylor in 1795, being preserved in the local pronunciation. This gives us "Affleet" rather than Arfleet of the former map spelling.

Modernised as Steam Flour Mills when William Lucas was its Victorian miller.
(Placenames / Industrial archaeology / Corfe Castle)

Arklow – a 500-ton steamer, which became a total loss on Kimmeridge Ledges [19 November 1880].
(Shipwrecks / Kimmeridge)

Avanti – steamship, torpedoed and sunk by a German U-boat off St Alban's Head [2 February 1918].
(Shipwrecks / Worth Matravers)

Aves – see entry for **The Halves.**

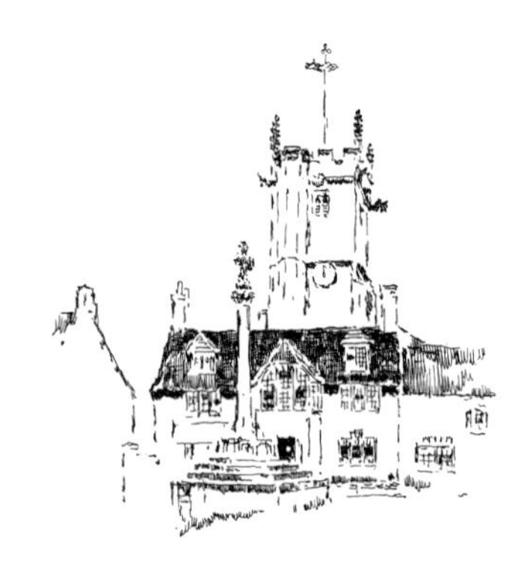

B

Ball clay – spawning three extensive mineral line systems, namely Fayle's Tramway, Furzebrook Railway, and Goathorn Railway, the extraction of some of the world's best clay has been a major Purbeck industry for more than two centuries. "Ball" is thought to take its name from the "tupal" or "tubal" which was the spade originally used in its cutting.

This became the favourite raw material of the Staffordshire potteries and the gargantuan operation that extracted it – via jetties at Middlebere Quay, Ridge Wharf, and Goathorn Pier – has slithered across almost the entire heathlands of the Isle of Purbeck, eight miles wide, from Povington at Tyneham parish in the west to Newton in Studland parish in the east.

As well as barges and tugs, at the shipment end, the industry has carried with it men, cranes, sheds, rails, and engines, to lift fresh seams from a combination of open pits and underground mines.

The operating companies eventually merged into Pike Brother, Fayle and Company Limited [1949], which celebrated a collective bicentenary in 1960, with a booklet looking back to its renaissance (forgetting the Roman predecessors): "Apart from the grading, turning and weathering, it is doubtful whether, in the early days, the clay was subjected to preparation. But it must be remembered that the blue clays of the Bagshot beds are the finest in the world. They fire a near white and their small and uniform grain size and consequent unequalled plasticity make them an important ingredient for bodies [mixtures] for the manufacture of most earthenware and pottery."

The white or near-white firings are achieved in an oxidising atmosphere, to between 1,000 and 1,400 degrees centigrade. Poole Pottery, for example, is thrown from a mixture principally of Dorset or Devon ball clay and Cornish china clay, crushed chalkland flint, and Finnish felspar. In 1973 the Purbeck connection lapsed for a time with the ball clay coming instead from Newton Abbot. "We take our clay from the best seam which English China Clays happen to be operating at the time," departmental manager Gerry Webb explained.

Traditionally, Purbeck ball clay used to be cut in chunks about one foot square, and was transferred at the head of the shaft into narrow-gauge railway wagons. Trains went to the weathering grounds, along the top of narrow ridges of clay, to tip their loads at the edge of the heaps. Here it stayed for six months, being turned over and aired, to improve the plasticity of the clay. This has been done away with by modern methods, simulating the process under cover, and truck movements are now by road and the mainline rail system.

Processing methods crush and shred the clay, removing moisture and putting it through various stages of dry mixing, pulverising it into a fine powder that is blown through air flotation mills. After shredding, blending, drying, and granulating the clay is then artificially weathered – subjecting it to alternate cutting, soaking, pressure sprays, moving, and further soaking. The effect of two years' weather on the clay is achieved in a matter of weeks.

The industry, which continues as a division of the great combine English China Clays, left behind a lunar landscape of sticky white hillocks that were soon reclaimed by the tough heathland flora and stand full of wild colour above the former workplaces. These, the claypit lakelands of Purbeck, having filled with water, now have their own unique charm, particularly in late summer when red, yellow, and white water-lilies flower across the shallows.

Geologically, as landform specialities, wonders such as the Blue Pool occur because the waters are translucent with turquoise light diffracted from particles of clay in suspension.

Local ownership of the Purbeck pits and Furzebrook Clay Works ended in 1968 when English China Clays [ECC] paid £30,000 cash and £1.2 million in shares to acquire Pike

Brothers, Fayle and Company Limited. The current operating subsidiary is ECC Ball Clays Limited, with mines and pits in four Purbeck parishes, works at Furzebrook, and offices in Wareham.

Late 20th-century production has been in the region of 125,000 to 150,000 tons a year, from an average of 15 to 20 workings, from a workforce numbering around 200.
(Industrial archaeology / Church Knowle, Corfe Castle, East Holme, Studland, and Tyneham)

Balloon *Gerard Heineken* – the world's largest hot-air balloon lifted off from Creech Barrow Hill, Church Knowle [evening of 25 July 1979] in an attempt at the international distance and duration flight record which ended half an hour later three parishes to the south-east at Coles Farm, Langton Matravers.

The basket of the 140-feet balloon snagged four power cables, 25 feet above a field, and plunged the village into darkness.

"It's a miracle we're alive." said Army balloonist Major Christopher Davey. "It was twilight and we couldn't see the cables until too late. Three cables broke and the other one wrapped itself around our flagwires. Then the basket swung like a pendulum until we were able to break free."

The fabric of the balloon was hardly damaged and pilot Don Cameron was talking of a second attempt within minutes of the unscheduled landing. Also in the basket was French balloonist Comte Jean de Costa Beauregard.

Half a million cubic feet of hot air had lifted the balloon for its passage across the four Purbeck parishes. They were attempting to beat the 334 miles record, in a 16-hour flight, set in the United States [1974].

People converged on Langton Matravers from miles around and police closed the roads to prevent any more from trying to see the huge but collapsed balloon. Major Davey, whose £1 million insurance had also escaped a close call, issued an apology to the villagers:

"We, the crew of hot-air balloon *Gerard Heineken*, would like to make a full apology to the people of Langton Matravers for the inconvenience and damage caused to them and their property as a result of our forced landing at the start of our cross-Channel voyage.

"We particularly regret breaking the high power tension cables that blacked out the area – and which probably saved us from careering over the cliff."
(Aviation / Church Knowle and Langton Matravers)

Bankes – lady of the manor **Lady Charlotte Bankes** is commemorated by the stained-glass east window in Corfe Castle parish church.
(People / Corfe Castle)

Bankes – barrister **Henry John Ralph Bankes** [1902-81], known as **Ralph Bankes**, was the last private owner of Kingston Lacy House and the 16,000-acre Kingston Lacy and Corfe Castle Estates, which he bequeathed to the National Trust, together with an extensive art collection. The Trust's "largest ever bequest" passed to it on 19 August 1982, a year to the day after his death.

Bankes arms: the family shield and motto, commemorated by two public houses in the Isle of Purbeck.

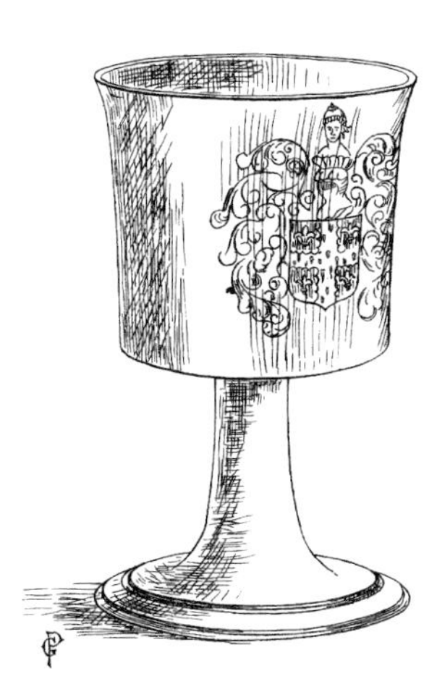

Bankes arms: on a chalice presented to Corfe Castle parish church, as a thanks offering from the family, when Richard Cromwell resigned the Protectorate in May 1659.

Ralph Bankes went to Eton and served in the Royal Navy Volunteer Reserve. He became High Sheriff of Dorset [1939]. With the death of his wife, Hilary [1966], he became a virtual recluse in his country house. He is buried towards the top end of the town cemetery at Wimborne.
(People / Corfe Castle and Pamphill)

Bankes – Attorney-General **Sir John Bankes** [1589-1644] acquired Corfe Castle [1635]. He had been the Chief Justice of Common Pleas and became the Attorney for Charles I.
(People / Corfe Castle and Pamphill)

Bankes – "Brave Dame Mary" **Lady Mary Bankes** [died 1661], the widow of Sir John Bankes, held Corfe Castle through its first Civil War siege [1643].
(People / Corfe Castle and Pamphill)

Bankes – for **Ralph Bankes**, see entry for **Henry John Ralph Bankes**.

Bankes – landowner **Walter Ralph Bankes** would be elected as the last Mayor of Corfe Castle [1881], as its historic administration would be abolished under the Municipal Corporations Act, 1883.
(People / Corfe Castle and Pamphill)

Bankes Arms Hotel – on the east side of the Square at Corfe Castle, it was rebuilt between the wars, transforming a typical but unostentatious Purbeck stone-roofed house into something much more stylish. A pair of columns support a projecting gabled porch and dormers were added to make attic rooms in the steeply-pitched roof.
(Placenames / Corfe Castle)

Bankes Estate – the Kingston Lacy and Corfe Castle Estates, being 16,000 acres of east Dorset and the Isle of Purbeck, bequeathed to the National Trust on the death of Ralph Bankes, its last private owner [19 August 1981]. It passed into Trust ownership a year later [19 August 1982].
(Placenames / National Trust / Arne, Corfe Castle, Holt, Langton Matravers, Pamphill, Shapwick, Studland and Worth Matravers)

Bare Cross – hilltop crossroads of two public roads, only one of which has been tarred, in the Purbeck Hills, above Cocknowle (SY 931 821).
(Placenames / Roads / Church Knowle)

Barnston Farm – former manor house and one of the earliest inhabited buildings in Purbeck, to the north of the Corfe River half a mile west of Church Knowle (SY 931 816). Locally known as the Mansion House, it incorporates a hall and solar wing of circa 1280 and the remainder of the building is little changed since the 1500s.

In all probability it was built by the Estoke family. Its estate extended to 1,000 acres, with six labourers' cottages, in 1564. There appears to have been a gatehouse, beside the lane on its south side, but the remains of this outbuilding were cleared away in the late-19th century.

Barnston is the only Church Knowle settlement listed in the Domesday Book [1086] that can boast a surviving mediaeval house; one which the Royal Commission on Historical Monuments commends as "a building of visual as well as archaeological note".
(Placenames / Mediaeval archaeology / Church Knowle)

Barnston Farm: incorporates parts of a manor house, circa 1280, making it one of the oldest inhabited buildings in Purbeck.

Barnston pillow mounds – beside Church Knowle footpath number 30, about 150 yards south-west of Bare Cross, (SY 929 819). Their first written records are by historian John Hutchins in 1773, and in a manuscript notebook of the 1870s, where Victorian antiquarian Charles Warne mentions "six oblong mounds" immediately at the foot of the Purbeck Hills, at Barnston, Church Knowle.

The Royal Commission on Historical Monuments gives their size as between 40 feet to 60 feet in length and 25 to 30 feet wide. They are about two feet high. Flanking ditches are a foot deep and ten feet wide.

They alternate in alignment from being either south-west to north-east, or set north-west to south-east. Probably of mediaeval date and perhaps built as rabbit warrens.
(Mediaeval archaeology / Church Knowle)

Barnston strip fields – fragments of the mediaeval West Field of Church Knowle survive as two strip lynchets, one 12 feet wide and the other about 50 feet wide, divided by a riser ten feet high (SY 927 818).
(Mediaeval archaeology / Church Knowle)

Barrows – see entries for **Long barrows** and **Round barrows**.

Battrick's Bakery – see entry for **Boar Mill**.

Baxter – missing scientist **Mrs Jean Baxter** featured in a media mystery when she disappeared from the Chemical Defence Establishment, Porton Down [February 1974]. Her badly decomposed body was found on the Purbeck cliffs near St Alban's Head [June 1974]. Little could be established from the remains, though dental records confirmed the identification, and personal documents were also present. The inquest heard [12 July 1974] that although she had access to classified material there had been no security aspect to the case.

Commander Arthur Simmons, who had worked with her, said Mrs Baxter had been "very depressed" two days before she disappeared. "She was a very gifted and artistic person. Her philosophy was that everything in life had to be perfect and because life, her colleagues and her circumstances were not perfect, some particular incidents could trigger off a reaction which could put her into a bout of depression. Her medical state worried her and she was planning to consult a specialist."

Although the implication is clear, there was no definite evidence of how she died, and the coroner, Nigel Neville-Jones, recorded an open verdict. This meant that the case remained unsolved as far as the press was concerned and it was mentioned several times during the spate of security revelations between 1979-82. A sad case was enveloped in national implications, though that is an occupational hazard for those on the secret side of public life.

(People / Worth Matravers)

Beecham – orchestral conductor **Sir Thomas Beecham** [1879-1961] lived on Round Island in the 1950s, where he wrote his biography of the composer Frederick Delius.

(People / Music / Corfe Castle)

Benfield – author and quarryman **Eric Benfield** [1902-1955], who is buried in Worth Matravers churchyard, wrote two classic Purbeck titles. He served his apprenticeship underground, but came up to work with words, and felt that the local society never forgave him.

Bachelor's Knap [1935] is a novel set in those workings, as is *Saul's Sons* [1938], and both are robust regional writing, with descriptions of mediaeval craft customs of men who "think in stone" mixed with an insight into their private lives.

In *Purbeck Shop* [1940], Benfield moved from documentary fiction into a factual account of mining. He never lost pride in his trade, describing the cleaving with wedges and the process through to finished sinks, troughs, staddles, kerb-stones, steps, hearths, setts for street paving, or whatever else was a product still within current demand or human memory when the world last went to war.

Southern English [1942] is an unusual product of that time. It has no sub-title inside but the dust-jacket was given one, perhaps as an afterthought: "Reminiscences of Purbeck country and people." This book, its subject found, was highly individualistic, both in selection of persons and their portrayal for wider attention. It presents the "Dorset mentality" of real-life characters who have "a little magic" in their lives. Some are hermits, one of whom could count his days of married life on his fingers. "Such things will out," they tend to sigh. Benfield had come through his own "quiet time" when he sat and thought, or just sat, and the resulting reflections lashed at the hypocrisy he saw all around.

It is as dispassionate an appraisal, warts included, as *England Your England*, the essay by George Orwell that analysed the inherent contradictions of our Englishness and was also the product of those anxious months of 1941 before the war had turned. Both show the same mistrust for authority.

Those who were branded the scum of the earth when they appeared before Wareham magistrates in the 1930s were now the saviours of the nation. Ditto the irresponsible mothers who used to be condemned for uncontrolled breeding. They were now to be complimented on having such fine sets of sons.

"Workmen out of work" had been seen as the epitome of "moral disintegration" but, Benfield wryly observed, the denouncement usually came from those who themselves enjoyed abundant leisure time:

"Often I have heard women whose sole sum of work was perhaps arranging the flowers in some church, explain that a man was bound to slip downhill unless all his days were coupled with useful labour. Such women should be ignored, as it is not feasible to take them aside and quietly knock them over the head; but there are many men with no first-hand knowledge of what the worker feels, yet who has held and expounded the same ideas."

It is Hardyesque but plus a dangerous added ingredient – a pinch of socialism. Benfield saw his roots in the *Town of Maiden Castle* [1947], "glad to know that I should be entirely at home watching an Iron Age pot simmering amongst the embers in the cosy bottom of a pit in the chalk. Undoubtedly it was a good life for those who could stick it, and we of to-day are the proof that they could."

Dorset, he wrote in the blurb for the cover of the volume of that title in the "County Book" series of 1950, "is a county where men appear to have little fear of themselves – a fact which has given rise to easy criticism that some Dorset literature is unreal. Dorset is not shy of being an emotion as well as a charming bit of England."

Benfield's exposition of the "Dorset touch" was out of tune with his host community and, ultimately, with himself. He was ostracised as the prophet in his own land though his philosophy was a general offensive against not merely "The Party" (there was only the blue one then) but attitudes as well. For that reason it was insidious and resented all the more.

I have met several of his contemporaries; none who claimed friendship. The mediaeval craft closed ranks to disown their self-appointed spokesman, and a quarryman told me that although Benfield had been buried at Worth Matravers the body had been sent back from London:

"There was nothing special about him, just that he was different. He wrote about us, but it was in London that he belonged, in that kind of living. He ended up killing himself. He wasn't one of us."

(People / Literary / Worth Matravers)

Bituminous Shale Company – established at Kimmeridge to extract shale for the production of varnish, grease, pitch, naphtha, dyes, wax, fertiliser and other coal by-products at its works beside the Backwater at Weymouth. The company obtained an Act of Parliament [1847] and built the first tramway on the eastern side of Kimmeridge Bay.

The company was registered in the new year [27 January 1848] and almost immediately ran into litigation. James Young sued the firm for infringing his patent for refining oil-shales to extract paraffin wax. After a protracted case it was ruled that "manufacture of offensively smelling and unmarketable oils from Kimmeridge shales should not be held to be an anticipation of Young's patent".

Though the company won the case, it proved to be a Pyrrhic victory, accompanied by substantial costs, and it then found itself in an environmental battleground over public health fears aroused by the Weymouth factory. This was condemned as a public nuisance because of the same sulphurous smells that had failed to impress the judge. The company went into liquidation [1854] and left a site polluted with heavy metals that has continued to be associated with carcinogenic clusters, particularly for bladder cancers, throughout the 20th century.

(Industrial archaeology / Kimmeridge)

Blashenwell Farm – has the distinction of being the earliest virtually continuous inhabitation in Purbeck, with a Mesolithic "ethnological storehouse" under the field east of the tarred road leading from Corfe Common and up into the farm (SY 952 805). The description was that of Clement Reid in 1896.

He found that a spring emerging from the limestone beds, and flowing across Wealden clay, deposited water containing calcium carbonate, which had created a tufaceous deposit eight feet deep. It had spread across about 20 acres. The tufa, by a happy coincidence, had covered and preserved a site of Mesolithic habitation complete with its flint debris and other rubbish. That, apparently, is unique. As well as the midden and a few flint implements, the presence of hundreds of flint flakes, plus a sharpening device, showed that tools were cut and worked at the site. Only a small area was excavated.

Bones from it have given a recalibrated radio-carbon date of about 5300 BC. Later prehistoric, and Roman pottery, have also been found on the ploughed slopes below the farm – indicating that this spot has hosted human habitation for thousands of years.

(Placenames / Prehistoric archaeology / Corfe Castle)

Blue Pool: transformed by man and nature, from claypit into beauty spot.

Blue Pool – the best known abandoned claypit in Britain, at Furzebrook (SY 935 834), was dug by Watts, Hatherley, and Burn of Newton Abbot [circa 1846-50]. The boys who removed the overburden of sand were paid twelve shillings a week and given a hot meal each day. Their wheelbarrows, called "rubblers", had to be pushed up planks to the top of the pit.

Clay from the Blue Pool was supplied to Royal Worcester, Minton, Wedgwood, and other leading pottery manufacturers of the day. A railway was built across the heath from Furzebrook to a quay on the tidal section of the River Frome at Ridge.

Henry Hatherley was still trading as a clay merchant at Wareham in 1851 though he sold some of his pits to William J. Pike who took up residence in Westport House. Meanwhile, the hole that would become the Blue Pool passed to the Brown family, who had been digging clay in Purbeck since 1669, and sold it to Walter Pike [1874]. Once use and drainage failed, the great man-made pit filled with water, and its sandy sides gradually sprouted heather and scrub.

Its present role as a beauty spot amid the pines began when T. T. Barnard opened it to the public [1935]. Three acres of water, 50 feet deep, are surrounded by 25 acres of heather, gorse, and woodland.

The vivid and ever-changing turquoise and blue colour of the pool is caused by diffracted light passing through the minute particles of clay that are permanently suspended in the water. Miss J. S. Barnard, who inherited the pool from her father, pointed out to me on a dull day in November 1972 that at such

overcast times, when there is no sunlight, the blueness is stronger, when there is no light refracted off the surface of the pool. She also told me that the water is dead; high concentration of minerals and an absence of oxygen prevents decomposition, and for this reason the Blue Pool has no vegetable or animal life.
(Placenames / Industrial archaeology / Church Knowle)

Blumlein – electronics inventor **Alan Blumlein** [1903-42] filed 128 patents, including technology for the world's first television system, which the BBC used for transmissions from Alexandra Palace [November 1936]. He came with the Telecommunications Research Establishment [TRE] to Worth Matravers [May 1940], where he made "seminal contributions" to airborne interception radar and proved himself in the words of Sir Bernard Lovell as "one of the best electronics engineers which Great Britain has ever produced".

He would be lost while testing the magnetron of H2S ground-mapping radar, pioneered at Langton Matravers, with a joint team from TRE and EMI. Their adapted Halifax bomber, V9977, suffered engine failure followed by a fire and crashed six miles from Ross-on-Wye [7 June 1942]. The magnetron was the only piece of electronic equipment to survive.
(People / Aviation / Langton Matravers and Worth Matravers)

Boar Mill, also known as **Battrick's Mill** – nestling beneath the south-east side of Corfe Castle and shown on a 1585 map by Ralph Treswell, though the present buildings date from the 18th and early 19th centuries. They are, nonetheless, ancient and characterful in appearance, as is the setting itself with leats and ponds on the Byle Brook. In the mid-Victorian era it was George Battrick who was the baker and miller and into the 1950s its faggot-heated ovens were Charles Battrick's Bakery.

The mill was bought by the National Trust in 1993, to preserve castle views and provide an alternative access path for some of the 160,000 people who visit Corfe Castle each year.

They may be in for a surprise, in that villagers claim the eastern slopes are haunted, by a headless white lady who drifts about between the castle and the mill. One sighting, straying into the middle of the road at 02.20 hours on a July morning saw John Seager braking to avoid collision with a ghost [1967]: "It moved on and down the path at the foot of the Castle Hill, near the bakery. I trembled and came over cold, in fact I felt frozen. It was an experience I would never want again."

What makes his story different from other sightings is that when he retold it to inevitable leg-pulling in the lounge bar of the Bankes Arms Hotel he felt that something would happen if they refused to believe him. Time was then being called at 22.30 hours and by 22.45 that Thursday night the room was cleared of customers and locked.

Moments later the whole ceiling collapsed. It filled the lounge with half a ton of plaster and rubble.
(Placenames / Folklore / National Trust / Corfe Castle)

Borough status – a borough by prescription, though not incorporated until the 18th year of Queen Elizabeth's reign [1575-76], Corfe Castle enjoyed privileges equal to those enjoyed by the Cinque Ports. A charter granted by Charles II constituted its administrative corporation as a mayor and eight barons.

The "rotten borough" lost its right to elect Members of Parliament with the Reform Act. The historic borough and its Mayor were abolished by the Municipal Corporations Act, 1883.
(Politics / Corfe Castle)

Boshards Green – being 0.82 acre of registered common land beside Church Knowle footpath number 20, south of Church Farm (SY 941 816). Given that it appears as "Beshard Green" on the parish tithe map [1842] it

should probably have been claimed as a village green rather than common land (registered unit CL 13).
(Placenames / Common land / Church Knowle)

Botteridge Pool – the historic name of Kimmeridge Bay, as given on Ralph Treswell's map of the Isle of Purbeck [1585-86].
(Placenames / Kimmeridge)

Bower – for **William Jeremiah Bower**, see the entry for **Billy Winspit**.

Bradle – former village with chapel, immediately south-east of the junction between Church Knowle and Kimmeridge (SY 932 806), now reduced to Bradle Farm (SY 930 806). Both East Bradle, which became grassland at East Mead, and West Bradle were listed in the Domesday Book [1086]. The "West" was subsequently no longer necessary for the surviving Bradle.

In 1327 a Subsidy Roll showed it as a tithing with ten households, but by the time of the Hearth Tax Assessment of 1664 it had expanded considerably, to 47 houses. Decline followed, with it dropping over the course of the next century to twelve tenancies in the Bradle Manor Rent Roll of 1784, and its old manor house was destroyed by fire.

By the early 19th century Bradle Farm, then in the occupation of the Voss family, was something of a local target for labouring discontent, suffering twice as agricultural unrest erupted during George IV's reign, aimed against the Duke of Wellington's administration.

Arson attacks burnt down a large barn and its contents [4 December 1830] followed by a second fire [20 December 1830] which destroyed much of the property removed from the proximity of the first blaze. Some landowners attempted to reduce the tension by lowering the rents of farmers, who were asked to pass on the benefit by increasing the wages of their workers.
(Placenames / Politics / Church Knowle)

Brenscombe Roman Villa – discovered at the foot of the Purbeck Hills, on the 150-feet contour north of Brenscombe Farm, to the east of Corfe Castle (SY 979 827) in 1961. Pieces of roof-tile, flue-bricks, chalk and sandstone cubes from tessellated pavements, and potsherds, were scattered over the site after the initial excavations.

These revealed a damaged mosaic floor of geometric pattern, with parallel lines and a central panel, inside a chevron border. A second mosaic, of higher quality with a foliate scroll, was later partially uncovered in an adjoining room [1967]. The latest date for fragments of pottery was in the latter part of the Roman period, in the 3rd or 4th centuries.
(Roman archaeology / Corfe Castle)

Brickworks – the local pit and kilns for Corfe Castle, in Victorian times, stood beside the stream just north of Lower Lynch (SY 962 805). In the 20th century the Purbeck supply has come from Godlingston at Swanage, from a works remarkable in still producing hand-made bricks.
(Industrial archaeology / Corfe Castle)

Bridge Cottage – see entry for **Brook Cottage**.

Brinscombe Farm – local Purbeck pronunciation of the Brenscombe placename, a mile east of Corfe Castle (SY 978 824). It is justified by "Bryncecomb" as the 1286 spelling though the name is "Brunescume" in the Domesday Book [1086]. The present farmhouse is a 16th-century building.
(Placenames / Corfe Castle)

British Inventor – tanker blown up by a German mine off St Alban's Head [13 June 1940]. She shipped water badly but was put in tow, unsuccessfully as the crippled ship began to list. The line was released and she was abandoned to sink.
(Shipwrecks / Worth Matravers)

Brook Cottage and **Bridge Cottage** – semi-detached cottages on the south side of the junction of Sandy Hill Lane with the main road into Corfe Castle, beside the Byle Brook.

Stone plinths and Flemish bond brickwork, rising into a massive chimney-stack with three offsets. Dating from the early-18th century.
(Placenames / Corfe Castle)

Brontosaurus – fossilised footsteps of this great dinosaur were reportedly discovered in the Purbeck stone beds at a quarry near Langton Matravers in 1986.
(Geology / Natural history / Langton Matravers)

Brown – guinea pig dairymaid **Abigail Brown**, buried in Worth Matravers churchyard, was the first person known to have been inoculated with cow-pox, by her father Benjamin Jesty in 1774, as a vaccination against smallpox.
(People / Medicine / Worth Matravers)

Brown – describing himself as "a near resident" **John Brown** was the anonymous author of *An Historical and Architectural Description of Corfe Castle* [1829]. It runs to 80 pages, with five prints by T. Wadham, and is the earliest guidebook to Corfe Castle.
(People / Literary / Corfe Castle)

Bucknowle – Domesday Book hamlet [1086], as Chenolle which was held by William de Broase, now centred on a mid-Victorian Tudor-style mansion with extensive outbuildings and five-acre grounds (SY 949 813). Its notable occupant, in the 1930s, was Air Vice-Marshal Sir Philip de la Ferte Joubert [died 1965], then Air Officer Commander-in-Chief of Coastal Command.

The grounds are skirted to the south, towards the Corfe River, by Church Knowle footpath number 17.
(Placenames / Church Knowle)

Burberry Lane – east of Blashenwell Farm, being the now overgrown mediaeval marble industry sledge track from Kingston to Corfe Castle (SY 953 801 to 954 807). This central section is no longer part of the rights of way system, north from the junction of public paths between Blashenwell Farm and West Lynch to the sharp bends in the public road across Corfe Common.
(Placenames / Mediaeval archaeology / Corfe Castle)

Burnham's Lane – see entry for **Tom Burnham's Oak**.

Burning shale – the one use of Kimmeridge shale into recent times. "It burns very strong and bright; and emits a sulphurous smell," wrote William Maton in his Observations on the Western Counties. "When exposed to the atmosphere, it soon falls into pieces; but in the cliffs, or under water, it is very hard. The price is about eight shillings per ton; it is chiefly used in ovens and by the poor people."

Shale is a high-gas tar-smelling solid fuel, which burns as readily as coal, without spitting. If it is added to a fire that is already hot, with a reasonable draw, the odour is not then so noticeable. The residue cools to an orange-brown, with little flaking, and the spent shale is sulphurous in its smell, like a used firework.

Some Kimmeridge people remember its regular use as fuel. Winifred Legg of Puddletown was in conversation with a former visitor to Kimmeridge: "Jack Mears said that when his grandparents and their big family lived at Kimmeridge they dug shale on the beach and burnt it instead of coal. It was very smoky but granny used to cook with it. Farm wages were then 12 shillings a week, after 3 shillings had been deducted for house rent."
(Industrial archaeology / Social history / Kimmeridge)

Bushey Stone Circle – this minor instance of modern eccentricity amongst the Purbeck landed classes came to light in 1977, two years after it had been built. An archaeological society reported that Major D. C. D. Ryder had constructed "a new circle of sandstone uprights" beside the drive to his new house.

This is beside Victorian gravel pits near the corner of the B3351 with the lane signed to Rempstone (SY 988 824). It is a phoney 1970s

Modern folly: Bushey Stone Circle was created in the 1970s.

stone circle of 19 sandstone boulders that might have looked a little more convincing without a suburban weeping willow planted at the centre.

Ryder already owned one genuine, 4,000-year-old stone circle, further east beyond Rempstone Hall. "Things might have been worse," I wrote at the time. "It could have been a pyramid."
(Follies / Corfe Castle)

Butavant Tower – also known as Dungeon Tower, being the western extremity of Corfe Castle which was constructed in King John's major rebuilding of 1201-04. It was a three-storey octagonal tower projecting from the walls, partially demolished in the 17th-century, with the lower part of the batter, with walls ten feet thick, encasing a newel staircase.

A crack let in the weather, causing it to collapse in a gale [11 July 1866], as Thomas Bond of Tyneham House reported in the Southern Times: "Into this rent the rains of more than two centuries have found their way, and have gradually sapped the strength of the mortar. The extraordinary wetness of the present season has augmented the mischief, and thus the masonry was rendered less able to resist the force of the wind. Parting at the rent above mentioned, the greater portion of the fragment which remained was blown down by the gale of Sunday last – a gale of unprecedented severity – and thus a structure which had withstood the vicissitudes of six centuries, had resisted the efforts which had been made to overthrow it with the help of the most powerful agency [gunpowder], and which so greatly enhanced the beauty of the majestic ruin of which it formed a part, has at length been hurled down from its proud and lofty eminence and now lies a mass of shapeless rubble in the valley below."

He went on to lament "the state of neglect into which the stately and magnificent ruin of Corfe Castle has been permitted to fall". Debris from the fallen Dungeon Tower included quantities of worked stone which might be used "for supporting some crumbling part of the building; but I am informed that it is intended to make use of them for building a 'sheep wash'!"
(Placenames / Mediaeval archaeology / National Trust / Corfe Castle)

Byle Brook – the eastern tributary of the Corfe River, flowing through Boar Mill, at Corfe Castle.
(Placenames / Corfe Castle)

Byle Brook Bridge – carries the main road up into Corfe Castle village, above the mill-pool at Boar Mill (SY 961 822). It has two semi-circular arches of the 17th or 18th century.
(Placenames / Bridges / Corfe Castle)

Castle gateway: Corfe Castle and the National Trust together proving that first impressions count.

C

Caernarvon Castle – a cutter, became a complete loss at Clavell's Hard, Kimmeridge [25 September 1856].
(Shipwrecks / Kimmeridge)

Calcraft – libertarian politician **John Calcraft** [1726-72] bought the Rempstone Estate from the Rose family [1757] and proceeded to acquire most of the buildings in Wareham. Nationally, he was said to have "the best head for intrigue in the whole party" of William Pitt's followers. He was Member of Parliament for Rochester, Kent, from 1768, until his death; which thwarted his ambition of a peerage – the Earl of Ormonde being the title he coveted. Politically, his aspirations were for "the liberty of the individual and Parliamentary reform". His monument is in the chancel of Lady St Mary parish church at Wareham.

Calcraft was reputedly the illegitimate son of Henry Fox, 1st Lord Holland, under whose patronage he became Deputy Paymaster for the Army raised by the Duke of Cumberland [1745-47]. As a result of this and other regimental assignments he accumulated a fortune and property in Brewer Street and Parliament Street, London, as well as the estates of Ingress Abbey, Holwood Hall, and Leeds Abbey. He had a total of six children by two mistresses, Mrs George Anne Bellamy, and Miss Bride, both highly fashionable actresses.
(People / Politics / Corfe Castle and Wareham)

Calcraft – reformer **John Calcraft** [1765-1831], eldest legitimate son of John Calcraft, was elected Member of Parliament for Wareham [July 1786] at the age of twenty. By then his father owned most of the town. He sat until the 1790 dissolution and was re-elected from 1800 to 1806. Then he took his father's old seat, the city of Rochester, from Admiral Sir Sidney Smith, until 1818. He then sat for Wareham, again, until shortly before his death.

The end for Calcraft was a political suicide, literally, which would be caused by the reproaches of his Tory friends after he reverted to his old Whig principles and was the single changed-mind vote that carried the Reform Bill [22 March 1831].

Initially, "the ardent reformer of Wareham" had a great success against the local Tory establishment when he went on to take one of the two county of Dorset seats, against Henry Bankes, in the subsequent general election [May 1831]. A crowd of 12,000 were on the edge of a riot at the hustings in Poundbury Camp hill-fort, Dorchester, when Calcraft's Corfe Castle labourers joined with horsemen provided by John Samuel Wanley Sawbridge Erle Drax of Charborough Park to charge and rout the pro-Bankes mob. Insults also flew in election leaflets:

"Pride shall have a fall.
Old Bankes' pride is nothing fresh;
He is a lump of proud, proud flesh.
What mortal can endure him?
Then let us drive him from the Poll.
Back, back, to Corfe's most rotten hole.
And try if that will cure him."

They had their wish. At the end of the contest Edward Berkeley Portman had won the first seat with 1,699 votes; John Calcraft took the second with 1,542 votes; and Henry Bankes (an MP since 1780) was the loser with only 1,176 votes.

The reformers had taken the House of Commons, though they still faced resistance from the House of Lords (including 21 Anglican Bishops). Calcraft despaired at his treatment from old Tory friends through July and August, though politically he was flowing with the tide, personally as well in that he successfully re-introduced a Divorce Bill which passed through the Commons.

One Sunday morning he killed himself at his Whitehall Place residence [11 September 1831]. He was buried in the chancel vault of St James's Church, Piccadilly, and also has a memorial in St Mary's Church, Wareham.
(People / Politics / Corfe Castle and Wareham)

Cemetery gateway: sculpted by Francis Newbery as Corfe's memorial to its Great War dead, with dialect words by William Barnes

Calcraft – heir **Captain John Hales Montague Calcraft** died suddenly at Rempstone Hall after winning the Wareham Parliamentary seat by 13 votes [November 1868].
(People / Politics / Corfe Castle and Wareham)

Calcraft Boundary Stones – estate boundary stones, otherwise known as "mere-stones" (mere = boundary) mark the limits of the Rempstone Estate. Some are now visible from National Trust land. One is set in the hawthorn hedge next to a "BP Pipeline" marker beside Corfe Castle bridleway number 3 to the north of Scotland Farm (SY 963 842).

The stone has a rounded top and is cut on its east-facing side with the letters "C. C. C." for "Calcraft Corfe Castle" and shows the north-west corner of an enclave of the Calcraft family's lands which stretched 400 yards into what were otherwise Bankes-owned fields on the west side of the Corfe River.

Others, amid stones for "N. B." (Nathaniel Bankes) and "R. B." (Ralph Bankes), mark the corners of strip fields at West Hawes, off West Street in Corfe Castle village (SY 958 817).
(National Trust / Corfe Castle)

Calcutta – sank, somewhere between Kimmeridge and the South Western Approaches, following a collision with a Prussian barque, according to a message in a bottle washed-up on the Chesil Beach at Abbotsbury [1869]: "Ship *Calcutta* going down; run into a Prussian barque – I think the *Emilie*, John McNeil. Been bailing two days. John Wells."
(Shipwrecks / Abbotsbury and Kimmeridge)

Caplestone Cottage – now Westacre (SY 979 803), 500 yards west of Harman's Cross, which was the only human habitation in the vicinity of what is now a hamlet, until the early 20th century.
(Placenames / Corfe Castle)

Cartridge – master mason **Derek Cartridge** has carried out quality restoration work for the National Trust, and has the distinction of being commemorated by a stone head set in a wall of Scotland Farm Barn [1990].
(People / National Trust / Corfe Castle)

Castle View – National Trust Interpretation and Educational Centre, opened in 1993, with a car-park in the former·quarry at the rear, at North Castle, Corfe Castle (SY 959 825). Battle of Britain crash-site of Hurricane P3984 of 238 Squadron from RAF Chilbolton, Hampshire [10 October 1940]. Pilot Officer Bob Doe, though wounded by gunfire from Messerschmitts, parachuted safely and landed on Brownsea Island.
(Placenames / National Trust / Corfe Castle)

Cemetery Gates – stone gateway in moulded stone with a pointed arch, beside East Street at Corfe Castle, designed by Francis Newbery in the 1920s. Built as a memorial to the dead of the Great War, it is surmounted by the words of Victorian dialect poet William Barnes: "DO'SET MEN DON'T SHEAME THEIR KIND."
(Placenames / Corfe Castle)

Challow Hill – eastwards from Corfe Castle, with a Bronze Age round barrow crowning the dome-shaped summit known as East Hill (SY 964 824). Further east the chalk downland is covered by 35 acres of a Celtic field system of Iron Age or Romano-British date (SY 969 823).

The latter map reference is at the point where the fields terminate at a lynchet that crosses the ridge. This cultivation terrace is four feet high, and other lynchets are up to eight feet high. On the other hand most of the field boundaries have been reduced to traces and much of the area is smothered in gorse scrub.

There are also two surviving ancient fields, each roughly square – being about 180 feet by 200 feet – on the steep north-facing slope above Rollington Wood (SY 966 825).
(Placenames / Prehistoric archaeology / Corfe Castle)

Chapel Cottage – former Methodist Chapel on the northern side of Kingston Hill (SY 958 801).
(Placenames / Churches / Corfe Castle)

Chapman – prolific Tudor biographer **Hester Chapman** [1899-1976] was born at Durnford House, Langton Matravers, which was then Durnford Preparatory School for boys. She was Hester Wolferstan Pellatt, the daughter of the master, Thomas Pellatt. Her initial fame would come from the novels *She Saw Them Go By* [1932] and *To Be a King* [1934].

She would have a variety of war experiences and excitements, helping the Free French, the American Red Cross, and then a canteen waitress for Combined Operations. Meantime she produced *Long Division* [1943], *Will Be Good* [1945], and *Worlds Apart* [1947], before embarking on the string of historical biographies for which she is remembered.

They began with *Great Villiers* [1949] and went on to deal with *Mary II* [1953], *Queen Anne's Son* [1954], *The Last Tudor King* [1958], *Two Tudor Portraits* [1960], *Lady Jane Grey* [1962], *The Tragedy of Charles II* [1964], *Lucy* [1965], *Privileged Persons* [1966], *The Sisters of Henry VIII* [1969], *Caroline Matilda* [1974], and *Four Fine Gentlemen* [1976]. The last, with impeccable timing, was being printed as she died.

Hester Chapman, who had been twice married but was childless, was complimented by J. H. Plumb on her "rare insight into the

Chapman's Pool: framed by Emmetts Hill to the left and a brave steer, in a photograph by Ted Legg, the author's father, circa 1935.

vagaries of the human heart". It was, he noted, a quality frequently lacking in historians.

Between the flow of solid histories, almost as light relief, there came a secondary sequence of novels: *Ever Thine* [1951], *Falling Stream* [1954], *The Stone Lily* [1957], *Eugeine* [1961], *Fear No More* [1968], and *Limmerston Hall* [1972].
(People / Literary / Langton Matravers)

Chapman's Pool Lifeboat Station – announced in a newspaper of 1866, which commented that "the great loss of life and property on this part of the coast have at length aroused the attention of the Government and we are happy to say that preparations have commenced for placing a lifeboat in this little bay". The boathouse was built in 1867 only a few yards from the spot where the French barque *Georgiana* had been driven ashore and broken-up by the sea [11 July 1866]. The lifeboat station was short-lived, however, and closed in the 1880s.

There was no settlement near the water to provide men for the boat with the speed that an emergency demanded. The Chapman's Pool station is now an ordinary boathouse, unusual for its position beneath the tumbling undercliff and the 400-feet contour of Emmetts Hill, buttressed along the top by a curtain of yellow stone. Below on the boathouse slipway in the 1970s were the lobster pots of Percy Wallace, who had two boats there. He retired into shell-fishing after serving as a Coastguard at St Alban's Head.
(Placenames / Shipwrecks / Worth Matravers)

Charing Cross – the most central and best known monuments in mediaeval London, erected by King Edward I, was sculpted in Purbeck marble [1291]. An item of account

Chapman's Pool: beneath the crags of Emmett's Hill with beach buildings ranging from a Victorian lifeboat station to wartime pillbox (foreground).

Lifeboat station: in retirement as a boathouse, at Chapman's Pool, with Houn's Tout Cliff rising behind the semi-sheltered inlet.

survives: "To William of Corfe for marble for the Eleanor Cross, £7. 19s."

This bill was for the original Charing Cross in the Strand which was the last of a series of memorial crosses for Queen Eleanor of Castile, along the route of her final journey from Lincoln to the capital.

It was destroyed by the Puritans, by order of the Long Parliament at the start of the Civil War [1641].

(Mediaeval archaeology / Corfe Castle / Dorset in London)

Chough – the demise of this member of the crow family was recorded by J. C. Mansel-Pleydell in 1888: "Fifty years ago it used to be abundant on the Purbeck coast, but has gradually become scarcer, and is now quite a rare bird."

It used to occur in scattered colonies along the limestone shore and nested in crevices on the cliffs. One was shot by John Stainer, at Swanage, on 21 January 1881. Five were trapped there in 1885. It was certainly present about that time at Seacombe and Winspit. There are also records from chalk downland at Studland. By the early 20th century, however, there were only a handful of sightings and none after 1925. It also declined to extinction on the Cornish coast; the nearest surviving colonies are in Wales.

(Natural history / Studland, Swanage and Worth Matravers)

Once abundant: the chough was a distinctive bird of the Purbeck cliffs, drawn here by J. C. Mansel-Pleydell.

Church Knowle – the clue to the village and parish name being the location of its church. The knoll is in fact the rounded mound on which it stands. This, in all probability, was a Bronze Age burial mound (SY 941 819).

Church Farm is opposite St Peter's Church [see its entry] but otherwise most of the village has migrated eastwards from the church, to the far side of a double bend. Here it developed in the late Middle Ages into a separate linear street. The parish extends to 2,900 entries and its entries include:

Air crashes; Ball clay; Balloon *Gerard Heineken;* Bare Cross; Barnston Farm; Barnston pillow mounds; Barnston strip fields; Blue Pool; Boshards Green; Bradle; Bucknowle; Cocknowle; Cocknowle Tramway; Cotness;

Crack Lane; Creech Barrow; Creech Barrow Hill; Creech Barrow Hunting Lodge; Creech Brick Works; Dobson's Farm; East Creech Farm; East Creech Roman Villa; East Orchard; Furzebrook Clay Works; Furzebrook Railway; The Gwyle; Horcerd; Hutchings; Killwood; The Lake; Long barrows; Mizmaze; National School; New Inn; Old Cottage; Old Rectory; Old School House; Orenstein and Koppel; Post Office; Puddle Mill Farm; *Quartus*; *Quintus*; Reading Room; Round barrows; *Russell*; St Peter's parish church; *Secondus*; *Sextus*; Snug's Farm; Stonehill Down; Strange-Boston; *Tertius*; Three Lords' Barrow; Village Hall; West Bucknowle House; West Orchard; Whiteway Farm; Wicken Stream or River Wicken.
(Placenames / Prehistoric archaeology / Church Knowle)

Churches – see under the cluster of entries for **Saints**.

Clavell – gentleman robber **John Clavell** [1603-42], nephew of Sir William Clavell of Smedmore House, Kimmeridge, was a gentleman and a highwayman, who boasted of both pursuits. The latter funded the financial needs of the former. In 1628, as "John Clavell, Gent." he published a volume of poems as "A Recantation of an ill-led Life; or a Discoverie of the Highway Law, in verse."

It is dated "from my lonely chamber in the King's Bench, October 1627". He had been captured earlier that year and sentenced to death, but was saved through his connections as a gentleman, by a royal pardon from Charles I.

The poem, he writes, is "approved by the King's most excellent majesty and published by his express command". It was a success, being reprinted in 1628 and 1634.
(People / Literature / Kimmeridge)

Clavell – alum-manufacturer **Sir William Clavell** [died 1644] of Smedmore House gave up the furnaces beside Kimmeridge Bay after the initiative was beset by litigation. His next venture was glass-making, with Abraham Bigo, using shale instead of wood as the fuel for producing green drinking glasses [1617]

Clavell Tower: Kimmeridge's 1831-built clifftop folly, erected by Rev. John Richards, who adopted the Clavell family name.

Clay mine: working an underground seam on the heath between Wareham and Corfe Castle.

but again attracted disputes [1621] and lost more than £20,000.
(People / Industrial archaeology / Kimmeridge)

Clavell Tower – picturesque folly on Hen Cliff overlooking Kimmeridge Bay from the east, built [1831] by Rev John Richards who had assumed the name Clavell upon inheriting the Smedmore Estate [1817]. The circular tower is a three-storey lookout, of brick and stone rubble, faced with stucco and ashlar. It is surrounded by a colonnade.

Though not built as such, it was used in the mid-19th century as a Coastguard lookout. Several old cannon were placed around a flagpole, each being set into the ground at an angle, to hold its stays. The last of the gun barrels was removed in the late 1960s.

The tower has proved to be of both use and ornament, as it has enabled at least one crew to make last minute corrections to their course and escape the clutches of the notorious Kimmeridge Levels.
(Placenames / Follies / Kimmeridge)

Clavell's Hard – named for a landing beach on the Clavell family's Smedmore Estate, but suitable only for small vessels, being immediately below a headland at the centre of the projecting Kimmeridge Ledges (SY 920 777). A brig, the *Olive Branch*, was stranded here but floated free [20 April 1838] and an unidentified brig, laden with coal, repeated the achievement a couple of years later [11 April 1840]. The cliffs have seasonal waterfalls and are riddled with late Victorian shale-mining tunnels.
(Placenames / Shipwrecks / Kimmeridge)

Clay-mining – of top quality ball clay, to supply the Staffordshire potteries, has been a major Purbeck industry for several centuries. Much is extracted by mining but one of the best accounts of a traditional open pit is that by C. E. Robinson, in the 1870s, who visited workings that were clearly Fayle and Company's, at Norden, for he mentions what can only be Fayle's Tramway, "having a flange to retain the wheels of the trucks". His description is vivid:

"Here is a wide uncovered excavation, the rubbish [over-burden] overlying the clay not being many yards in thickness. The steep sides are being cut away in steps by men with spades, and are charmingly tinted, light pink, bright yellow, grey, and white, according to the

varieties of the clay. As they are cut, the square lumps of the plastic material are slid in a wet state along a smooth plank, towards a truck, into which they are lifted by a man with an iron prong. From the ground level above a [stationary steam] engine hauls the loaded trucks up an inclined tramway, and when it has leisure from this employment, is busily engaged in sawing out timber props and sleepers. The whole scene, on a fine day, is animated and pretty; but in wet weather there must be pleasanter occupations than the constant handling and treating of slippery adhesive clay."

Bill Stockley [born 1874] retired to Corfe Castle where he recalled old-time clay mining beneath the Purbeck heaths: "We used to go down ladders, 80 feet or more, straight down the shafts in my day. Candles to see with underground, we had; and every bit of clay had to be cut by hand. It all had to be pulled out by hand-winches too."

Foreman Fred White of Norden Mine was a Purbeck clay-miner for the entire first half of the 20th century. He recalled the pre-1905 horse-drawn tramway to Middlebere, where the clay boats came in on the tide to meet the end of the line beside a harbour inlet. "But that's all changed now," he said. "Our clay goes off by rail and road, some of it to the Staffordshire potteries, and quite a lot for export."

See also random entries throughout; especially those for Ball clay, Blue Pool, Fayle's Tramway, Goathorn Railway, and named mineral railway locomotives.
(Industrial archaeology / Corfe Castle)

Coal money – formerly believed to be an ancient currency, shown by John H. Austen [1856] to be core-waste from Roman lathe-turned armlet production from Kimmeridge shale.
(Roman archaeology / Kimmeridge)

Coastguard graves – in Kimmeridge churchyard there is a line of gravestones which catalogue the misfortunes of a small band of Coastguards [1811-41]. Nearest to the sea is

Goathorn Railway: branching eastwards (left) from Eldon Sidings, Norden, seen from Will's Bridge in 1971.

Norden railways: narrow gauge clay line westwards (right) across the standard gauge branch line (below) at what is now Norden Station.

the headstone of John Lavery, a boatman in the Coastguard, who died aged 26 after "accidentally falling over the cliff in the execution of his duty" on the night of 7 October 1839. His headstone, like the next which is to John Perren, was erected by "fellow officers and boatmen". Perren was a boatman who drowned whilst on duty, at the age of 26 in Kimmeridge Bay, on the night of 14 April 1838. Boatman Alexander Simpson also died aged 26, "killed by his own firearms" in the execution of his duty on the morning of 9 February 1841. Finally, there is a stone to boatman Henry Plomar who died (the stone does not say how) on 13 January 1811, again at the age of 26.

The "old" Coastguard Station was on the east side of Kimmeridge Bay and the centrally-placed "new" Coastguard Cottages at Gaulter Gap were built in the late 1820s.

(Shipwrecks / Kimmeridge)

Coastguard misadventures: gravestones at Kimmeridge record a series of accidents, ranging from drownings to discharged firearms.

Coastguard Stations – in the west at Gaulter Gap, Kimmeridge, and in the west on St Alban's Head, where there is still a Coastguard lookout. This was always the larger operation, with its Victorian staffing, fully occupying the range of Coastguard Cottages, being 13 men. Station officer in the 1880s was Thomas Bailey. Rocket Life Saving Apparatus number 300 was issued to the station. Six men were employed at Kimmeridge, under chief officer John Macgillicuddy.

Their modern replacement [1948] is a mile inland, on the south side of Weston Farm, Worth Matravers.
(Placenames / Shipwrecks / Kimmeridge and Worth Matravers)

Cocknowle Chalkpit – operated by English China Clays on the opposite side of the combe and lane from the Victorian incline railway (SY 931 823). The chalk is used at Furzebrook Clay Works as part of the mixing and preparation processes.

As for the shape of the pit, it has moved westwards and up the valley, towards Stonehill Down, after the present author was the first to publicly voice concerns that if it were allowed to break through the rim of the combe it would cause a great white gash in the northern side of the Purbeck Hills.
(Placenames / Industrial archaeology / Church Knowle)

Cocknowle Tramway – serviced extensive marl pits along the top of the Purbeck Hills, eastwards for nearly half a mile from Bare Cross, which supplied chalk to Wareham Cement Works at Ridge, in the parish of Arne. Its products included Portland cement, ground lias lime, white stone lime, and agricultural manure lime. The Victorian workings along the southern side of the ridge above Church Knowle had a horse-drawn tramway from a point south-west of the Six Ways path junction (SY 936 822).

Towards the western end of the quarries it then turned northwards (SY SY 932 821) the tramway became a cable-operated incline railway down the slope of the hill. Loaded drums descending hauled the empty ones back to the top. Below, beside the lane from Furzebrook, there was a large weathering heap (SY 933 823).
(Placenames / Industrial archaeology / Arne and Church Knowle)

Commodore – brigantine from Caernarvon, carrying Welsh slates up-Channel, destination Hamburg, stranded on the ledges off Freshwater, Encombe, in thick fog [18 August 1877]. The crew escaped in their rowing boat but she became a complete loss.
(Shipwrecks / Corfe Castle)

Company of Marblers and Stonecutters of Purbeck – the mediaeval trade guild that

National Coastwatch: archetypal setting for a maritime lookout, on St Alban's Head.

Old Hall: site of the Saxon 'domus' of Corfe Castle, re-using its stone, in what is probably the oldest surviving late 11th-century fragment on Castle Hill.

controlled the stone industry, electing two Wardens and Stewards to control the Isle of Purbeck. They remain in existence, holding an annual gathering and elections at the Town Hall, Corfe Castle, on Shrove Tuesday.

Tradition is maintained by adjourning to the Fox Inn on the opposite side of West Street and from there kicking a football to the ancient stone port of Ower. They also carry a pound of pepper.

The custom preserves the memory that the once vital right of way to the shore of Poole Harbour was secured by the payment, literally, of a peppercorn rent. Indeed the section beyond Rempstone Heath to Ower is, or was, known as Peppercorn Lane. The agreement was made with John Collins of Ower in 1695 and has been maintained ever since, though now instead of being handed over the football is kicked into the water and the pepper sprinkled over it.

Now more or less institutionalised as a media event, the practice has at times lapsed into a token effort, such as in 1969 when only one marbler arrived at Ower on the evening of Shrove Tuesday, with the pepper but without a football.

(Mediaeval archaeology / Corfe Castle)

Congregational Chapel (Corfe Castle) – built as an "Independent Chapel" [1835] on the west side of East Street (SY 961 819). Its first minister was Rev. George Hubbard [1780-1870], "having secured, though at an excessive price, the only available bit of freehold," after the room where his Day School met "was closed against him and pulled down".

The British School continued in "the old leasehold chapel" which the new building replaced. It is of course Purbeck stone with a slate roof.

(Churches / Corfe Castle)

Cooper – incorrigible smugglers **Reuben Cooper** [born 1801] and **Charles Cooper** [born 1813] both made assize appearances at

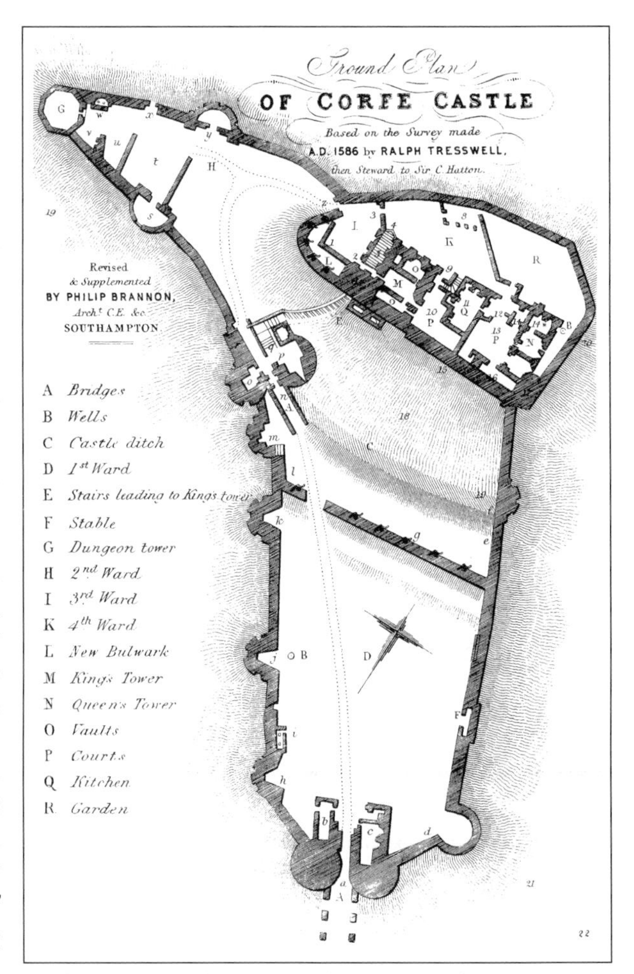

Corfe Castle: Ralph Treswell's survey of 1586, as re-drawn by Philip Brannon, circa 1860.

West Bailey: clockwise from the Keep are the South-West Gatehouse, South Tower, Old Hall (site), Butavant Tower, and New Bulwark, overlooked from West Hill.

West Mills: rustic foreground (centre) dating the picture to the turn of the 20th century, and showing a key element of the Corfe Castle setting that has been lost.

Boar Mill: ancient building remembered locally as Battrick's Bakery, acquired by the National Trust to secure the stunning setting of the ruin seen from the road.

Dorchester. Reuben was fined £100 [1821] and Charles was imprisoned for six months [1840]. When the Cooper family finally came to hang up their grappling hooks and half-anker spirit cask these were to pass to the Dorset County Museum in Dorchester.
(People / Smugglers / Kimmeridge and Dorchester)

Copper Bridge – stone-built packhorse bridge, at a crossroads of public rights of way, across the Corfe River at the northern extremity of Corfe Common, west of Corfe Castle village (SY 956 816). On National Trust property, having being inherited with the Bankes Estate [1982].
(Placenames / Bridges / National Trust / Corfe Castle)

Copper Bridge Roman Villa – immediately west of the Corfe River, between Corfe Castle and Bucknowle (SY 955 816). The first Roman villa to be discovered south of the Purbeck Hills, found [1974] by antiquities collector P. A. Brown of Eastgate, beside the entrance to Corfe Castle.

He had thought pieces of pottery found on the surface were only chance debris that had accumulated at a river crossing used for a long period. A trial trench, however, exposed a rubble wall with facing blocks of limestone. Probing showed the floor was ten feet across, and less than a foot below the surface.

Subsequent finds may indicate the presence of a domestic shrine though others have jumped to the conclusion that the building may be a Romano-Celtic temple. The spot is on National Trust land, inherited with the Bankes Estate [1982], opposite the north-west tip of Corfe Common. It is reached by two public paths from Corfe village, less than half a mile away.
(Roman archaeology / National Trust / Corfe Castle)

Corfe – the core placename of this book, with the entry for Corfe Castle following, and the name also applying to one of Dorset's largest parishes. This sprawls across some 10,400 acres, from the English Channel to Poole Harbour, and is covered here by multiple entries on almost every page, with too many for a listing to serve any practical purpose.

"Corfe", in Old English, meant "The pass" and applied here to the cutting through the Purbeck Hills that was known as Corfe Gap into the Middle Ages.
(Placenames / Corfe Castle)

Corfe Castle – Purbeck's world-class monument has stood on Castle Hill for more than a thousand years (SY 959 823). The setting is magnificent, with the two forks of the Corfe River – known locally as the Byle Brook below the east side, and Wicken Stream to the west – having cut the single break in the central massif of the Purbeck Hills. The strategic position is superb, commanding the passes on each side, and the visual splendour of the ruins is the equal of anything in Europe.

Herring-bone walling and the windows of the Old Hall, a Norman Conquest period structure, stand on the site of the previous Saxon royal house and pre-date the rest of the ruins. This masonry can be found between the Butavant Tower and the South Tower on the south side of the West Bailey.

It was on the entrance to this, at Edward's Gate [now the South-West Gatehouse, beside the Keep] that the boy-King Edward was assassinated by members of his step-mother's household [18 March 978].

The great central Keep at Corfe is an immense Norman structure [1095-1105] on the site of earlier 11th-century defences. Despite demolitions it still stands in part to 80 feet in height. It is one of the earliest mediaeval fortresses in Britain, with a general design and style well ahead of its time. It is built upon and otherwise surrounded by earlier walls, about nine feet thick, which stood nearly 30 feet high on the outside.

John Hutchins, Dorset's county historian, wrote that "its structure is so strong, the ascent of the hill on all sides but the south so steep, and the walls so massy and thick, that it must have been one of the most impregnable fortresses in the kingdom before the invention of artillery".

It did just that by surviving an abortive siege when King Stephen failed to oust one of his rebel barons, Baldwin de Redvers [1139].

The West Bailey, around the site of the Old Hall, was re-fortified with its three towers when Corfe Castle was King John's notorious state prison [1201-04]. In 1202 the dungeon held Savaris de Mauleon, a baron from Poitou on the edge of the disputed Aquitaine. He had taken John's mother, Eleanor, prisoner at Vienne. John rescued her.

Of the 25 French prisoners held at Corfe – "where there was never food nor drink" – 15 starved to death. Savaris, however, was "turned" as we would say, not only surviving but thriving, after his return to France as an English agent.

The Great Ditch between the Keep and the vulnerable Outer Bailey, to the south of it, was quarried out of the hill when John made Corfe his treasury [1207] for the store of confiscated church funds and other finances, gathered for the coming war against France. A great convoy of carts was needed to move the cash from Corfe to Portsmouth, the port of embarkation [1214].

Known as the "Gloriette", the King's Hall and John's State Rooms were built at this time [1205-08]. The east wall stands to two storeys and has pointed-arched moulded windows in elaborately mullioned stone. King John enjoyed hunting in Purbeck, where he could also keep an eye on his money.

Timber palisades protected the Outer Bailey until the process began of gradual replacement in stone [after 1212] and the main perimeter defences date from half a century later [circa 1170]. These comprise the First Tower, South-

Model village: dominated by an intact Corfe Castle in a garden behind the Square, with the real thing rising for comparison in the background.

Classic view: the Corfe Castle skyline from the Church Knowle road, with the thatched Vinceyard Cottage and its smoking chimney in the middle distance (centre right) captured by Colin Graham.

Norman Keep: silhouette of one of the most spectacular ruins in Europe, forming Dorset's best known skyline.

Corfe Square: a pre-1897 photograph from the church tower, datable by the steps of the ancient market cross, and the absence of the replacement commemorating Queen Victoria's diamond jubilee.

King's Hall: built as King John's Purbeck palace (centre and right) inside the fortress at Corfe, with the stairs (left) having led to the King's Presence Chamber.

West Gatehouse, Plukenet Tower, Horseshoe Tower, Outer Gatehouse, and its Outer Bridge.

Deposed King Edward II would be held prisoner at Corfe, by Sir John Maltravers, before his assassination in Berkeley Castle [1327].

History finally caught up with Corfe Castle in the Civil War between King Charles and his Parliament. On May Day in 1643 the traditional Isle of Purbeck staghunt was used as a pretext for a troop of Parliamentary horsemen to attempt entry into Corfe Castle. Lady Mary Bankes had the gate shut against them and they and their comrades would continue to be defied for almost the entirety of the conflict, through a series of sieges from the nearby Rings of King Stephen's time, as the main action ebbed and flowed across middle England from Marston Moor to Naseby Field.

Somerset fell to the cavalry of Sir Thomas Fairfax in 1645, and by 1646 the castles at Corfe and Portland were the only two token Royalist garrisons still holed-up in Dorset. They were by now merely an irrelevance but the inevitable finale came to Corfe through treachery rather than force of arms.

A Royalist officer, Lieutenant-Colonel Thomas Pittman, conspired to let a group of the enemy into the castle, under the guise of reinforcements. At dawn the defending garrison found themselves pinned down under impossible crossfire, from the intruders inside and the main body of attackers outside. The final 48-day siege ended with the surrender of the Governor, Colonel Henry Anketell [08.00 hours, 27 February 1646].

A few days later the House of Commons ordered the demolition of Corfe Castle [4 March 1646]. Even with tunnelling and explosives it was no easy task and the process of reducing it to ruins took many months. Some of this undermined masonry has slipped down the sides in subsequent centuries, including part of a northern tower that destroyed my father's parked motor-cycle in the 1920s.

Corfe Castle is still one of the greatest English castles, for even in total ruin it remains one of Britain's most important historic buildings. The romantic ruin is now in the care of the National Trust. Both in size and for the importance of its story, this was the principal single treasure bequeathed to the Trust by Ralph Bankes, who died in 1981. Conservation and consolidation has been sympathetic, to the extent of sparing some ivy on the walls, which has been gardened by the Trust "to maintain and enhance the romantic quality of the castle".

It is the subject of an old couplet, from the days of oil painting:

"The castle of the feudal victor,
now serves for nought, but for a picture."

(Mediaeval archaeology / National Trust / Corfe Castle)

Corfe Castle Band – the Yeovil Gazette of November 1864 reported an encounter between an exuberant bandsmen and a livid Purbeck clergyman: "A resident writes to complain of the arbitrary and unreasonable conduct of one who, to be consistent with his profession, ought to set an example of forbearance and gentleness. One night, as the Corfe Castle Band returned through a neighbouring village on their way home, they struck up a lively tune; whereupon the parish priest rushed from his house in a rage, asked the musicians what business they had there at that time of night, and actually proceeded to pull the instruments from the players' hands by main force. The Isle of Purbeck is a place where very strange things are occasionally done – things which, before long, we will publish to the world."

It does not seem, sadly, that the promise was kept.

(Social history / Corfe Castle)

Corfe Castle Borough – archetypal "rotten borough" electing two members of Parliament [from 1572] as did nearby Wareham as well [from 1302]. Disfranchised by the Reform Act of 1832, when Corfe was included in the borough of Wareham, with new limits extended to cover 50 square miles. These 31,560 acres stretched from Milborne St

Andrew to the sea at St Alban's Head, with a population of 6,694 [1861].

Of these, the total number of male occupiers of property was 1,159 [1866] with voters among them numbering only 898.

(Politics / Corfe Castle)

Corfe Castle Cemetery Gate – moulded stone in a pointed arch, designed by Francis Newbery who lived nearby in East Street, to commemorate the village's dead in the Great War. Above it is cut a quasi-dialect version of the words of Victorian parson-poet William Barnes:

"DO'SET MEN DON'T SHEAME THEIR KIND."

(Placenames / Memorials / Corfe Castle)

Corfe Castle census – a remarkable private census of Corfe Castle was compiled by William Morton Pitt of Encombe [1796] and incorporated by editor Richard Gough into his first volume [1796] of the second edition enlargement of John Hutchins's History of Dorset. It gives the names, addresses, ages, and incomes of the 1,239 inhabitants of Corfe Castle parish. They were living in 261 dwellings (4.75 persons per household).

The census goes much further than the official state versions which it predates, in that the personal information extends to wages and was printed in full detail the year after its compilation; presumably without asking anyone for agreement to the publication of this gross invasion of privacy.

It is accompanied by a call for a national census: "From such returns great parochial advantages would be derived wheresoever they might be adopted, and if they were general, great national benefit would result therefrom."

Certainly a great national outcry would result if it were to appear contemporaneously in this form today.

Jane Umby, for example, was aged 31, knitting in Back Street to a earn a shilling and sixpence a week, and the remarks column adds: "Husband ran away."

William Bailey, at 72 and on parish pay, living at Little Woolstone, had seen better days: "He was formerly a Farmer, and Overseer of the Poor of the Parish."

Clay-cutter Thomas Norman's household had problems: "This family on parish pay. Thomas Norman foolish, Martha Norman a cancer on her face."

"Ann Smith, a Dwarf, on parish pay . . .

"Jane Barfoot's husband absent."

Labourer William Chaffey "has Cows on the Common."

Michael Hayward is described as "almost an Idiot" although he was earning the average weekly wage of ten shillings a week [£0.50].

"Abner Crocker is blind. He is maintained by his children, &c."

All the males in the parish are categorised and appear to have been generally kept busy, in that a lot of the work was long and hard, and those in the self-employed support trades mostly held the local monopoly.

INDUSTRIES

Claycutters 55; Stonemasons 16; Quarries 10; Ropemakers 6; Twine spinners 3; Flax dressers 2; Manufactory superintendent [at Kingston] 1; Stonecutter 1; Lime burner 1; Woolcomber 1 = 96 total.

AGRICULTURE and FISHERIES

Labourers [mostly in farming] 64; Farmers 18; Dairymen 12; Fishermen 14; Farmers' and Traders' sons 9; Shepherds 4; Merchants 3; Fellmongers [dealers in furs and skins] 2; Hurdler 1 = 127 total.

SERVICE TRADES

Servants, apprentices 42; Shoemakers 16; Carpenters 14; Carters 11; Blacksmiths 10; Boatmen 6; Publicans 5; Tailors 4; Breechmakers 3; Butchers 3; Other shopkeepers 3; Millers 2; Tallow chandlers 2; Bakers 2; Sadler 1; Barber 1; Thatcher 1; House painter 1; Glazier 1; Furze cutter 1; Mole catcher 1 = 130 total.

PROFESSIONS

Writing clerks 2; Clergy 2; Schoolmasters 2; Of Independent fortune 2; Surveyor 1; Bailiff 1 = 10 total.

EXCLUDED

Boys under 15 years 241; Too old to work 4; Boarder 1 = 246 total.

Vintage porches: extending out into the highway from the Greyhound at Corfe Castle, with the western one still a thoroughfare with columns supporting it, and the vehicle dating the photograph to the 1920s.

The figures show a stable and self-sufficient rural coastal community. A 21st century observer must first note the complete absence of a category for the unemployed, and secondly that the number who are age-exempted in what we would call retirement is minuscule, at four out of 609. If people were old – and the parish registers show that many did survive into advanced old age – they carried on working for as long as they were fit.

The third revelation is that even in 1795 the service trades were numerically the largest single sector of the economy, though they would take another two centuries to outnumber all the other areas of employment added together.

The other 19th and 20th century growth area would be in the socially preferred professions, which had not at that time found much sustenance in country communities. In 1795 the overwhelming bulk of the adult male population was in work and doing something useful with its hands.

The elite of the old Purbeck working class were the quarrymen and the fishermen. Those born inside these families made a closed shop of such crafts; the way of life was hard and demanding but it offered a security denied to the lesser classes. Life was much tougher and offered less on the northern side of the Purbeck Hills which separate the rich limestone landscape from the arid barrenness of the heaths that spread across the thin sandy soils to the backwaters of Poole Harbour.
(Social history / Corfe Castle)

Corfe Castle marble industry – in mediaeval times, marble was brought from the Purbeck quarries, to workshops in Corfe Castle village on heavily-laden sledges, hauled by horses, down deeply cut lanes from the hills to the valley. Such tracks, with thick hedgerows either side, overhanging and meeting across the middle, can be followed, with difficulty, in the rough countryside south of Corfe Common.

Burberry Lane, east of Blashenwell Farm, is one of the ancient marblers' routes. Another runs from west of Afflington Barn to Woodyhyde, If you bend and untangle the brambles that get constantly in the way, it is possible to walk stooped beneath the canopy for a considerable distance. It, and the other old roads in these parts, head eventually for West Street at Corfe Castle.

The old layout of the tracks came about because from the Middle Ages up to the making of the turnpike roads the main street at Corfe was West Street. This is now hard to believe as the old street is a dead-end that disappears on to the common, where an unfenced drive that heads for Blashenwell Farm and East Orchard is still a public road.

In West Street, stone was stacked in "bankers" along the wide verges. The leading stone merchant was based at the other end, beside the Square, at Chaffey's, and the entire road thronged with people connected with the trade.

There is no evidence that marble was carved on the quarry floor, but having reached Corfe in rough-hewn blocks it was prepared for onward transit as squared blocks, and some was partially carved. Other work, however, was taken through the full process and finished by Corfe masons. That included many of the monumental effigies which were at the top of the status stakes for would be immortals.

Next in terms of prestige, and produced in much greater quantity, brasses were a common form of memorial in churches, throughout the mediaeval period. These were always set in a stone slab. The most favoured stone, yet again, was Purbeck marble. Considering the numbers that exist, and allowing for the proportion of such slabs that have disappeared through natural attrition combined with puritan disapproval, it is likely that production of this product in the Isle of Purbeck was, in total, well in excess of 10,000 slabs.

With so much work passing out of Corfe, it is to be expected that a little would remain in the village. Two carved panels, intended for tomb chests, are built into the walls of cottages in West Street, and in the church some mediaeval marble work survives, including a hard reddish 15th-century font.

More important in showing the scale of the work done on marble in Corfe village is the fact that for much of West Street the road is built on a core of marble chippings several feet thick. This debris includes fragments of foliations and mouldings and other work that was fractured and discarded. When it came to fine stone it was usually the mistakes that stayed in Dorset.

(Mediaeval archaeology / Corfe Castle)

Village focus: Oliver Vye's Lane, weaving below a sketchy castle, with Corfe as a place centre-stage in this study by Sir James Pelie in 1882.

East Street: dominated by the Keep of Corfe Castle, with the chimneys of the Greyhound glimpsed between the brow of the hill and the curtain wall.

Stone streets: aother driver's eye view of passing through Corfe Castle, climbing towards the Square (right) and Swanage (left).

Corfe Castle parish church – see entry for **St Edward the Martyr parish church**.

Corfe Castle Town Hall – see entry for **Town Hall**.

Corfe Castle village sign – see entry for **Village sign**.

Corfe Common – the mediaeval open landscape south of Corfe Castle village, registered as common land [CL34] and now in National Trust ownership, having been inherited with the Bankes Bequest [1982].

Not having been cultivated in the past millennium its scrubby 309 acres of Wealden Bed sands are covered with three-dimensional archaeology. Earliest and most conspicuous is a Bronze Age cemetery of between 2100 BC and 1500 BC, which is the easiest to visit of such monuments in Purbeck, and comprises eight round barrows. It straddles the bracken-covered ridge that runs from west to east across the centre of Corfe Common (SY 962 809). The largest of the mounds is 55 feet in diameter and about eight feet high.

Iron Age or Romano-British Celtic fields cover some 15 acres of the south-facing slope at the middle of this ridge. Six of these small fields, taking up only two acres, are particularly well-preserved (SY 957 809).

Gouges in the sides and crest of the ridge are the ruts of mediaeval sledge tracks, along which the stone for cathedrals and effigies was dragged from the quarrylands to the south, into West Street at Corfe Castle. Lesser tracks head westwards to the Copper Bridge where a Roman villa has been discovered under the arable field beyond the Corfe River.

Grazing with cows and ponies takes place as has been traditional for centuries. Those holding rights in common can turn out specified numbers of animals. Notices point out that non-qualifying stock can be impounded. It is still an elemental landscape, perhaps never more so than in the severe thunderstorm of a September afternoon in

The Square: with the 1897-erected shaft on the steps of the ancient Market Cross, and the Town House behind, dwarfed by the parish church, at Corfe Castle, pictured in the 1920s.

Northern view: taken in 1948, showing the church and ruin at Corfe Castle with a concrete telephone kiosk of the type preserved at Tyneham.

1891, when two cows were struck by lightning and killed instantly.
(Placenames / Commons / Prehistoric archaeology / Mediaeval archaeology / National Trust / Corfe Castle)

Coryton – high flyer **Air Chief Marshal Sir Alec Coryton** [born 1895] retired to Two Leas at Langton Matravers. He had been Air Officer Commanding of the Bomber Group at the Air Ministry [1942-43] and Air Commodore of the Third Tactical Air Force, in Bengal and Burma, for South East Asia Command [1944-45].

In Purbeck his pride and joy was the restoration of a 1903 De Dion Bouton which was almost a total wreck. The car was bought in Italy by Daniel Hanbury of Castle Malwood, Lyndhurst, who brought it back to England in 1910. Hanbury's daughter, Philippa, married Alec Coryton.
(People / Aviation / Langton Matravers)

Cotness – picturesque cottages and a mobile pattern of claypits that have woven a jigsaw amid

Southern view: West Street at Corfe Castle begins with the Town House and Town Hall, in the shadow of the church tower.

Corfe cottage: characteristic courtyard architecture of low-level stone roofs and flagged floors.

heathland woods and pastures comprise this hamlet on the north side of Creech Barrow Hill (SY 925 830).
(Placenames / Church Knowle)

Court Pound – 18th-century drystone-walled enclosure, on the south side of the Mount Misery stone mines, north of the main road at the western end of Langton Matravers village (SY 991 787). Court Pound Cottage stands 70 yards to the south.

The pound has 4-feet high sides, forming almost a square, about 27 feet by 29 feet. It is quite likely on the site of the mediaeval enclosure used for impounding straying sheep and other stock, either on the highway or those illicitly turned out on the parish's common lands. In post-enclosure times, however, it became the convenient compound for donkeys that were employed to turn the capstans in the nearby underground quarries.

With their closure, the gate was sealed and the compound pensioned off, becoming a walled garden protecting roses from the wind.
(Placenames / Commons / Mediaeval archaeology / Langton Matravers)

Court Pound Cottage – formerly an L-shaped pair of dwellings, dating from the 18th century, on the north side of the main road at the top end of Langton Matravers village (SY 991 787).

It is on or beside the site of the mediaeval Court House of the Wallis family; probably it was just to the south, around a courtyard beside the well, between the present cottage and the B3069. This was the hub of the western manor of Langton Matravers, which owned an offshoot block of land on the other side of the Purbeck Hills, at Langton Wallis in the moorlands of Arne parish, between Norden and Middlebere.
(Placenames / Mediaeval archaeology / Arne and Langton Matravers)

Crack Lane – originally known as Creek Lane, being the road from the eastern end of Langton Matravers (SZ 000 792) down to the former backwater which flowed inland from Swanage to Herston.
(Placenames / Langton Matravers)

Hunting lodge: the foundations of King John's building, on the summit of Creech Barrow Hill.

Creech Barrow: the heathland summit seen from the pastures of East Creech.

Creech Barrow – there is an actual ancient barrow on the otherwise natural Creech Barrow Hill, being a round mound of the "ditched bowl" type, on the twin peak of the southern spur of the summit at the 600 feet contour (SY 921 823). It is about 75 feet in diameter and six feet high, with a depression in the centre, probably being the barrow digging hole of antiquary John H. Austen.

Just west of centre it is crossed by the boundary bank with Steeple parish; as with the hill itself, most of the mound is in Church Knowle parish.
(Prehistoric archaeology / Church Knowle and Steeple)

View eastwards: just about the entire line of the Purbeck Hills are visible from the top.

Creech Barrow Hill – the volcano-shaped summit of the Tertiary formations of the Purbeck heaths, between Wareham and Church Knowle (SY 921 825). In fact it comprises two almost equal peaks. Here the sands, gravels and clays of the heathland scenery rise to an unprecedented 634 feet and actually overlook the adjoining chalkland ridge of the Purbeck Hills to the south.

Creech, or "Critch" as the cottagers call it in the foothills, is one of Dorset's few pure descendants from a Celtic word. Only about twelve Celtic placenames have been discovered in the country. This example is almost the pure Old English "cryc" (from the British "cruc") meaning a "hill or barrow". By 1280 the name was written as "Crich" and the fact that the local tongue has virtually preserved this sound (against the long-standing advice of the maps) is a fine example of the purity of popular etymology.

As the meaning of the words became blurred it picked up duplicate forms in the subsequent language, with the present Creech Barrow Hill meaning repetitiously "Hill Hill Hill".
(Placenames / Landform geology / Church Knowle)

Creech Barrow Hunting Lodge – on the summit of Creech Barrow Hill (SY 921 824). One of the three royal lodges of Purbeck Chase, from the time of King John to that of Sir Christopher Hatton who alleged that damage had been done to the building [1583], when it was depicted by a round tower on a contemporary map by Ralph Treswell [1586]. It is also shown on John Speed's county map [1610].

Stone footings survive in the grass and the bracken, in places four feet wide and 18-inches high, and can be traced to form a rectangle 30 feet from north to south by 25 feet west to east.

The Royal Commission on Historical Monuments [1970] describe a surrounding setting of banks, of some complexity, though the western side of the square is now almost invisible: "The tower remains are at the centre of a symmetrical arrangement of ditched banks, up to three feet high, which together outlined a Greek cross, the arms running downhill, within a square, measuring about 110 yards each way."
(Mediaeval archaeology / Church Knowle)

Creech Brick Works – Arthur Cobb combined brick-making with farming on the north-eastern slopes of Creech Barrow Hill, on the clayey spring-line halfway between the summit and Cotness (SY 924 826). All signs of his Victorian works and their pits have now been absorbed into the undergrowth of Cotness Wood.
(Placenames / Industrial archaeology / Church Knowle)

Creech Barrow: "from the Wareham Road", sketched by Alfred Dawson in 1882.

Crime – Purbeck people were generally credited in the county with being the authors of their own crime. Encombe House was burgled in August 1880 when about £15,000 of jewellery, silver, and gold were stolen from Lord Eldon's study. In suggesting it was the work of a local person, the Dorset County Chronicle made the point that Purbeck was still a remote land: "A stranger prowling about would certainly be noticed, for the population of the whole of the Island of Purbeck is exceedingly sparse, and the unfamiliar face is as a rule pretty well scanned by the man in blue as well as the more general inhabitant."
(Social history / Corfe Castle)

Crocodiles – common in the Isle of Purbeck, some 130 million years ago. Countless thousands of their teeth are now in Dorset County Museum, Dorchester. "They were unbelievably abundant," says scientist Paul Ensom.
(Fossils / Purbeck parishes)

Cromwell Cottage – tucked between the Manse and the railway bridge, on the north side of Sandy Hill Lane at its junction with the main road into Corfe Castle. The sometime home of Simon Regan of *Scallywag* magazine fame and a withdrawn libel action from Prime Minister John Major.
(Placenames / Politics / Corfe Castle)

Cromwell's Battery – see entry for **The Rings**.

The Cross – in the Square at Corfe Castle, inscribed for the "V.R. 1837-97" diamond jubilee of Queen Victoria, "ERECTED ON THE STEPS OF ANCIENT MARKET CROSS".
(Placenames / Memorials / Corfe Castle)

Cuckoo Pen – corner of woody scrub on the north-east side of the corner on the road into Wytch Farm where the track branches off to Wytch Passage (SY 977 856). Preserves the widespread Purbeck belief that cuckoos hibernated in such habitat.
(Placenames / Folklore / Corfe Castle)

Cuckoo Pound – Purbeck traditionally receives the first cuckoos in the country, often in the first week of April and dependably in time for Wareham Spring Fair [17 April] where, it was said, "he buys hisself a pair of breeches". Most parishes in south-east Dorset have their Cuckoo Pen or Cuckoo Pound, attaching to small and often wooded enclosures.

These date from the 18th century or earlier and seem to be close to former areas of extensive common grazing rights. There is one south of Verney Farm, on National Trust land a hundred yards west of the Swanage boundary, in the parish of Langton Matravers (SZ 008 776). The Cuckoo Pound has the only trees on the central stone plateau of southern Purbeck, midway between South Farm and Blackers Hole, half a mile from the sea.

It was a common belief, before and indeed after Gilbert White's time, that cuckoos and swallows hibernated in hollow trees. Logically – always a perilous commodity to bring to folklore – they were first heard from the Cuckoo Pound and therefore believed to have over-wintered there.

Another bit of reasoning is that before falling into disuse and becoming overgrown, these enclosures were stock pounds for sheep, bullocks, and hogs being gathered for the "Cuckoo Fair," as it was called, at Wareham. Cuckoo Fair Pounds became Cuckoo Pounds as the stock element of fair-going declined. The bird's association with the event came about because it was the reliable audio clock for the first couple of weeks in April.
(Placenames / Commons / Folklore / National Trust / Langton Matravers)

Culliford family – owners of Encombe House, from its purchase by Robert Culliford [1552] until the estate was overwhelmed by the debts of William Culliford who obtained a special Act of Parliament to enable its sale [1734]. Their old home would then be pulled down and entirely rebuilt by John Pitt [circa 1736].
(People / Corfe Castle)

D

Dancing Ledge – romantic name for its sea-level ribbon of waves, extended into a wider upper platform by 18th and 19th-century quarry workings, south of Langton Matravers (SY 998 769).

Originally quarried by the Hayward family, they came into the ownership of schoolmaster Thomas Pellatt of Durnford Preparatory School [circa 1880-1930] who rented the quarry to the Webber family. He had the quarrymen cut a swimming pool in the lower ledge for use when conditions were unsuitable for the boys' usual dip. They would strip and queue, completely naked, to take their turn in jumping off the cliff for their daily swim in the sea.

Pellatt's notable contribution to the study of English history was to be the father of Tudor biographer Hester Chapman [1899]. By about 1930 the quarry's distinctive tripod-style "whim" – the derrick or crane used to lower cut blocks into boats which carried stone to Swanage – had been removed to the slightly-inland St Aldhelm's Quarry on St Alban's Head.

An artistic footnote for what had now become one of Dorset's best loved beauty spots was its use in the filming of risqué movies by Derek Jarman who would entitle his autobiography *Dancing Ledge* [1982].

It came into National Trust ownership with the acquisition of Spyway Farm [1992]. The cliffs and limestone grasslands are floristically rich, with many rare species of orchids, as well as maritime plants. It can also claim the last of the Dorset auks and puffins. (Placenames / Natural history / Literary / National Trust / Langton Matravers)

Morning ritual: boys from Durnford School, Langton Matravers, started the day with a walk to Dancing Ledge where they stripped for a swim.

Dinosaur traces – the dinosaurs of the Purbeck Limestone Group, which have left footprints and other fossil remains across the stone plateau from Kingston and Worth Matravers to Swanage, show the presence of an exceptionally complete and diverse range of Mesozoic terrestrial animals. Their footsteps must have been unearthed for centuries, but the knowledge was then known only to masons and regarded as witchcraft rather than science, until Samuel Husband Beckles first published their existence, as a footnote in his study of Sussex Wealden fossilised footprints [1854]. He had discovered two large three-toed footprints in a slab of Purbeck marble – not a true marble, but smooth limestone – in the collection of the London Geological Society.

Purbeck has since eclipsed Beckles's Wealden specimens in number and importance. They are the only British examples of multiple trackways, much better than finds in the Jurassic limestones of Yorkshire, Sussex, and the Isle of Wight. They have established the three parishes of south-eastern Purbeck as one of the prime sites in international palaeontology. These finds on the south Dorset coast usually come from the Middle Purbeck layers which represent the earliest Cretaceous period, spanning the Late Jurassic and Early Cretaceous boundary of 145 million years ago. Some were claimed for the slightly earlier Lower Purbeck strata, in the 19th and early 20th centuries, but revisionist thinking now tends to put these into the later period, which is now bound to be disproportionately represented given that it is

Dancing Ledge: National Trust ownership of this descriptively named beauty spot completed a jigsaw of coastal acquisitions.

the only level currently being worked. Open quarries, excavated from the surface, are now the only type of workings, since underground operations became uneconomic and started to be regarded as too risky for modern times.

The fossils resulted from the deposition of mud and silt on the shoreline at a time when sea levels were falling, thereby filling the moulds left by dinosaur prints, and the preserved samples of fauna and flora also include fish, turtles, amphibians, insects, lizards, dwarf-crocodiles, rat-kangaroo mammals, pterosaurs, cycad trees (as preserved at the Fossil Forest east of Lulworth Cove) and ferns. Teeth have also survived, probably because they are often resistant to decomposition, and include those of theropod and iguanodon species. Few track-sites across the world can claim such a wide range of dinosaur types and other vertebrate fossils.

The best ever British find of fossil footprints was made by quarryman Kevin Keates, at his

Swimming pool: cut in the shelf of Dancing Ledge by quarrymen in the 1890s, so that public schoolboys could still enjoy their morning dip when the sea was rough.

working on National Trust land east of Worth Matravers village, when he drove a digger and was in the process of removing unwanted Freestone from the top of a level of the Middle Purbeck beds which he was intending to cut and lift. This was the Bottom Freestone (known to geologists as the Intermarine Member of the Lulworth Formation) and it revealed a remarkable collection of prints, running for about 200 metres, which fellow quarryman Trevor Haysom, who operates St Aldhelm's Quarry, confirmed as being those of dinosaurs. Word reached the National Trust and a professional palaeontologist was commissioned to study the site.

Dr Jo Wright's report for the National Trust on the dinosaur footprints found at Keates Quarry, Worth Matravers [1997], shows their immense significance: "It is the biggest dinosaur tracksite found in Britain, and as such, is of international importance. The site was excavated and investigated with the support of the National Trust. The footprints were made by sauropod dinosaurs and the present track surface is the actual layer on which the animals walked. The tracks were made by more than one individual – probably more than 12. At the time of track formation this site was a shelly beach beside a freshwater lagoon. The tracksite is the only evidence for the presence of sauropod dinosaurs in the Purbeck Limestone Group because no skeletal remains of these dinosaurs have been found in these sediments. The discovery of this site means that all the major groups of dinosaurs around in the Cretaceous are now known in Purbeck from footprints."

She found that 1.8 metres of Freestone and Roach beds were above the footprint surface and an estimated one metre of Freestone below. The prints were preserved "in a typical

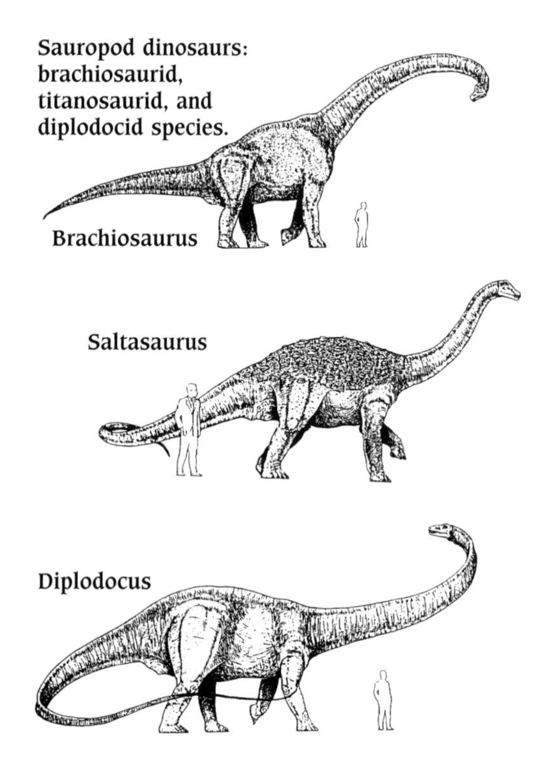

Sauropod dinosaurs: brachiosaurid, titanosaurid, and diplodocid species.

Purbeck shelly limestone" largely comprised of broken freshwater bivalve shells mixed with less quantities of oyster fragments, "agitated by waves or currents". This led her to conclude that the sediments were deposited on the beach beside a freshwater lagoon which was separated from the sea by a bank of oyster shells. The protective overlying bed had shells "chaotically orientated" with "closed, fully-articulated bivalves" which was evidence of rapid deposition, possibly during a storm. Roughly either oval or D-shaped, their maximum external length is 1,560 by 350 mm with an internal length of 1,060 by 300 mm, "and the limestone surface now preserved is the actual surface on which the dinosaurs walked". It had probably been exposed above the water level and consisted of very wet coarse-grained shelly sand that "slopped around the sides of the footprints but had enough cohesiveness to retain the rims as relief features". These sediments had probably spread during the track formation, before becoming cemented after burial, because otherwise the Purbeck sauropods would be among the largest known to science. Even allowing for that, "some of the sauropods that made these tracks were very large". The leading track-maker was therefore probably a brachiosaurid sauropod as they were commoner and larger than either diplodocid or titanosaurid sauropods during this period. The Keates Quarry prints are unique in Britain as a collection of sauropod footprints preserved in situ; and of a period where such prints are also uncommon worldwide.

The National Trust's Purbeck property manager, J. C. Homer, says that the Trust is committed to preserving the prints, though they may be treated much like the Roman mosaic floor at Woodchester in Gloucestershire which is only occasionally put on public view: "At the moment the prints are covered and we have some consultants advising on how best we can preserve the prints. Equipment is being installed to record temperatures and moisture levels. The most likely scenario appears to be for the prints to remain covered with some of them being periodically uncovered for public viewing. Periodically might mean every ten years or so. However, we have made no decision in this respect at the moment."

Purbeck quarrymen have long known of the typical three-toed footprints, about a foot across, of tridactyls, and would say: "He has been this way." A fine set of double tracks was exposed at Herston in 1961 when E. W. Suttle reopened an old quarry at Mutton Hole. There were 26 separate footprints, attributed to a megalosaurus, and in 1963 the British Museum of Natural History intervened to excavated a further 70 feet of undisturbed strata with prints across it, part of which is now displayed in the museum forecourt, in South Kensington. Prints found at Queensground, Langton Matravers, between 1963 and 1965 were unusual at the time in coming from the Freestone beds rather than the Roach bed about four feet above.

As for the catastrophe that put an end to the 140 million year reign of the dinosaurs, which met their sudden extinction at the end of the Cretaceous period 65,000,000 years ago,

evidence continues to point to an asteroid having slammed into the Earth. It seems to have plunged into Yucatan Peninsula, Central America, where the oceanic crust slides westwards, and even a large crater could have literally disappeared under the surface, subducted by plate tectonics and lost beneath the Latin American continent. There would have been nuclear-style blast waves, firestorms, and winds gusting at hundred of miles an hour. Endless steam would then cloud out sunlight from the planet for months, causing plants to die as well as organisms in the upper waters of oceans, and trigger a major ice-age. Temperature is critical for reptiles, as can be shown today by the American alligator which flourishes in 36 degrees Centigrade but soon reaches lethal limits, between 38 and 40 degrees. The mass extinction at the end of the Cretaceous killed all animals of Earth that were heavier than 25 kilograms. One hopes it is purely coincidental that the first scientific report to be commissioned by the British Government in the third millennium is a study into the chances of another asteroid hitting the planet.
(Geology / Natural history / National Trust / Worth Matravers, Langton Matravers and Swanage)

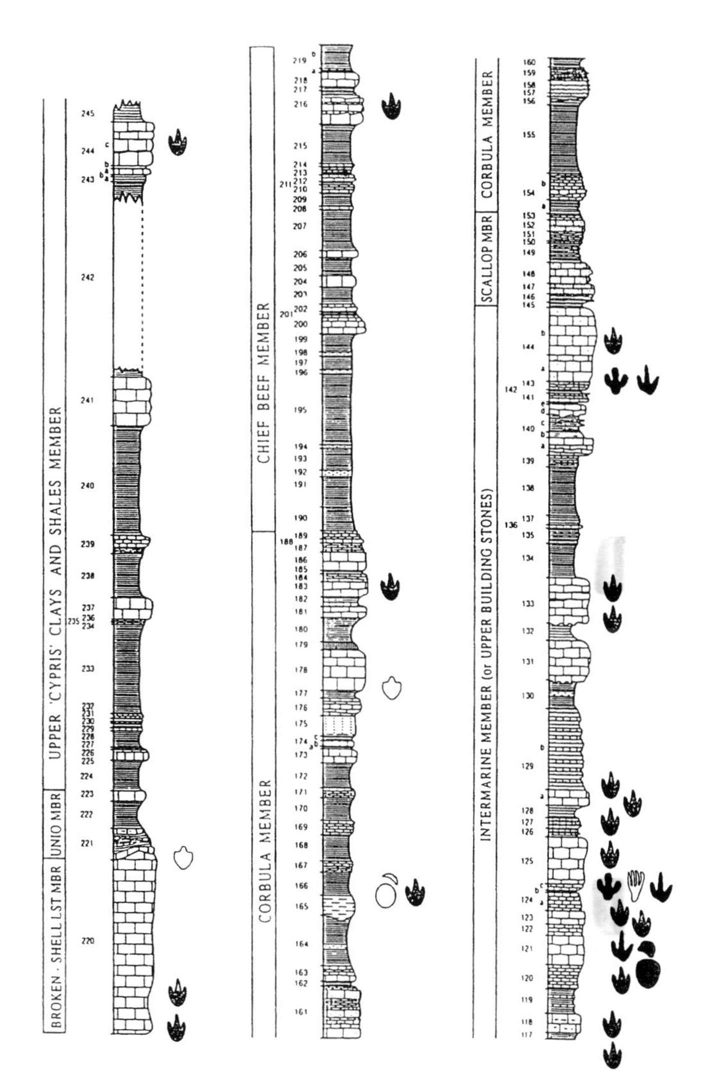

Footprint bearing: the Intermediate Bed at Keates Quarry.

Diplodocus – fossil reptile, the first British footprints of this dinosaur being discovered in a Purbeck stone quarry near Langton Matravers in 1986.
(Geology / Natural history / Langton Matravers)

Dodson's Farm – 19th-century heathland farmstead, on the east side of the lane at Creech Bottom (SY 909 842).
(Placenames / Church Knowle)

Don Pedro – Belfast schooner, lost on the ledge beneath Rope Lake Head, east of Kimmeridge [14 March 1841].
(Shipwrecks / Kimmeridge)

Drury – village physician **Dr Godfrey Dru Drury** [born 1880], the son of Colonel Edward Dru Drury of Blackheath, moved to Corfe Castle and became Purbeck's top medical man

Chaotic layout: plan of the dinosaur footprints at Keates Quarry.

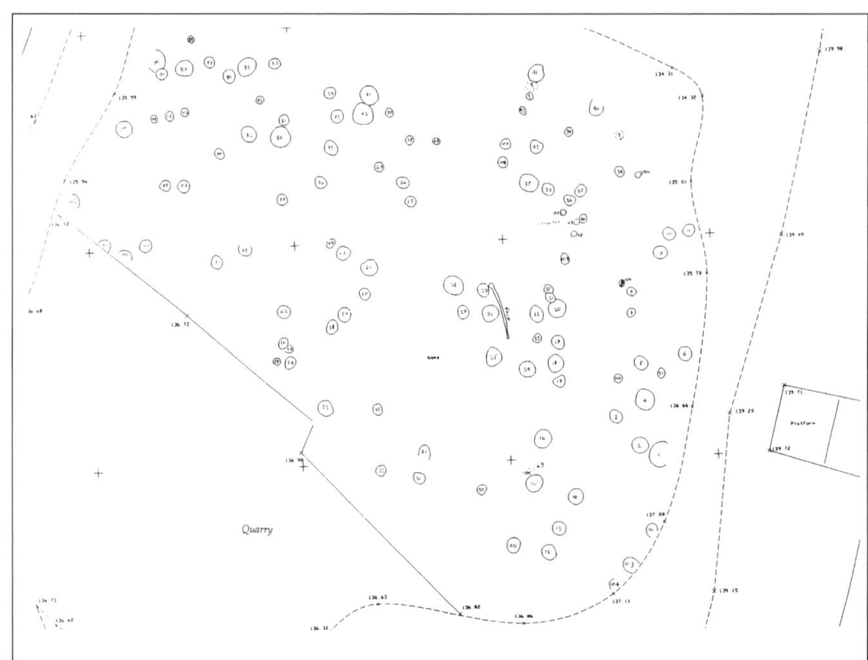

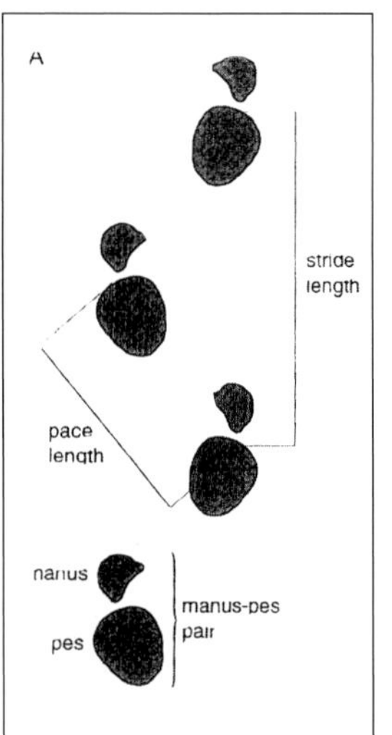

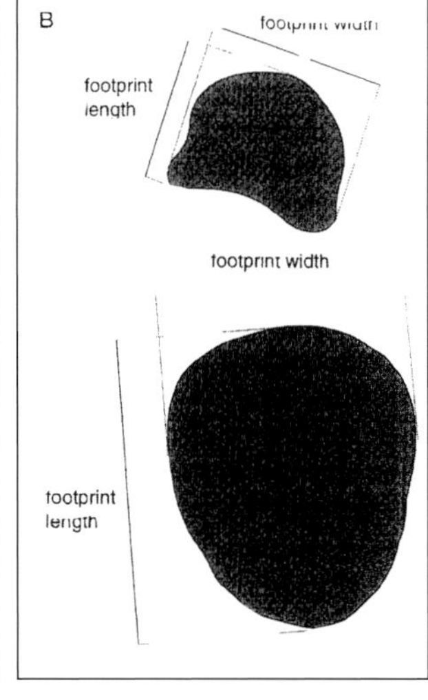

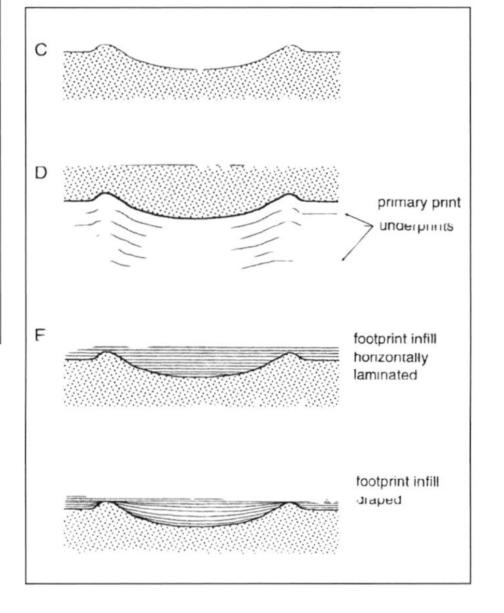

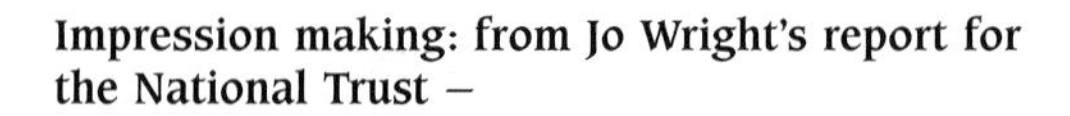

Impression making: from Jo Wright's report for the National Trust –

- (A) trackway terminology
- (B) footprint measurements
- (C) vertical cross section through a footprint showing the raised rim
- (D) illustration of the loss of detail in progressively deeper underprints
- (E) horizontal laminae infilling primary print
- (F) draped laminae infilling primary print

of the first half of the 20th century. He was Medical Officer and Public Vaccinator for the Wareham and Purbeck Union, and honorary Medical Officer to the Cottage Hospital at Swanage.

His pastime was archaeology, as the local officer for the Society of Antiquaries, and a leading member of the Dorset Natural History and Archaeological Society. In his younger days his sport was rugby football and in his mature years he captained Corfe Castle Cricket Club [1906-30].
(People / Medicine / Corfe Castle)

Dungeon Tower – see entry for **Butavant Tower**.

Dunshay Manor – 17th-century house, partially rebuilt in 1906 (SY 981 797), on the presumed site of the mediaeval home of Alice Breuer who donated marble from the nearby quarries for the building of Salisbury Cathedral. An "I A D 1642" inscription was for John Dolling, who had the house built, and "M G M 1906" for its re-builder, Commander Guy Montagu Marston RN.

For the remainder of the 20th century it was the home of the Spencer Watson family, with painter George Spencer Watson being succeeded by sculptor daughter Mary Spencer Watson. Its earlier notable inhabitant was pioneer vaccinator Benjamin Jesty, at a time when the past and present name had been corrupted into Downshay.
(Placenames / Mediaeval archaeology / Worth Matravers)

Durnford House – mediaeval farm of the Durneford family, on the north side of the High Street at Langton Matravers (SY 997 789). Converted into a small country house by the Serrell family [1725] who held it until the 1890s. The last member of the family to live there was Captain Serrell Rogers.

It then became Durnford Preparatory School, for boys, with its notable contribution to English literature being the birth there of Tudor biographer Hester Chapman [1899]. She was the daughter of the schoolmaster, Thomas Pellatt.

During the Second World War it was requisitioned by the Telecommunications Research Establishment [1940-41]. By the end of the war, having visibly suffered from occupation by boys, scientists, and soldiers, it required almost complete rebuilding, though this was done with much of the original masonry including stone-mullioned windows and door mouldings. It became the home of Lady Savage.
(Placenames / Langton Matravers)

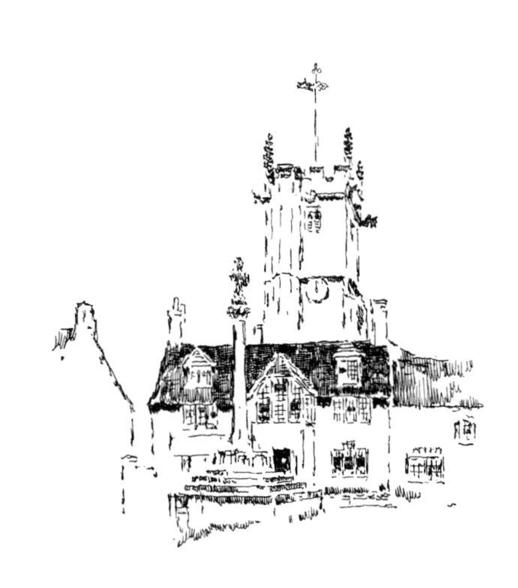

Sea view: looking inland, across Dancing Ledge, to Spyway on what is now a National Trust skyline.

Dunshay Manor: then known as Downshay, in this 1882 sketch by Alfred Dawson, with a horse-mounting block being the detail to spot (far right).

E

East Creech Farm – characterful farmyard setting on the north side of the Purbeck Hills at Church Knowle, with its pond and ducks being balanced by an unusual architectural mix on the other side of the lane (SY 929 825). There is a conventional low-level stone and brick block on the east side, dating from the late 17th century, which rises into a lofty stucco-faced 18th-century wing to the west.

The juxtaposition may be unintentional, the Royal Commission on Historical Monuments suggests, as "a projecting bay stepped forward from the south front has the appearance of having been intended for the centrepiece in a symmetrical composition" of what was to have been "a whole rebuilding scheme". Opposite, on the other side of the road, is a Georgian style gateway with mouldings and rebates.
(Placenames / Church Knowle)

East Creech Roman Villa – a tessellated floor and other substantial remains of buildings, including a Tuscan column four feet high, were found between East Creech and Norden Wood, Church Knowle (SY 935 828), after deep ploughing in 1869. Lawrence Warburton Pike, the clayfield operator of Furzebrook House, took possession of the antiquities.

The area is still arable and the Royal Commission on Historical Monuments was able to trace what seemed to be "an artificial platform" for the footings of buildings, running for 180 feet along the long axis of the field.

To the north are wooded former clay workings stretching to the Blue Pool and the area to the south, between the village and the Purbeck Hills, was also dug for ball clay in the 1960s.

Walls revealed in 1869 had internal plaster. A further mosaic floor, with a lattice design of red and white tesserae, was discovered in 1888. A sunken area of walling some distance to the north appeared to be "the basement of a hypocaust". Later surface finds have included flue-tiles, pottery, coins, and lathe-turned shale armlet cores, dating from the late 1st century through to the 4th century AD.

As for the Roman column, probably one of several supporting a veranda, its last known address was Leymore, Parkstone, Poole. This was the suburban retirement home of the clayfield-operating Pike family from Furzebrook House; since demolished with its grounds sub-divided for housing development.
(Roman archaeology / Church Knowle)

East Hill – the summit of what is otherwise known as Challow Hill, overlooking Corfe Castle from the east, with a Bronze Age burial mound at its summit (SY 964 824).
(Placenames / Prehistoric archaeology / Corfe Castle)

East Man – see entry for **Winspit strip lynchets**.

East Orchard – valley farm south of the Corfe River just inside the Church Knowle parish boundary to the south-west of Corfe Castle (SY 945 808). Listed in the Domesday Book [1087], it belonged to Shaftesbury Abbey until the Dissolution of the monasteries [1536] and then became part of the Encombe Estate until being sold by Robert Culliford to George Hayter for £1,300 [1694].

George Clavell also sold two parcels of the Smedmore Estate [1770]. Lord Eldon recovered East Orchard for the Encombe Estate, by purchasing it from Betty and William Voss [1837].
(Placenames / Church Knowle)

East Street – the present main road through Corfe Castle village, taking the traffic from Wareham to Swanage, used to be a backwater before its turnpiking in coaching days. The bog at its south end had to be filled and a new road then continued across the common.

That turned East Street into a bypass to the principal part of the town, around West Street, and virtually all fresh development then occurred around East Street until that, in turn, became the new main street.

Assassination site: the Saxon King Edward was knifed on the site of what is now the South-West Gatehouse (centre left) of the extended Norman fortress.

Town's End, as it was called with meaning, became an area for expansion with several side streets. As new building retreated from the growing traffic, there was some danger of the common suffering, but it came through unscathed into National Trust ownership and East Street's cottages still cease at Town's End, as they did in 1700.
(Placenames / Corfe Castle)

Edouard – French schooner, struck the High Ledge, Kimmeridge, in a violent gale at 23.00 hours {29 November 1842]. Ten men, one woman, and a child were drowned. Only a Newfoundland dog reached the shore.
(Shipwrecks / Kimmeridge)

Edward – assassinated **King Edward the Martyr** [960-978, reigned from 975] was murdered at Corfe Castle by members of his stepmother's household. Tradition holds that the deed was committed at the entrance to the West Bailey where the later South-West Gatehouse [the one beside the Keep] was historically known as Edward's Gate.

Seventeen-year-old Edward was the eldest son of Edgar the Peaceful and the natural heir to the throne which he took on his father's death [July 975]. He defended the Church and its religious houses against growing anti-monastic pressures, but was unpopular among the nobles, and notorious for violent outbursts of rage that shook his own household.

On the fateful evening [18 March 978] he returned from hunting in Purbeck and called at the "domus" where his stepmother, Elfthryth (commonly known as Elfrida), and her son, Ethelred, were living.

According to what appears to be an accurate account of the killing, it happened as the King was mounting his horse to leave, when an assailant seized his left hand and stabbed him with a knife. At the same moment another assailant, on the other side, put his right hand on Edward's shoulder "as though to give him a kiss" and drew the King towards him.

This unbalanced the King from his saddle and he cried out: "What are you doing,

Church statue: Edward the saint, martyred at Corfe.

Village sign: featuring the teenage King assassinated at Corfe Castle.

breaking my right hand?" His left hand had already been broken. The King's horse then broke away and he fell to the ground. He was knifed in the stomach, "his bowels being ripped open so as to fall out".

Alternatively, in the words of William of Malmesbury: "The King, finding himself hurt, set spurs to his horse, thinking to recover his company, but the wound being deep, and fainting through the loss of much blood, he fell from his horse, which dragged him by one stirrup, until he was left dead at Corfe Gate."

Professor F. M. Stenton, the authority on Anglo-Saxon England, says that the "circumstances of abominable treachery" shocked men who were conditioned to tolerate any crime of open violence. He adds: "So far as can be seen the murder was planned and carried out by Ethelred's household men in order that their young master might become king [Ethelred II]. There is nothing to support the allegation, which first appeared in writing more than a century later, that Queen Elfthryth had plotted her stepson's death."

Miraculous things were being claimed. A blind woman, at a house where Edward's body had lain, was said to have awoken at midnight with her eyesight restored and the building radiant with light. The body is then said to have been hidden "in a well at a marshy place" where it would be discovered after "illumination by a pillar of fire". The traditions came to be associated with St Edward's Fountain, a clear trickle issuing from the eastern side of Castle Hill above the Byle Brook, which became a sacred "eye-well" reputed to have healing qualities especially powerful in the treatment of failing sight.

The body was said to be uncorrupted when it was exhumed from the church at Wareham and taken to the nunnery of Shaftesbury Abbey [981] for veneration and saintly transition. The "long thin knife with which he was stabbed" was preserved in the abbey church of Faversham until the suppression of the monasteries by Henry VIII.

As for Edward's bones, allegedly, these were excavated by Wilson Claridge in the ruins of Shaftesbury Abbey [January 1931]. A small lead box was found ten inches below the ground; jammed into a recess at the base of an abbey wall. It had apparently been hidden at the dissolution. The box contained ancient bones – the skeleton of a youth – that were obviously highly regarded relics. Edward was the obvious original owner and the bones would be displayed as his until changes in the ownership of the ruins. They then went into a bank vault.

Thomas Stowell, a pathologist, had already given them a post mortem, which was reported in The Criminologist [1970], and annotated for me by Dr J. J. O'Reilly of Ferndown.

Damage to the bones fits perfectly into the accounts of Edward's death. This was a summary of the findings, with our comments in parenthesis:

"Greenstick fractures [confirm they belong to a young person of about 17]. Comminuted fracture of the left radius. Transverse fracture of ulna immediately below elbow joint. Fracture of left humerus just below shoulder joint. Transverse fracture of left femur, and running from it a greenstick fracture with separation of the head. Fracture of the upper end of the left tibia with an associated greenstick fracture. [The injuries are consistent with him having been forced back over the saddle by his assailants, and then damaged by the weight of his own body as he fell from the horse.] Fracture of neck of right shoulder blade. Upper part of humerus missing but almost certainly fractured. Fracture of right radius at lower end [due to the arm being violently twisted by an assailant]. Fracture of right hip socket. Oblique fracture of lower end of right femur."

These injuries show that the King fell heavily on his right shoulder and hip, with the head of the right femur being driven forcibly into the socket.

There was no longer any reasonable doubt that the Shaftesbury bones are those of the assassinated King Edward, though those in the town who could have stopped them being offered to the Russian Orthodox Church failed to respond to the evidence and preferred historic scepticism to modern evidence. No one explained quite why it should have been that worthy institution, the heirs to St Basil, but at least it showed someone wanted the relics. As is always the case, once someone shows an interest in acquiring an object, the rest then awake to its existence.

(People / Politics / National Trust / Corfe Castle)

Edward II: penny from the reign of 1307-27, that ended with imprisonment at Corfe being followed by his barbaric assassination.

Edward – assassinated **King Edward II** [1284-1327; reigned from 1307] spent his penultimate spell of illegal imprisonment at Corfe Castle. One of the prime conspirators was Sir John Maltravers [1290-1364], a Knight of the Shire of Dorset. Maltravers had been forced to flee the country after the defeat of Lancaster at the Battle of Boroughbridge, in Yorkshire, in the War of the Roses [1322]. He returned to England and Dorset in 1327, to talk treason with Edward's wife, Isabella (the daughter of Philip IV of France). She resented Edward's homosexuality and had taken a lover, Roger Mortimer. The trio wanted freedom and power; they conspired to hold Edward prisoner at Corfe.

Having deposed the monarch, Maltravers and his brother-in-law Thomas, Lord Berkeley, then took Edward to the family seat of Berkeley Castle in Gloucestershire, where Thomas was paid £5 a day for the King's keep. He seems to have been less keen on the ultimate act which took place when Berkeley was away from his castle.

The regicide would be carried out by Sir John Maltravers and his aide William Gurney [September 1327]. The King was held down on a table and a red-hot poker pushed into his anus.

In the almost quaint words of a contemporary chronicler, Higden, the King "was sleyne with a hoote broche putt thro the secret place posteriale". His death shrieks were said to have resounded through the castle. Not only had they regarded this as an appropriate method of killing him – revenge for his sodomy – but it had the important advantage of leaving no obvious mark, which is why it is used for killing fur-skinned animals such as cheetahs. A natural death was claimed and the body put on view to refute suspicions of foul play.

The outcome was that Mortimer and Isabella, now the Queen Mother, ruled the country in the name of the late King's son, Edward III, who was only 15-years-old.

Ian McQueen investigated the Dorset links with Maltravers in the Transactions of the Monumental Brass Society for 1966. He writes

Regicide remembered: being recorded by Philip Brannon in his caption to this 1862 print, "Edward the Martyr's or Second Gate & Great Sunken Tower, Corfe Castle".

that Sir John was given the task of inducing the dead King's brother Edmund, Earl of Kent, to plot against the new regime and provide an excuse for Edmund's disposal.

This Maltravers achieved by lying to Edmund that Edward was still alive and held at Corfe Castle. It appears that Edward was transferred to Corfe for only a short time during his imprisonment but that elaborate pretences were staged to indicate that he continued to be held there. These extended to the hosting of a dinner party at which the King was impersonated.

Edmund then fell into the trap of scheming to achieve his brother's escape. He was convicted of high treason and beheaded.
(People / Politics / National Trust / Corfe Castle)

Edward – future **King Edward VII** [1841-1910; reigned from 1901] first visited Dorset at 14, as Albert Edward, Prince of Wales, known to the royal family as Bertie. He came incognito, with two aides, on a walking tour [September 1856]. They stayed at the Bath hotel, Bournemouth [night of the 23rd] and next day walked along the beach to Sandbanks, were ferried to Brownsea Island, and walked through Parkstone to Poole, where they spent the night at the Antelope Hotel [24th]. They then went to Wimborne to see Wimborne Minster and stayed at the Crown hotel [25th].

Next day they reached Swanage and booked into the Royal Victoria Hotel [26th]. The following day they walked to St Alban's Head and inland via Kingston to join their carriage at Corfe Castle for the journey onwards to Wareham and Dorchester, where they stopped for two nights at the King's Arms [27th and 28th].

The 28th was Sunday and they attended morning service at St Peter's Church where the Prince was spotted. "The young Prince walked the streets with the jaunty independent air of an Englishman and chatted without the smallest restraint or without the slightest show of condescension with the poorest of the inhabitants," it was reported. "He had even entered into a personal negotiation with the owner of an extraordinarily sagacious dog with a view to the purchase of the animal."

Without the said canine they walked the Roman road to Eggardon Hill and descended to Askerswell and Bridport, where they stopped for the night [29th] before going on to Honiton for the following evening [30th]. The tour was then cancelled [2 October 1856] because the secret was out and it was stirring an embarrassing wave of public interest.
(People / Royalty / Askerswell, Bournemouth, Bridport, Corfe Castle, Poole, Swanage, Wareham, Wimborne, and Worth Matravers)

Edward's Gate – see entry for **South-West Gatehouse**.

Eldon, Earls of – see entries for the **Scott family** and **Encombe**.

Eldon Arms – stone-roofed public house in the centre of Kingston village (SY 957 797), now named the Scott Arms, for the family rather than its title. Giles Foot was the mid-Victorian publican [1851], followed by Charles Bartlett [1889], through to the Great War and 1920s, with Mrs Georgina Bartlett holding the licence during the 1930s and the Second World War.
(Placenames / Corfe Castle)

Eldon Seat – superb block of Purbeck stone, eight feet long and four feet wide, with another massive ashlar as the backrest, set on a raised podium in an outcrop of undercliff below the great inland escarpment of Swyre Head (SY 938 779). It has a delightful view of the sheltered mini-landscape of the Big Wood and the lake across to Encombe House nestling beneath its trees and the huge slope.

The first stone was laid by Lady Elizabeth Repton on 13 October 1835. Beside it there is a memorial to Pincher, the late Lord Chancellor Eldon's last dog, who outlived his master by two years and died in 1840.
(Placenames / Memorials / Corfe Castle)

Eldon Sidings – operational hub of the Fayle Company claypit operations at Norden from 1885 until 1970. The sheds were established on the eastern side of the standard gauge Swanage Railway (SY 957 828) with a narrow gauge mineral line to western workings crossing this by a bridge (SY 958 827). It then crossed the main road at a level crossing (SY 956 826).

Items of rolling stock lain abandoned and rusting on overgrown arms of the railway until the last remnants of the system were ripped up in 1971.
(Placenames / Industrial archaeology / Railways / Corfe Castle)

Elinor – a brig from Beer, Devon, stuck on the ledge beneath Rope Lake Head, east of Kimmeridge, but refloated [27 June 1842].
(Shipwrecks / Kimmeridge)

Encombe – as near perfection as any Dorset great house and estate, not only for the pleasantly simple south-facing frontage that was completed in 1770, but in its idyllic situation in an isolated coastal valley south of Corfe Castle (SY 945 786). This has a restrained opening seawards down the South Gwyle to a waterfall into Egmont Bight,

Encombe House: Scott family values and the politics of patronage turned it into the greatest of the Purbeck seats.

between Kimmeridge and Chapman's Pool, but is remarkable for its Golden Bowl, created by a swirl of hills from Swyre Head around to Houns-tout Cliff, that protects not only the house but also its lawns, lake and woods from all the drawbacks of a location 1,000 yards from the sea.

The main part of Encombe House was the creation of John Pitt, who had started rebuilding "the much decayed" ancient family seat of the Culliford family in 1734. The estate passed to his son and heir William Morton Pitt. Lost through his imprudent philanthropy, it was sold [1807] to John Scott MP, later created Earl of Eldon, for whom William Bushrod of Weymouth largely refitted the interior, with new marble fireplaces, moulded ceiling and cornices, in a series of repairs [1811-13] that followed a fire.
(Placenames / Country houses / Corfe Castle)

Encombe mushroom – an oversized mushroom, from Encombe Valley, is recorded by J. Britton and E. Brayley in their *Topographical Description of the County of Dorset* [1803]: "In the year 1753 was found on this farm a mushroom that weighed 8-lbs, was 15 inches long, ten round, eight deep, and about in the form of a figure of eight."
(Natural history / Corfe Castle)

Encombe Obelisk – 40-feet high, tapering in Egyptian needle-style, standing at the 425-feet contour above Quarry Wood at the landward end of Encombe Valley (SY 946 791). Built with blocks of Purbeck limestone, from the cliff-quarries at Seacombe, it was erected for Sir William Scott, first Baron Stowell [1745-1836] who was a close friend of Dr Samuel Johnson and the pre-eminent draughtsman of international maritime law. Inscriptions record the laying of the foundation stone by Lady Frances Jane Bankes [28 May 1835].

Sir William was still living and a stone states that it was raised "in honour of Sir William Scott, created Baron Stowell". The lettering gives Lady Frances's second initial as "I", there being no "J" in the Roman alphabet.
(Memorials / Corfe Castle)

Encombe Rock Bridge – primitive-style megalithic construction over a gully in the wooded ravine 450 yards south of Encombe House, carrying the farm track from the east into Encombe Dairy (SY 945 781). It is built in rustic fashion with great semi-tooled boulders of Purbeck stone, without cement, and has monolithic uprights to ensure it also looks bizarre from a distance.

It is said to date from the time of John Scott, second Earl of Eldon, and I take it to be a piece of fun by architect George Stanley Repton, the youngest son of landscape-gardener Humphry Repton. Having eloped with Lady Elizabeth Scott [1817] he made his peace with the first Earl of Eldon [1820] and henceforth, until his death in 1858, the estate had its own Gothic architect.
(Placenames / Bridges / Corfe Castle)

F

Fayle's Tramway – Dorset's first railway was the creation of Benjamin Fayle, a London potter, who bought the claypits at Norden which appear to have been established by a man named Chiffney in 1795. Fayle initially used an old cart-track, north-eastwards across the heath from Norden Farm, to Middlebere Lake inlet on Poole Harbour. He learned of horse-drawn tramways in the North, from his customers in the Staffordshire potteries, and would have been aware of the opening of the Surrey Iron Railway [1803], by which time he was contracting a railway engineer to bring modern methods to the Isle of Purbeck. It would be operational for 40 years before the first mainline railway crossed into Dorset.

The narrow-gauge New Line he cut across the heath, westwards from the valley of the Corfe River, had graceful sweeping curves, shallow cuttings, and low embankments. Its skilfully gentle gradient manoeuvred a gradual drop from the 100 feet contour to sea level.

It was built in 1806 at a cost of £7,500, pit manager Willis told agricultural surveyor William Stevenson a few years later. The wage of the clay cutters was then 3 shillings 6 pence per day.

As for the innovation, in improving efficiency it also brought unemployment, cutting Fayle's labour force of about 250 "before the iron railway was made" to "upwards of 100 men" in 1809. Their numbers stabilised at this lower level. Nearly a hundred went on Fayle Company's annual outing in 1876, which was from Swanage to Portsmouth, in the *Royal Albert* paddle steamer.

Production, however, increased as a result of the railway. It rose from 14,500 tons of ball clay in 1802 to 22,000 tons in 1808. That was 11,000 wagon loads.

Stevenson described the five-wagon trains that the horses hauled: "The clay is conveyed on small carriages with four iron wheels, carrying two tons each. Three horses draw ten tons to the sea-side three times a day, at the expense of about sixpence a ton weight."

The cuttings of the two original spurs of the line can still be seen at Norden, now carrying brackish streams from a ferny wood into culverts beneath a bypassed section of the A351. Narrow stone-arched bridges take them under a section of the old course of the main road, the northern being 50 yards south-east of the eastern end of footpath 75, and the other 150 yards south-east of this point – just around the bend which is now bypassed. The

Fayle's Tramway: "BF 1807" keystone on the northern tunnel (now blocked) of Dorset's first railway, at Norden

Central cutting: the clay railway from Norden dropping down through Middlebere Heath, east of Hartland Moor.

Stone sleepers: surviving on the approach to the harbourside embarkation point for Fayle's Tramway, at Middlebere Quay.

original arched underground lengths now join lower square-topped drains under the 20th-century carriageway. The northern of the little tunnels, six feet wide and 75 feet long, still has its dated keystone: "BF 1807". That of the other one has lost its inscription but it is said to have been "dated in 1848"; though that may have been a date of repair rather than building.

By 1811 there were three separate lines branching away from the business end of the railway. Two went into the early pits on the Middlebere side of the road that pre-dated the railway and would be exhausted by the 1930s. The third was the northern one that went under the turnpike road into what was becoming the main area for future exploration. It was duplicated by the southern tunnel in order to enable empty wagons to return to the pits without disrupting production. This was the only dual-line section of the railway; otherwise wagons coming the other way had to divert into en route passing loops at Langton Wallis Heath, Hartland Moor, and on the Middlebere peninsula.

Seth White, a driver on the tramway before 1850, remembered that the tops of the horse harnesses "had to be cut off to clear the roofs of the tunnels".

Mechanisation came to the line with the introduction of *Tiny*, a steam engine built by Stephen Lewin at his foundry in Mount Street, Poole. "S. LEWIN, ENGINEER, POOLE 1868" was the stamping on her original cylinders. The foundry had been established five years earlier and employed more than a hundred men in the production of his own distinctive style of miniature locomotives, as well as stationary engines, and boilers. By 1877 he was prosperous enough to retire to the Riviera. *Tiny* survived in regular use for 80 years.

Meanwhile, by 1880 the north tunnel at Norden was virtually out of use and then its line to the east was severed by the construction of the standard-gauge railway from Wareham in 1885. On the east side of this tunnel were the offices and repair sheds of Norden Clay Works, including a blacksmith's shop for wagon repairs and horse-shoeing. The coming of the steam railway caused the nub of the Fayle organisation to be moved half a mile south-eastwards to Eldon Sidings, and from there the lines again extended back across the Corfe road, though this time over a level crossing.

Fayle's Tramway was a so-called plateway, with the trucks having flangeless wheels. Instead the flange was on the rails. These were

L-shaped and in 3-feet sections, tongued at one end and grooved at the other, which slotted together. There was a small hole through which each was nailed to a stone sleeper.

There was a separate row of sleepers set in the ground on each side. These stones were 18-inches square and 9-inches deep, weighing about 70 pounds, with a "hole to receive an oak plug, to which the rails were fastened by means of a large-headed nail driven between the continuous ends, through a small cavity which is left for the purpose". The narrow groove that was cut in the sleeper was about 5-inches wide and is visible in the stones that survive at Middlebere Quay. Some retain the iron pegs that held the rails.

Originally there were more than 10,000 sleepers on the line. A few would be re-used as paving stones at Langton Wallis Cottage.

The gauge was 3-feet 9-inches, an unusual width, which would later be adopted for its successor mineral line, the Goathorn Railway of a century later [1905].

One operating difficulty on a plateway carrying such heavy loads was that the wheels ground "against the flange or rib on the bar" and needed incessant greasing. An inventor turned his mind to the problem. In 1811 the Collinge axle-tree was patented and put into immediate production at an engineering works in Westminster Road, Lambeth. They were already in use at Norden when Stevenson visited the pits to gather information for his survey, which was published in 1812.

It is possible to trace the line beside Norden Cottages, northwards into National Trust land at Hartland's Farm. From here the entire course is on Trust land which was acquired with the Bankes Estate [1982]. It passes New

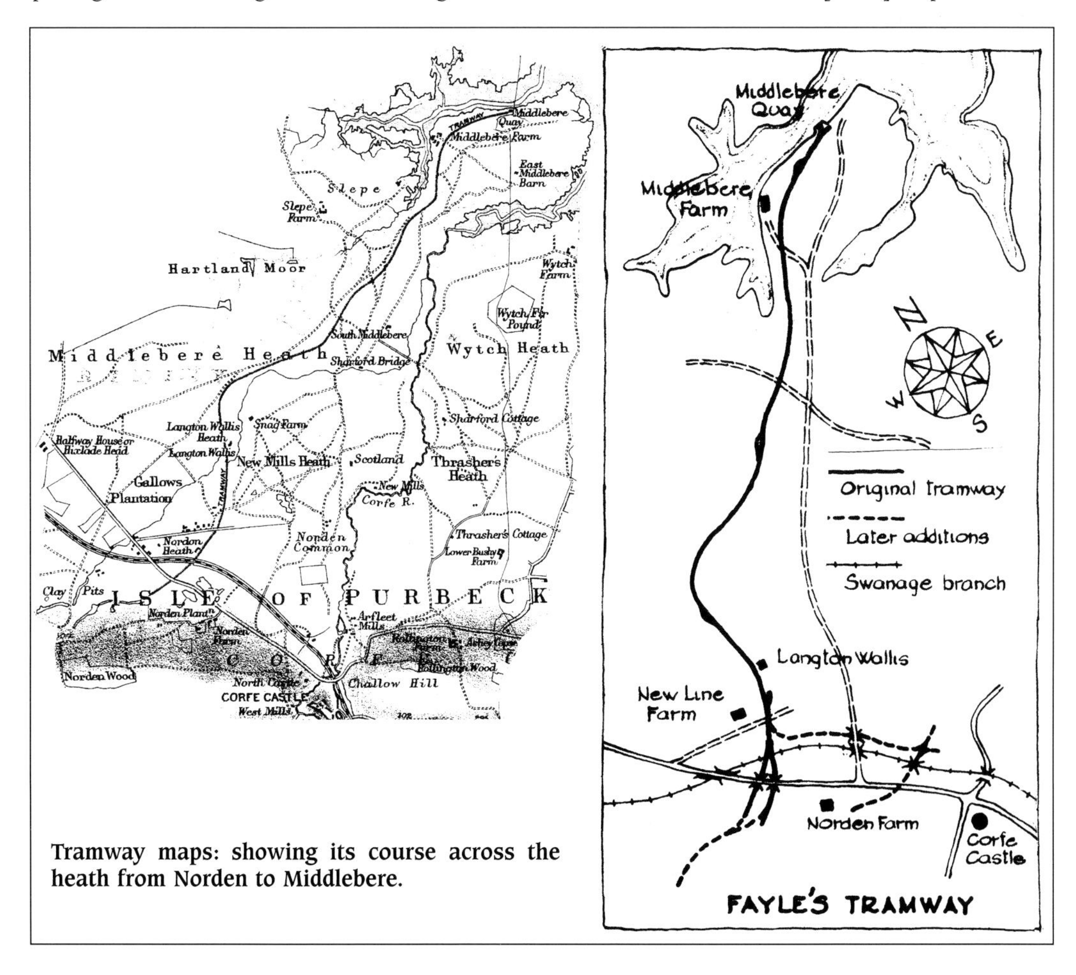

Tramway maps: showing its course across the heath from Norden to Middlebere.

Line Farm (preserving the original name of the railway) and Langton Wallis Cottage, where the gap in a short section of steep embankment was caused when the dam burst after the culvert had blocked, following closure of the line. The tramway then crosses Langton Wallis Heath and Middlebere Heath. On the latter, east of Hartland Moor, there is a well preserved cutting, and a long low embankment then carries the line across marshy ground. The gradual descent continues along a low ridge above Slepe, into its final curve east of Middlebere Farm, to a ruined building at Middlebere Quay and the decaying timbers of its jetty.
(Industrial archaeology / National Trust / Railways / Arne and Corfe Castle)

Ferguson and Muschamp – established a gas-works at Wareham, extracting fuel from Kimmeridge shale [1855-58], on the site at Sandford that later became Wareham Pottery and was re-developed for housing in the 1970s.
(Industrial archaeology / Kimmeridge and Wareham)

Ferry tragedy – the market boat from Corfe Castle to Poole, on its return trip across Poole Harbour to Wytch Passage, came to grief off Brownsea Island [9 March 1759]. Thirteen people drowned as it sank in the mud.
(Shipwrecks / Corfe Castle, Poole and Studland)

Fig Tree Cottage – typical stone-roofed Purbeck cottage of the 18th century on the south side of the High Street at Langton Matravers (SY 999 788). It has a low roof-line with the two upstairs windows being virtual dormers in attic bedrooms.

This was the home of 19th-century quarry operator Charles Hayward. He was also the village Sub-Postmaster and the tiny room to the right of the front door doubled as his sorting office and shop; stamps being sold through an arched opening in the wall to customers standing in the narrow flagstone passage.

Hayward also owned the squeezed "one up, one down" Little Fig Tree on the east side of Fig Tree Cottage, which was the home of his daughter and housekeeper, Mrs Mary Trupp [1823-94].
(Placenames / Postal history / Langton Matravers)

Firestone – a block of stone being cut by quarrymen at Winspit smoked and flamed when touched and gave several of the workers minor burns, in 1949. It was described as having glowed before dawn like "a huge lump of sugar lit from inside". It was believed to be impregnated with phosphorus.
(Geology / Industrial archaeology / Worth Matravers)

First Tower – projecting from the 14th-century curtain wall to the west of the Outer Gatehouse at Corfe Castle, being built between 1250-85. Adjoining is walling of 1212-15 and then the Second, Third and Fourth Towers, also of those earlier dates.
(Placenames / Mediaeval archaeology / Corfe Castle)

Fitzworth – the peninsula on the southern shore of Poole Harbour on the western side of Ower backwater, north-east of Corfe Castle (SY 990 870). The local name, Vitower, perpetuates several centuries of recorded forms, from "Vytower" in 1617 to "Vitt-Ower" used by Hutchins's editors in 1861.

The meaning, from "Fitoure" of 1545, could have been "disputed shore" but the alternative official form, first recorded in 1571, brings a compelling second choice. Fitzworth was a detached offshoot of the manor of Worth Matravers where the wife of Hugh Fitz Grip held land in 1068. Worth manor passed from the Fitz Paynes to the Fitz Alans in the 14th century. "Fitz's shore" therefore seems the much more likely name.
(Placenames / Corfe Castle)

Forge Cottage – 18th-century home of the blacksmiths of Langton Matravers, the last of the line being Harry Ryall, after whose death it

Clay works: as approached by what was still a working railway, at Furzebrook, in 1956.

was stripped and rebuilt [1955]. The premises stood on the south side of the High Street (SY 999 788), with the eastern part being a small tackle shop, and a passage on the west side led to the forge and yard at the rear.
(Placenames / Social history / Langton Matravers)

Fortitude – a London brig, which became a total loss on the rocks beneath St Alban's Head [14 January 1839].
(Shipwrecks / Worth Matravers)

Fourth Tower – between the Third Tower and the South-West Gatehouse, on the north-eastern side of the Outer Bailey at Corfe Castle, built in 1212-15.
(Placenames / Mediaeval archaeology / National Trust / Corfe Castle)

Fox Inn – on the west side of West Street, with its sign stating: "Reputed to be the Oldest Pub in Corfe Castle, circa 1568." The present building appears to be 18th century, with a long passageway to the deep recesses of the traditional meeting-place of the Company of Marblers and Stonecutters of the Isle of Purbeck.

It is from here on Shrove Tuesday that they kick a football and carry a peppercorn for the rent, to reassert their right of way across the heath to the mediaeval stone port at Ower Quay, on Poole Harbour.
(Placenames / Mediaeval archaeology / Folklore / Corfe Castle)

Fry – pastel artist **James Fry** [1911-85] moved with his wife Ivy from Horsham to Bay Tree House, at 130 East Street, Corfe Castle [1954]. Later they moved to the former barn of Dollings Farm, being 148 East Street, where he established a studio [1964]. He was a familiar figure on a butcher's bicycle, carrying his easel, paints, palet and camera in the baskets, until he fell off in his final decade. He would die at home, after refusing hospital treatment, and left a collection of several thousand Purbeck slides which would be donated to Dorset County Museum.
(People / Artists / Corfe Castle)

Furzebrook Clay Works – comprising Furzebrook Clay Store, Furzebrook Shredders, Furzebrook Drier, Furzebrook Mill, and the Control Laboratory of ECC Ball Clays Limited. Its evolution is described in the entry for Furzebrook Railway.
(Industrial archaeology / Church Knowle)

Furzebrook Railway – originally a horse-drawn tramway, constructed by claypit-operators Watts, Hatherley and Company [1838-39], northwards from the Blue Pool at Furzebrook (SY 935 835), in a straight line for two miles to Ridge Wharf (SY 938 871) on the tidal stretch of the River Frome downstream from Wareham. From here the clay was towed downstream in barges by the sail-tug *Purbeck*, until the steam revolution of the brave new world, brought about by the sensational and successful cross-Channel voyage of the tiny vessel *Sirius* in Queen Victoria's accession year [1837].

Purbeck would be replaced by the Ridge-built steam-tug *Frome* [1844] and a second paddle-steamer named *Purbeck* [circa 1850]. The latter crunched James Mussell of Wareham in an horrific paddle-wheel accident off Russell Quay, Arne [August 1852].

By now the Furzebrook clay workings were being bought out by brothers William and John Pike, with Pike Brothers being managed by William's son, William Joseph Pike, from offices in North Street, Wareham [1850s]. Sidings and Ridge Clay Works were built near Ridge Farm (SY 937 865).

Tramway wagons were at one stage allowed to run unattended across the heath, with gravity taking them down a one-in-30 gradient; as they approached Ridge a pair of catch-points at Nutcrack Lane triggered a sledge-brake in one of the wagons. Once the inevitable happened and a rake of five fully-loaded wagons came down the line before the brakesman reset the points. The train careered through Ridge at what was described as "hundreds of miles an hour" and ran off the ends of the rails, sinking a barge in the water below.

The gauge was 2-feet 8.5-inches (a section of rail is still embedded in the Arne Road) and mechanisation came with Purbeck's first steam locomotive, being 0-6-0T *Primus* [1866]. Her successors were *Secundus*, *Tertius*, *Quartus*, *Quintus*, *Sextus*, and *Septimus*.

Inland, the original course of the line turned west from the north side of the Blue Pool – as we know what was then an open pit – and headed for a series of workings north of Blackhills (SY 927 833). This barrow-studded ridge, now Blackhills Plantation, is north-east of Cotness. The Pike Brothers were moving westwards towards the rich deposits of Creech and Povington, while their main competitors, Fayle at Norden, were looking in the other direction, to Newton and Goathorn.

The last of the steam-tugs was the *Allen*, named for her Harry Allen, who was her builder at Ridge Wharf [1932]. By this time the sheds had moved to Furzebrook Clay Works (SY 932 841), with sidings on to the standard gauge Swanage Railway. Pike Brothers' own railway section employed three drivers, two fitters, three runner boys, four platelayers, and two carpenters. The livery was green. Wooden wagons were used throughout the Pike network and more than 100 were in regular use. One veteran carried the date "July 1880".

Contraction of the system followed during the Second World War, starting with closure of the original line from Furzebrook to Ridge [1943]. There was still an intricate, interwoven network extending three miles from Furzebrook to West Creech, with numerous offshoots and sidings, particularly around Cotness and East Creech.

In 1949, the historic rivalry of Purbeck's clay companies came to an end, when they merged into Pike Brothers, Fayle and Company Limited. The old wooden wagons were replaced with V-shaped, all metal, side-tipping trucks.

W. J. K. Davies examined more than 50 end-tipping wooden wagons at the close of the Furzebrook sector of the railway [1955]. They were built to carry clay from the pits to weathering beds: "The body is mounted centrally on the frame, but overhangs at one end with a corresponding clear section of the frame at the other end [for the next wagon to overhang it]. In service, these wagons always ran with the overhang nearest the weathering beds, to facilitate the dumping of clay. To enable the mine's locomotive to couple-up to these wagons, a small four wheeled flat truck was permanently coupled in front of the locomotive."

Davies also inspected ten side-tippers used between the weathering beds and the Furzebrook depot. There were another 30 "trap-door" wagons that either opened at the ends or the sides. Each of the wagons, of all types, had a supporting frame of oak and a box of elm.
(Industrial archaeology / Railways / Arne and Corfe Castle)

Furzey Island – the 35-acre sister isle to Brownsea, across White Ground Lake from the south-west corner of its much larger neighbour, where the former Branksea Pottery dwarfed its almost flat profile which is barely 30 feet in height (SZ 012 871).

The house was built by Lord and Lady Iliffe for their daughter [1935] to designs by Sir Edward Maufe, who was the architect of red-brick Guildford Cathedral. Fursey Island was given much more sympathetic treatment, with an extensive veranda facing Green Island to the south-west, though it also shows his penchant for innovation. Modern materials included silicate blocks, a form of reconstituted granite, and window glass an inch thick.

Lady Iliffe employed wartime sailor Alan Bromby [born 1923] and he worked on Furzey for a decade [1948-58] before moving on to Round Island and becoming almost a legend as head warden of Brownsea Island for the National Trust [1962].

Meanwhile, Furzey Island passed to Lady Iliffe's eldest grandson, during whose time the rhododendrons became a jungle, until its sale to Birmingham businessman H. Newton Mason for £46,000 [1969]. He carved out lawns on each side of the house, which regained its south-facing views across the South Deep to the conifers of Goathorn peninsula, and entertained his staff at a number of lavish functions.

Next, briefly but with some irony, its owner was oil magnate Algy Cluff [born 1940]. He sold it to British Petroleum plc [1983] who probed the northern extremities of their Wytch Farm oilfield from two sites drilled in its pine woods. The company is now discussing its future after oil, with ten acres already being formally designated as a nature reserve [1999]. The parish clerk at Corfe Castle, Stephen Yeoman, has urged that it should be kept for "community and environmental benefit" and cautions against its return to the previous "seaside gem" ownership of entrepreneurs or hideaway personalities. "We want to come up with a thumping good idea which BP Amoco will support. We couldn't

Furzey Island: oil amid the pines, bringing about the construction of a new jetty, in 1985.

afford to take on the island as a parish but perhaps the district or county councils could acquire it."

The Open Spaces Society, founded in 1865 and Britain's oldest national conservation organisation, has suggested that the National Trust would make the obvious owners, given that it could be wardened from Brownsea Island and incorporated into the round trips of pleasure boats operating from Sandbanks and Poole. The society suggest a similar mix of public access and nature sanctuary protection as on the sister island but Dorset Wildlife Trust expressed concern that Furzey is "too small and sensitive for uncontrolled access".

(Placenames / Industrial archaeology / Corfe Castle)

Oil owned: but British Petroleum are already preparing Furzey Island for a greener future.

G

Gee Chain navigation system – one of ten transmitting stations, nationally, was RAF Worth Matravers in Dorset [1942-70]. Operating in pairs, these provided accurately timed radio pulses for British aircrew, who used the signals to plot their aircraft's position by intersecting hyperbolic lines on a pre-printed lattice chart.

The system "revolutionised the effectiveness of RAF bombing raids" with "targets being found and bombed as never before". The first to use it operationally was a Wellington of 115 Squadron from RAF Watton, Norfolk, captained by Pilot Officer Jack Foster.

The stations continued in operation through the Cold War, but by the late 1960s the Ministry of Defence considered that other ground-based navigation aids and airborne systems had made Gee obsolete, causing the abandonment of the stations and demolition of their tall aerials.
(Aviation / Worth Matravers)

Georgiana – French barque of 400-tons, built at Le Havre in 1856, washed ashore in a south-westerly gale on the east side of Chapman's Pool [11 July 1866]. Her crew of 13 and two passengers were saved by a rocket-line fired from the shore by Coastguards. The master, Martin de la Barre, thought he had been driven on to the Isle of Wight; a not unreasonable assumption. He had aboard 160 tons of coffee, 40 tons of cocoa, and 60 tons of mahogany. A total of 2,400 bags of coffee and cocoa would be salvaged.
(Shipwrecks / Worth Matravers)

Ghost Army – see entry for **Phantom Army**.

Glebe House – the former Rectory in the Square at Corfe Castle, built in the late 17th century to replace its predecessor, on the same site, which was destroyed during the Civil War sieges of the castle.

The replacement was described as a "small mean structure" until it was extended and transformed by Rev William Bond, during his incumbency [1800-20]. Several original windows were blocked and the house was generally heightened. It was also given a symmetrical frontage with an octagonal bay projecting into the street. Stucco-covering concealed the blocked windows.
(Placenames / Corfe Castle)

Goathorn Pier – timber jetty on the northern tip of the Goathorn peninsula (SZ 016 863), then known as Goat Ord Point, permission for which was given by the Admiralty [1852] as the wharf for claypits being dug on Newton Heath, a mile to the south.

In its final working phase it extended about 250 feet, to the edge of the South Deep, having become the shipment point for Fayle and Company operations, with the construction of a six-mile railway across the heath from Norden Clay Works [1905].

This ceased working with the Second World War, when the peninsula was used as a bombing range and for live-fire military training, and post-war the pier decayed into a ramp of stones and half a dozen insubstantial posts. Conifers also spread to the shoreline, as the coastal extremity of Purbeck Forest, which had been planted inland across Rempstone Heath to within a mile of Corfe Castle [1948].
(Placenames / Industrial archaeology / Railways / Corfe Castle and Studland)

Goathorn Railway – the longest mineral line in Dorset, replacing Fayle's Tramway, built across five miles of heathland from Eldon Sidings at Norden (SY 957 829) to Newton (SZ 010 845) where it linked with an existing rail-track to Goathorn on Poole Harbour [1905]. It was the same, rare, 3-feet 9-inch gauge as the original horse-drawn tramway, though by the time of replacement that had long been mechanised. Steam engine *Tiny* [1868-1948] moved on to the Goathorn operation, and was joined by *Thames* [built 1902], bought from London County Council.

Years before, in 1852, the Admiralty had given permission for a wharf on Goathorn peninsula and by 1859 a fresh series of claypits at Newton were in full production and a railway ran from there to the South Deep of Poole Harbour at Goathorn Pier. Newton Clay Works (SZ 013 848) was a sizeable concern and with its opening the labour force of Purbeck clay workers reached a total of 350 men; earning between 12 shillings and 17 shillings per week, on piece-work. The quantity of clay being shipped through Poole reached 50,000 tons a year.

The Goathorn Railway linked the pits at Norden with those at Newton, with the site of the junction between the two lines being opposite Drove Island (SZ 012 851).

From Eldon Sidings, which had engine sheds for *Tiny* and the newly acquired locomotive *Thames*, the track crossed the Corfe River and passed through small fields on the edge of the heath to Bushey, where it ran to the north of Thrasher's Cottage and then stretched eastwards across the lonely pre-conifer wastes of Brinscombe Heath, Burnbake, Claywell, and Newton Heath. Having closed in 1939, the line here is now the main artery for oil exploration traffic and its low embankment doubles as a firebreak, between the conifer plantations which have transformed the region since 1948. Penultimately, at the eastern end of Purbeck Forest, the line continues into a sandy cutting through what was still a remnant of the heath in the 1960s, but is now smothered by wind-sown pines, hiding the traces of a siding and a limeworks.

During its short life the railway was worked with about 24 wagons and an improvised coach for taking children from Goathorn and Newton to school at Corfe Castle. On several occasions the railway was used to transport Purbeck stone. One operation continued for several years, when stone was carried from the Corfe road [1928-34] for the building of a mile-long spit extending south-eastwards into the sea from the eastern end of Shell Bay (SZ 043 860). It is known as the Training Bank and was devised to direct the high tides into the mouth of Poole Harbour to scour its sediment.

Each train had ten trucks, each of these carrying three tons. At high water the rubble was dumped from ships to form the middle core of the breakwater and settled on top of 10-ton blocks already lowered for the base.

Among the last of the old sailing ships that came to Poole Harbour for clay were graceful wooden vessels from Italy. The barquentine *Patria* and a brigantine, *Auvenire*, arrived in the 1920s to load ball clay for Savona in northern Italy.

W. H. Froud of Poole recalled the clay industry at Goathorn and Newton during the early 20th century:

"The Dorset Iron Foundry used to look after Fayle's two locomotives and my father and grandfather worked on them regularly. On some occasions in the years before 1914 I went to Goathorn with them. In those days the pier was regularly used by steamers that called to take the clay to London. They were generally Henry Burden's boats from Poole.

"There was one cottage at the pier, then occupied by the foreman, William Tubbs. This has now been modernised. The hamlet of Goathorn consisted of a number of cottages occupied by workers at Newton Clay Works, a small school, and a locomotive shed. There was a resident schoolmistress and the school was attended by the small number of children who lived at Goathorn. On Sunday afternoons a church service was conducted in the school by a visiting parson and organist from Swanage.

"The only communication with the outside world, except by boat, was along the railway to Corfe Castle, and I believe that on Saturdays the people were taken on the railway for shopping – and the nearest public house.

"The ships ceased to call at the pier in 1930 but the works continued some years longer. In the 1930s the school was closed, because of the decline in the number of children, and the remaining ones were taken to Corfe on the railway. One of the wagons was covered in, as a passenger coach, and the County Council paid the clay company for the service. The hamlet and the works, together with its railway, were abandoned by 1939."

Drinking water for this small community was imported by rail in a large barrel labelled "Oporto". It was taken on board to the north of

Golden Bowl: the romantic name for the sheltered setting that surrounds Encombe House.

Corfe Waterworks, at Arfleet, where an offshoot turned south to pits below East Hill and Rollington Wood. The school train, taking the children from Goathorn to Corfe, seems to have run both earlier and later than Mr Froud remembered. It appears to have been in operation from 1921 through to 1939.

Their passenger coach was known as the "Hen-house". This otherwise ordinary clay wagon had the additional protection of a low corrugated iron roof, leaving only a ventilation slit where this met the sides – providing more light than view during the 20-minute journey.

Gates had to be opened at Goathorn village, Churchill's Green, Fir Glen, Meadus's Lane, and Thrasher's Lane. The children were dropped at Arfleet junction and walked from there for the final half mile into Corfe village.

(Industrial archaeology / Railways / Corfe Castle and Studland)

Green Island: pine-clad part of off-shore Purbeck, in Corfe Castle parish, which extends far into Poole Harbour.

Golden Bowl – see entry for **Encombe**.

Great Ditch – quarried out of the rock of the Castle Hill at Corfe Castle, between the Outer Bailey and Inner Ward, in 1207.
(Placenames / Mediaeval archaeology / Corfe Castle)

Green Island – 46 acres of mud-fats, beaches, and pinewoods facing Goathorn peninsula in the southern archipelago of Poole Harbour (SZ 005 865). It lies off Cleavel Point, in the northern extremity of Corfe Castle parish, and used to be connected to the mainland by a stone-ramped submarine causeway that partially emerges at low tide.

This was probably surfaced with stone flags and is broken by a gap in the centre of the channel. There are extensive traces of Iron Age and Roman occupation, including evidence that it was used for the manufacture of shale armlets.

Modern communications, to a timber cottage and nearby chalet, tends to be by yacht or helicopter. The wooded summit rises to 68 feet above harbour-level and is the preserve of a colony of red squirrels.

The island was leased to Mrs Ella Barratt [1922-37] who became an almost total recluse, reading her books and listening to gramophone records, and employed Fred Churchill as her handyman and gardener. They created a small market garden in the benign microclimate of the sheltered south-eastern corner of the island which was fertilised by seaweed dragged by a donkey from the nearby shore. Despite being drenched with seawater, to everyone's surprise, the landlocked harbour waters are well diluted by the River Frome, and the combination made for a highly productive soil. Produce included tomatoes, strawberries, raspberries, and figs, plus Morello cherries from an avenue of trees flanking the path to Mrs Barratt's bungalow. "Twice a week Fred took the launch to Poole to sell the produce," Richard Blomfield recalls.

In their time Chinese golden pheasants joined the native avian fauna, such as ringed plovers and green plovers, and continue to breed on the island.

It was owned by S. L. Fowler, followed by Tim Hamilton-Fletcher from 1961 until its sale in 1987. From 1968 he rented it to Guy and Joan Sydenham who established the Quay Pottery on the northern tip of the island, and built a cedar cabin, known as Greensleeves Studio [1971], at the end of a 100 yards avenue of sweet chestnuts that were planted by Wareham naturalist Charlton Xavier Hall early in the 20th century. The Sydenhams had already established their reputation for salt-glazed stoneware on Long Island. It was a two-decade idyll, marked by such harmless fun dressing up as pirates, to raid neighbour Ted Foster on Round Island, with the odd bizarre incident such as a huge bonfire on the salt-marsh burning itself free from the island and floating like one of Drake's fire-boats amid clusters of moored yachts.
(Placenames / Prehistoric archaeology / Roman archaeology / Corfe Castle)

Greyhound Hotel – two 17th-century cottages in the Square at Corfe Castle were merged by "I.C." in 1733 and given a grand frontage with two sets of three elegant Tuscan columns erected across the pavement to support rooms projecting above.

The western porch is still open, as built, but two of the three columns supporting the east porch have been encased in 19th-century brickwork, causing the footway to be diverted around the front.
(Placenames / Corfe Castle)

The Gwyle – Isle of Purbeck name for a wooded glen. The best known example is between Tyneham and Worbarrow, where its origins are said to be Cornish, attributed to the Williams family from Probus who bought Tyneham House [1567].

Gwyles in Corfe Castle parish lie north and south of Encombe House (SY 944 786) and immediately north of Rempstone Hall (SY 993 826). Another is at Church Knowle, to the north-east of Bucknowle House (SY 951 815), along the parish boundary with Corfe Castle.
(Placenames / Church Knowle, Corfe Castle, and Tyneham),

H

H2S – airborne "Town Finder" radar for blind-bombing of German cities, devised by Group 8 of the Telecommunications Research Establishment, working from a wartime Nissen hut in the grounds of the scientists' eastern out-station, Leeson House at Langton Matravers [1941-42]. Given its "chemical" formulaic code-name after Winston Churchill's chief scientific adviser, Professor Frederick Lindemann, snapped "It stinks!" upon hearing excuses on why it had not been developed earlier.

Tested above the Bournemouth conurbation by aircraft of the Telecommunications Flying Unit, initially from a Blenheim bomber flying from Christchurch Aerodrome and then on a specially adapted four-engined Halifax from RAF Hurn [17 April 1942].

Put into production in a top-secret factory beside Northbourne Golf Links at West Howe, Bournemouth. First used operationally, by Pathfinders, to drop flares for the bombers to follow in a major raid on Hamburg [30-31 January 1941]. Enabled carpet-bombing at night of the correct target cities – previously Bomber Command had "attacked Hambourn in mistake for Essen" – for the duration of the Second World War.
(Aviation / Bournemouth, Christchurch, and Langton Matravers)

Halsewell – Purbeck's worst shipwreck, an outward bound East Indiaman, which foundered [6 January 1786] on the cliffs between Winspit and Seacombe (SY 981 764). A total of 168 passengers and crew were drowned, the Gentleman's Magazine reported: "The few men who escaped were most terribly bruised, and some had their limbs broken from being dashed on the rocks. The East India Company's loss is valued only at about £60,000. Captain Pierce was the oldest captain in their service, and proposed to retire, had it pleased providence to permit his return from this voyage."

Its premature end was recorded by Rev. M. Jones, the vicar of Worth Matravers, in his parish register: "On the fourth, fifth, and sixth day of January, a remarkable snow storm,

***Halsewell* tragedy: dramatic end to the outward-bound voyage of an East Indiaman, in a January blizzard in 1786.**

Halsewell Rock: leaning against the cliff between Winspit and Seacombe, from which shipwreck survivors were hauled.

sometimes a hurricane, with the wind at south. On the latter day, at two in the morning, the *Halsewell* East Indiaman, 758-tons burthen, commanded by Captain Richard Pierce, bound for Bengal, was lost in the rocks between Seacombe and Winspit quarries in this parish. Never did happen so complete a wreck. The ship long before day-break was shattered to pieces, and a very small part of her cargo saved. It proved fatal to 168 persons, among whom were the captain, two of his daughters, two nieces and three other young ladies. Eighty-two men, by the exertion and humanity of the inhabitants and neighbouring quarriers, at the imminent hazard of their own lives, were saved. The East India Company, to reward such merit, sent 100 guineas to be distributed among them."

In 1967, three Swanage divers found a cannon from the wreck and recovered coins, cannon balls, lead shot, tackle and glass. Further seabed finds, in 1973, included the pintle; the bronze hinge which held the rudder.

Contemporary salvage and loot comprised a green hour-glass (in Dorset County Museum), a mirror (Worth Matravers parish church), a cupboard (Town Hall Museum, Corfe Castle), and the captain's private cabinet, with glazed doors and a semi-circular top (fitted in the bedroom of a house near the New Inn, Swanage).

The dead from the *Halsewell* were buried in four trenches cut on level ground in Seacombe Bottom (SY 985 767), and the graves marked by guns recovered from the ship, but these had disappeared within 50 years of the shipwreck. Digging took place in 1972, without success, to rediscover the site.

Oliver W. Farrer described the spot in 1858: "One other sad memorial remains; on the little patch of flat grass where the cliffs divide, and the stream, when there is a stream, falls over the cliff, may yet be seen the traces of four long graves. The spot is appropriate. As you stand by the almost obliterated mounds, the eye wanders over little but sea and sky, and the wild solitude of the spot accords with the sadness of the tragedy here played out."

It provided the inspiration for a novel by Charles Dickens, *The Long Journey*, which appeared half a century after the disaster. The folk memory was absorbed by generations of quarrymen, with last of the line having been Billy Winspit. He told me [1964] to walk round East Man, along the clifftop path, to the first stile and there stop and look down through the blackthorn, more than 100 feet, to the Halsewell Rock on to which the survivors climbed and clung. It rests against the base of the cliff immediately to the east, and came into National Trust ownership with its Bankes Estate inheritance [1982], now with the approach from East Man also having been purchased by the Trust [1999].

(Shipwrecks / National Trust / Worth Matravers)

The Halves – locally known as Aves, this was the mediaeval open field on the west side of West Street at Corfe Castle. It was called "West Hawes" on a plan of 1585.

"Middle Hawes" lay between West Street and East Street. "Hawys" or "Hawes" was the name of a landowning family at Corfe from the time of Edward I.

"Haw" is also an archaic word applied to closes and yards in towns, although this definition does not describe these two open fields. Whichever is the origin, as "w" used to be pronounced "v" and Dorset speech drops the aspirate, the current form of Aves preserves the original word perfectly. It came into National Trust ownership with the Bankes Estate [1982].
(Placenames / National Trust / Corfe Castle)

Harman's Cross – formerly known as Harman's Cross Roads, where Haycraft's Lane from the south and Tabbit's Hill Lane to the north were intersected by the 19th-century turnpike road from Corfe Castle to Swanage (SY 984 804). Coplestone Cottage, 500 yards to the west, was then the only inhabitation in what by the mid-20th century had became a hamlet of 70 homes. The northern gardens end at the ancient ditched hedgerow of the Worth Matravers parish boundary.
(Placenames / Worth Matravers)

Hatton – statesman **Sir Christopher Hatton** [1540-91], Lord Chancellor of England [1587-91], was given Corfe Castle by Queen Elizabeth [1575]. He was known as "the Dancing Chancellor" as a result of his appearance at a court masque when he first attracted the monarch's attentions. In 1585 he bought the Wollaton Hall, Nottinghamshire, as his main country estate, and brought his personal papers up-to-date with transcripts that included his Purbeck property deeds.

Remarkably, a contemporary conveyance was bound into a re-cycled vellum leaf that had come from one of the most famous pre-Conquest great bibles, assembled on the instructions of the Venerable Bede in about 712. Bede asked Ceolfrith to make three identical manuscripts, for each of his monasteries, at Jarrow and Wearmouth, and with the third being a gift to the Pope.

That copy went with Ceolfrith to Rome, in 716, but the abbot died in France though his bible did reach Italy, later coming into the possession of the monastery of Monte Amiata, near Florence. It was eventually placed in the Laurentian Library in that city [1786] and is known as the "Codex Amiatinus".

The two Wearside bibles were considered to be completely lost but in 1909 Canon Greenwell of Durham came across a leaf in a junk shop in Newcastle. His discovery led to eleven more leaves being found, re-used as binding for deeds, in the muniments room at Wollaton Hall. These were acquired by the British Museum in the 1930s.

The additional page from one of Ceolfrith's Wearside bibles was spotted after the National Trust found itself owning the Corfe Castle Estate [1982], in a deed box at Kingston Lacy House, by Nicholas Pickwoad, the Trust's consultant on book conservation. He passed it to John Fuggles, the Trust's literary adviser, though at that time neither realised they were handling Saxon parchment. Christopher Hatton's staff had stripped apart one of the Wearside bibles to use its vellum as folders for title deeds and other legal documents.
(People / Politicians / National Trust / Corfe Castle)

Hawes family – see entry for **The Halves**.

Hawtrey – for **Louisa Hawtrey** see entry for **Mary Palgrave**.

Hayward – quarrier and smuggler **Charles Hayward** [1796-1879] of Fig Tree Cottage, in the High Street at Langton Matravers, rented the cliffside Dancing Ledge workings from Mrs Frances Serrell of Durnford House. His grandson would recall that the family quarries here and "Balston Quarry" to the west (probably Topmast Quarry) did night duty for smuggling towards the end of the free-trade era and that after the rebuilding of the parish church [1828-29] it was used for the hiding of kegs.

Stones were removed from the tower wall, from the newel staircase below the bell

Hedbury cannon: rescued from Legg-mentioned obscurity and turned into a coastal display piece, in a quarry the Ordnance Survey doesn't bother to name.

chamber, to give access to the roof space above the domed ceiling of the nave.

Hayward, like so many of the smugglers, became a pillar of local society. He was Parish Clerk [1846], village Sub-Postmaster [1860], and the rector's Churchwarden and Sexton [1870].
(People / Smugglers / Social history / Langton Matravers)

Stone cliffs: eastwards from Hedbury towards Topmast Quarry (another placename the Ordnance Survey does not give) and Dancing Ledge.

Heath-croppers – the peasant stock of northern Purbeck, existing as crofters in isolated cottages on the heath. Their homes had walls of mud, the yellow cob of east Dorset, under thin roofs of ageing wheat thatch or reeds they gathered themselves from the harbour backwaters. Each dilapidated hovel was set in an oasis of small fields and sparse grass standing by a stream or pool amid the empty desolation of the great heath.

This provided their rough grazing, peat for fuel, and furze-faggots for the oven. It also pressed relentlessly at these pockets of civilisation, questioning with a combination of gorse and bracken. As the occupant aged and withered the heath would win back its former property and the walls of the cottages were known to crumble to nothing in only three years.

Such a way of life struggled into the 20th century but many of the solitary habitations were finally evacuated in 1943, when Army ranges extended over much of heathland Purbeck and live-firing took place from Lulworth and Povington across to Arne and Studland.
(Social history / Purbeck parishes)

Hedbury Quarry – 18th and 19th-century cliffside workings, 200 yards west of Topmast Quarry, at Langton Matravers (SY 992 768). Its name, which has evaded the Ordnance Survey – lamentably many do – is correctly Hedbury rather than "Headbury" as given in the parish Tithe Award [1838], because it takes its name from the Eidbury family. They opened the quarry in the mid-18th century and it expanded into the fourth largest along this coast; after Seacombe, Winspit, and Dancing Ledge.

It has long been something of a time-warp, never reached by road, with a discarded reminder of the French Wars on the ledge overlooking the sea. Ironwork set directly above the waves shows the site of the "whim" derrick used to lower stone into boats. These off-loaded at Swanage.

The French connection, either from anti-invasion defences or lifted from a contemporary shipwreck, is a 12-pounder cannon which used to lie among abandoned blocks of cut stone [1960]. It was then hauled out, and mounted on a stone plinth [1970s], to point seawards.

The workings and the surrounding coast came into National Trust ownership as an outlying corner of the Bankes Estate [1982] but conservation ownership has since been consolidated with the acquisition of the cliffs

Hill Bottom: described as a "Village up Renscombe Valley" by Alfred Dawson in the caption to his 1882 print, this hamlet lies a kilometre inland from Chapman's Pool.

to the east, at Topmast Quarry and Dancing Ledge [1992].
(Placenames / Industrial archaeology / National Trust / Langton Matravers)

Hildegarde – steamship, registered in London, carrying Spanish iron ore destined for Newcastle, wrecked off Freshwater, Encombe [10 November 1900].
(Shipwrecks / Corfe Castle)

Hill Bottom – the hamlet for the fishermen of Chapman's Pool, situated beside what is still a public road in the deep-cut valley a kilometre north-east (SY 962 778). Described as a "village" by artist Alfred Dawson [1882] but now reduced to four surviving buildings, including Mermaid Cottage, Bakehouse Cottage, and Hill Bottom Cottage.

A Victorian Coastguard station was sited in this gully, with Thomas Austin being its chief boatman [1889], with six men as his crew.
(Placenames / Shipwrecks / Worth Matravers)

Holland – newsagent **Charles Holland** [1911-89] created the replica intact Model Castle and Village in the garden behind his shop in The Square at Corfe Castle, which looks across a deep-cut valley at the ruins of the real thing.
(People / National Trust / Corfe Castle)

Horcerd – mediaeval "lost" hamlet in the parish of Church Knowle, north-east of West Orchard Farm (SY 941 808). It is mentioned in the Domesday Book [1086]. Only fragmentary traces survive of banks and ditches, in what became known as Oakley Close.
(Placenames / Mediaeval archaeology / Church Knowle)

Horseshoe Tower – projecting north-east of the Outer Gatehouse at Corfe Castle, dating between 1250-85.
(Placenames / Mediaeval archaeology / National Trust / Corfe Castle)

Hutchings – novelist and topographical writer **Monica Hutchings** [mid-20th century] lived at Broad Mead, Church Knowle (SY 943 818). She had made her name nationally with "doctor-nurse romances" in the 1950s and locally, in the late 1960s by trespassing on the Lulworth Ranges to expose animal welfare abuses and take evocative photographs of its out-of-bounds scenery and ruins.

These became a slide show which she toured around Women's Institutes. Retired to Scotland in the mid-1970s, suffering breast cancer and failing sight, which caused her suicide by drowning, in the sea off Argyll.
(Literary / Church Knowle)

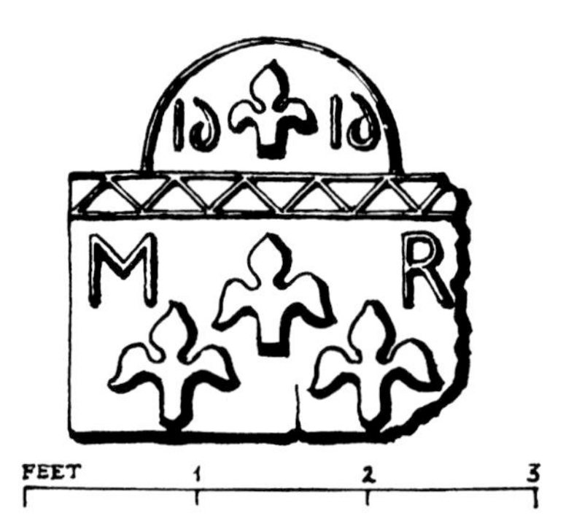

Worth fireback: 17th-century ironwork in the possession of Commander J. R. Strange, drawn by G. Dru Drury, curator of Dorset County Museum and inserted in his personal copy of the 1927 volume of their *Proceedings*, which is now in author Rodney Legg's collection.

I

Iliffe – insurance and provincial newspaper magnate **Edward Mauger Iliffe**, 1st Baron Iliffe [1877-1960] owned Furzey Island in Poole Harbour.
(People / Corfe Castle)

Isle of Purbeck – name of the south-east corner of Dorset, justified visually and historically, rather than geographically. The area of 70 square miles is bounded to the north by the River Frome and Poole Harbour. Eastwards is Poole Bay. To the south is the English Channel. On the west there is a land link, at East Lulworth, from which Luckford Lake stream flows northwards to the Frome.

Since extended as a concept, with the creation of Purbeck District Council [1974]. Its boundaries, westwards, include Chaldon Herring and Moreton, and to the north Affpuddle, Bere Regis, Bloxworth, Morden, Lytchett Matravers, and Lytchett Minster.
(Placenames / Purbeck parishes)

Ivinghoe – somehow the **Prioress of Ivinghoe**, a nunnery near Leighton Buzzard, Bedfordshire, came to lose her seal in the heart of the Isle of Purbeck [circa 1375]. She could only have come to such a remote spot to arrange for the purchase of marble, most likely for an effigy. The seal has the bust and head of St Margaret encircled by lettering: "Sigillu Priorisse de Iuyngho". It was discovered during digging of the foundations for the National School at Langton Matravers [1845]. This is now St George's Hall.
(People / Mediaeval archaeology / Schools / Langton Matravers)

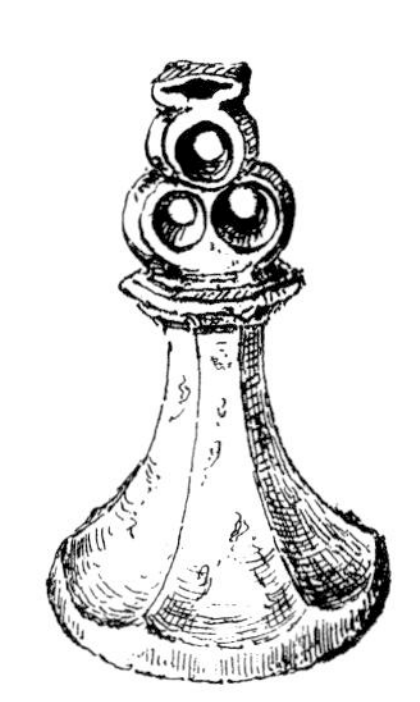

Ivinghoe seal: lost by the Prioress of its nunnery, circa 1375, and found during the digging of foundations for a new school-room at Langton Matravers, in 1846.

Interesting inscription: recording the restoration of a well in West Street, Corfe Castle, "to commemorate the wedding of H.R.H. Princes Charles and Lady Diana Spencer, 29th July 1981".

Entering Kingston

J

Jarman – film director **Derek Jarman** [1942-97] entitled a volume of his autobiography *Dancing Ledge* [1982] after the rocky Langton Matravers beauty spot where he and his friends and lovers used to take movies of each other, invariably without their clothes. He was best known for *Caravaggio* [1986]. His own mother appears posthumously in *The Last of England*, described as "the most startlingly original film of the year" [1987] with a "versatile and visionary" mix of "power and politics, dancing, violence, and gratuitous sex".

Blatantly homosexual, and openly admitting to having been diagnosed HIV-positive, the impending onset of terminal illness gave Jarman's work an almost manic urgency as he continued to follow his mother's advice: "Break all the rules, Derek."

This was achieved in abundance with anarchic paintings and rebellious films. One of the former unflatteringly portrayed a female British Prime Minister, while savouring a vampiric meal, so it was perhaps understandable that the conventional film industry was reluctant to finance his projects. As a result, Jarman's final work had to be shot "economy class" on Super 8 that was then transferred through video to a 35-millimetre cinema print.

"I see it as an allegory," he said of *The Last of England*. "It's a wonderful thing to have made a film like this. Everything I think is in it."
(People / Artists / Langton Matravers)

Jenkins – farmer **William Jenkins** [born 1782] of Knitson Farm, north of Langton Matravers, was called by John Calcraft MP to give evidence to a Parliamentary committee on hardships caused by the salt tax (two shillings per bushel) which was being considered for abolition [1825].

He came to London dressed in a long smock, buckskin breeches, and gaiters. His appearance brought a touch of humour to the day which was preserved in Purbeck folklore by the apocryphal tale that some wag attached a notice to his back: "Varmer Jenkins, up from the County."

It was, however, a successful performance, as the tax was duly repealed and a block of salt as large as a brick fell in price to a penny.
(People / Folklore / Politics / Langton Matravers)

Jesty – farmer and medical pioneer **Benjamin Jesty** [1736-1816] of Yetminster and then Downshay Farm, Worth Matravers, was claimed to be the first person known to have inoculated cow-pox, in 1774, as a vaccination against smallpox, although the credit would go to physician Edward Jenner who did not publish his results until 1798. Jesty's experiment was on dairymaid Abigail Brown.

The case is complicated by the fact that neither could have discovered the principles of immunisation because these were in widespread practice before either man was born. Errors have arisen in the debate because we loosely call any kind of immunisation "vaccination". This introduces an immediate problem because the word is derived specifically from cowpox (known as "vaccinia").

The knowledge of inoculation against smallpox was brought to Britain from Turkey by Lady Mary Wortley Montagu in 1717. "The New Practice of Inoculating the Small-Pox" was condemned in a pamphlet of 1722. From 1727 Dr Hans Sloane was inoculating members of the royal family. The College of Physicians endorsed the practice in 1755 and Stroud weaver George Ridley "inockilated" 200 to 300 people in Gloucestershire in the next two years; "and but two or three of them died".

The inoculation was with serum taken from someone with a mild bout of the disease but the danger was that sometimes instead of inducing immunity it was passed on with full virulence. Nature's answer to the threat was a rural resistance that first found its expression in print in the words of a Cotswold dairymaid: "I shall never have the smallpox for I have had

Jesty graves: recording that Benjamin, buried at Worth in 1815, had "made the Experiment from the Cow on his Wife and two Sons in the Year 1774".

cowpox. I shall never have an ugly, pock-marked face."

Here Benjamin Jesty enters the story, in 1774. Using cowpox serum from diseased cattle at Chetnole, near Sherborne, he successfully vaccinated his wife and two children, when they were living nearby, at Upbury Farm, Yetminster. Jenner "found the vaccine matter first in the West of England", it was later reported to the House of Commons, though he faced the disbelief of doctors when he self-published the results in 1798. He had tested the theory by vaccinating eight-year-old James Phipps, with pus from a milkmaid's cowpox sore, and then tested the boy's immunity six weeks later with an inoculation of active smallpox pus.

It was to the general exposure of rural Britons to endemic cowpox that relatively low losses from smallpox in the American War of Independence could now be credited. Their low level of incapacity, not that it would prove militarily decisive, could be compared with colonial problems of plague proportions, with 5,500 incapacitated out of a force of 10,000.

Despite Benjamin Jesty and Edward Jenner it was a lesson that was still only half learnt. Although vaccination became widely used from 1800 onwards it did not become a necessity of national life, for the next century until eradication, after 162,000 died in the epidemic at the beginning of the 1870s.

Benjamin and Elizabeth Jesty enlarged their family to four sons and three daughters, by 1785, and in about 1797 moved from Yetminster to Downshay Manor, in the corner of Worth parish between Langton Matravers and Harman's Cross. It is now known as Dunshay – its ancient name.

When in 1802 the House of Commons was petitioned on Jenner's behalf, seeking a State reward to mark his achievement and defray his expenses, it was admitted that others carried out vaccinations, "particularly a farmer in Dorsetshire who inoculated his wife and children". Jenner's contribution was regarded as paramount, because he had published his findings and risked his professional reputation, and he was awarded £10,000.

Dr Andrew Bell, the new vicar at Swanage, took up Jesty's case in August 1803. He told them of the Chetnole experiment (yokelising its name as "Chittenall") with the result that the Secretary of the Vaccine Pock Institute eventually wrote to Benjamin Jesty, in 1805, inviting him to London to sit for a portrait.

It turned into more than a painting; Benjamin was vaccinated with cowpox and his two elder sons were inoculated with live smallpox serum, without result, to show they were still immune. A testimonial recorded the vigorous state of their health and praised Benjamin's "exemption from the prevailing popular prejudices and his disregard of the clamorous reproaches of his neighbours" which "entitle him to the respect of the public for his superior strength of mind".

Jenner submitted a further petition to Parliament and received a further £20,000 in 1806. His is the name that would be remembered.

(People / Medicine / Chetnole, Worth Matravers, and Yetminster)

John – English monarch **King John** [1167-1216, reigned from 1199] adopted Corfe Castle as a hospitality suite complete with dungeon for his political prisoners [1201], and then had the Great Ditch dug to protect the Keep when it was in use as his treasury [1207-14]. He also enjoyed staghunting across Purbeck Chase, using lodges such as that on Creech Barrow Hill, with a tower on the summit from which he could continue to keep an eye on his money.

His tomb, in Worcester Cathedral, has double distinction of being topped by the first effigy of an English monarch, appropriately carved in Purbeck marble [circa 1240].

(People / Politics / Corfe Castle)

John Richard – struck the Kimmeridge Ledges and became a total loss, though the crew and some of the cargo were saved [29 September 1826].

(Shipwrecks / Kimmeridge)

Joseph Desiri – stricken French chasse-maree wrecked in Kimmeridge Bay, from which its crew of eight men and a boy were hauled ashore [28 November 1838]. She had orientated herself to the west of the Clavell Tower landmark and had managed to beach on the shingle in the bay with the sea breaking around her.

Lieutenant Smith, RN, the chief officer of the Coastguard at Kimmeridge, was awarded a gold medal for gallantry by the French Government and the members of his crew received silver medals for their part in the rescue.

(Shipwrecks / Kimmeridge)

Jubilee monument: the Market Cross at Corfe, erected in 1897, commemorated the sixtieth year of Queen Victoria's record reign.

Thatched street: Kimmeridge is a rarity in Purbeck, being an exception to the stone-roofed norm.

Kimmeridge Bay: its inlet at Gaulter Gap, with Coastguard Cottages, defended by a 1940 pillbox.

K

Keates Quarry – east of Worth Matravers village, this working on National Trust land is famous for its dinosaur footprints. A splendid array of more than a hundred sauropod prints up to 44 inches in diameter, discovered in 1997, is described in our entry **Dinosaur traces**.
(Placenames / National Trust / Worth Matravers)

The Keep – the great centrepiece of Corfe Castle, where timber was replaced by stone, apparently by the year 1100, and was then standing 80-feet high and fully utilising the potential of Castle Hill which rises 150 feet from the streams below. Even if it is a little later, it is still one of the earliest mediaeval fortresses in Britain, and militarily it was well ahead of its time.
(Mediaeval archaeology / National Trust / Corfe Castle)

Killwood – former lonely cottage amongst some small and ancient fields on the mixed soils of sand and chalk to the north of Knowle Hill (SY 939 825). Boundary stones mark the boundaries of Bond family lands and the Encombe Estate.

Killwood seems to have disappeared, early in the 20th century, as a result of the general extinction of heathland crofters, rather than through the ramifications of nearby pits and shafts, with extensions of Fayle Company's Norden claypits from the east and Pike Brothers' East Creech workings and mines south-west of Killwood Coppices (SY 935 825).
(Placenames / Industrial archaeology / Church Knowle)

Kimmeridge – linear coastal village of a single short street southwards from its parish church, set a mile inland between Kimmeridge Bay and Smedmore Hill. Traditionally, being on clay and shale bed-rock rather than Purbeck stone, the cottages have tended to be thatched rather than stone-roofed. Entries here for the 995-acre parish include:

Air crashes; *Arkow*; Bituminous Shale Company; Botteridge Pool; Burning shale; Caernarvon Castle; Calcutta; Clavell family; Clavell Tower; Clavell's Hard, Coal money; Coastguard graves; Coastguard Stations; Cooper family; *Edouard*; *Elinor*; Ferguson and Muschamp; *John Richards*; *Joseph Desiri*; Kimmeridge multiple entries; New Inn; *Olive Branch*; St Nicholas's parish church; Saltpans; Sanitary Carbon Company; *Robert S. Shaw*; HMS *Skylark*; Smedmore House; Tank targets; Wanostrocht and Company; Wareham Oil and Shale Company.
(Placenames / Kimmeridge)

Kimmeridge coast: landmark pines, with the Clavell Tower as the distant speck on the cliffs.

Treacherous coast: just one of the infamous Kimmeridge Ledges of shipwreck notoriety, thrusting out into the English Channel.

Kimmeridge alum works – Lord Mountjoy discovered that land at Kimmeridge was "full of allom myne" and he obtained a patent to manufacture alum there [1560s]. In this usage the word "mine" has its older meaning as the "ore" of a material and refers to "alum shale". Alum is a double sulphate of aluminium and potassium which is widely used in medicine and the arts.

Mountjoy's plan was unsuccessful but it was taken up again by Sir William Clavell, the owner of Kimmeridge, around 1600. When Clavell had perfected the production process, his alum works was seized by a group of London merchants who had been granted King James I's sole patent for making alum. They took possession of Clavell's "houses, furnaces, and coal pits" and left only when he agreed to pay them £1,000 "rent" each year.

Months later, however, they returned and systematically ransacked all the alum houses and sold-off all Clavell's chattels. Sir William retaliated by spending £4,000 on litigation, at the same time as turning Kimmeridge into a port by building a pier 100 feet long, 15 feet high, and 60 feet wide. The height of the quay is given in one document as 50 feet, but that is obviously a mistake as a structure of such height would be totally unusable as a pier or anything else. The pier was described in the 1620s as a "little key in imitation of that at Lime" (the Cobb at Lyme Regis) and it was apparently allowed to fall into disrepair, being finally destroyed by a storm [1745]. Its remains, comprising large blocks of squared stone, can still be seen in the south-eastern corner of the bay, together with a ruined section of sea wall that was also built by Clavell. A later wall, built in the 19th century, has survived in better condition.
(Industrial archaeology / Kimmeridge)

Kimmeridge Clay – the grey oil-bearing shales extending north-eastwards across England to the Yorkshire coast, which are named for their famous exposures in the cliffs of Kimmeridge Bay.
(Geology / Kimmeridge)

Kimmeridge coal money – thought to have been ancient currency, but in fact the core waste from Roman lathe-turned armlet production, as was first deduced by antiquarian John H. Austen in a "Purbeck Paper" read at Creech Grange [1856].
(Roman archaeology / Kimmeridge)

Kimmeridge glass-making – began when Admiral Sir Robert Mansel established a prototype furnace [1615] and sold a concession to Abraham Bigo, glassmaker, allowing him to set up a glass-house to make green drinking glass in the Isle of Purbeck [1617]. He went into business with Sir William Clavell, who had been making alum beside Kimmeridge Bay. Nationally, coal was being used instead of charcoal, for smelting, and Bigo and Clavell used shale as their substitute fuel. This may have caused them to abandon Mansel's furnace as "unuseful", perhaps because it had been based on a design for a wood-burning furnace and failed to take into account the difference in flame lengths between the two fuels.

The air passage of an alum-producing furnace and the foundations of a later, shale-fired glassmaker's furnace, were discovered by the late Dr David Brachi [early 1980s] near the slipway at the southern end of Kimmeridge Bay (SY 909 788).

This was intended for burning shale, with the fire-box set at its centre, rather than having the longer fire-passage of the conventional wood-fired furnaces. Fragments were found of the crucibles, as well as bits of drinking glasses – mainly beakers and wine glasses – that had been made there, in "varying shades of green".

Clavell operations tended to struggle at the edge of the law, and he was soon challenging the terms of the concession [1621]. Royalties were unpaid; products were sold in London against a restrictive covenant; workers were "seduced" from Mansel's Newcastle works to one Clavell had become involved with, in Scotland.

After two periods in prison, Clavell was released with a free pardon [1626], conditional on him giving up glass-making. His losses were in excess of £20,000 and he died in 1644 without recovering his financial position.
(Industrial archaeology / Kimmeridge)

Kimmeridge Ledges – one of the most treacherous sections of the central South Coast, second only to the Chesil Beach at Portland for its tally of shipwrecks, are the succession of shale outcrops that stretch out to sea for two miles eastwards of Cuddle at Kimmeridge (SY 911 782). The strata is set in parallel waves, extending south-eastwards from the base of the cliff, with up to 300 metres being visible at low-water and a similar distance remaining lethal beyond that at all stages of the tide. The final cluster are off Freshwater at Encombe. Most of the wrecks were driven into the ledges by gales, or just prevailing south-westerly winds, but others were own-goals caused by navigational error.

Those with entries in this book include *Welfare* [1371], *John Richard* [29 September 1826], *Joseph Desiri* [28 November 1828], *Tyne* [13 January 1837], *Olive Branch* [20 April 1838], *Don Pedro* [14 March 1841], *Elinor* [27 June 1842], *Edouard* [29 November 1842], HMS *Skylark* [April 1845], *Sarah Park* [3 October 1854], *Caernarvon Castle* [25 September 1856], *Commodore* [18 August 1877], *Arklow* [19 November 1880], *Hildegarde* [10 November 1900], and *Treveal* [10 January 1920].
(Placenames / Shipwrecks / Kimmeridge)

Kimmeridge Lifeboat Station – in a gully at Charnel, beside Kimmeridge Bay, in the south-east corner of Tyneham parish (SY 901 791). Established after a spate of shipwrecks along this shore [1868] with William Stickland of Stickland's Cottage, South Egliston, being coxswain of its boat, the 28-feet *Mary Heape*.

He was the hero of the rescue of 17 men crewing the stricken Norwegian vessel

Stralsund, which wedged on the Kimmeridge Ledges in ferocious seas [8-9 December 1872].

Immediately after William Stickland's death [March 1881] the boat was replaced by the 32-feet *Mary Heape II*. She saved three seamen from the cutter *Ceres*, from Poole [21 March 1886] and continued in service until 1887.

The next and final boat was the 34-feet *Augustus Arkwright* which would succeed in refloating the brigantine *Lythemore* [26 June 1892].

The station had its limitations, particularly because of the distance from the far-flung dwellings of this sparsely populated shore, and shortage of manpower caused its closure [1896].

The large shed and slipway became a boat-building yard, operated by Louis Stickland, son of the late William. It now lies inside the Lulworth Ranges [since 1943] and has been reduced to footings and the remains of rails and the winch. Fresh-water trickles into the sea, out of the cliff to the south-east, and was intercepted by a stone-built culvert.

There is a path down through the gully from the main coast path of the Lulworth Range Walks, when these are open, or alternatively across the rocks from Kimmeridge Bay.
(Shipwrecks / Kimmeridge and Tyneham)

Kimmeridge Oil and Carbon Company – Wareham-based, growing out of the Sanitary Carbon Company [1876], operating the underground shafts east of Kimmeridge Bay and producing shale by-products towards the end of the Victorian era [1890s].
(Industrial archaeology / Kimmeridge and Wareham)

Kimmeridge Oil Well – on the low shale cliffs above Kimmeridge Bay, actually in the parish of Steeple, beside the coastal footpath (SY 904 793). Immediately outside the south-east corner of the Lulworth Ranges, beside red flag No. 56.

British Petroleum's "nodding donkey" or pump-jack oilwell was the first successful drilling in what is now the Purbeck oil-field. It has been pumping since 1959, from the Cornbrash limestone at 1,790 feet, and the cumulative production is now in the region of half a million tons.
(Industrial archaeology / Kimmeridge)

Kimmeridge shale industry – the drab grandeur of Kimmeridge is of industrial interest because of a thin layer of bituminous shale less than three feet in thickness that runs through the greyish masses of the bed known to geologists as Kimmeridge clay. This shale is known as blackstone or Kimmeridge coal and the story of its exploitation makes for a chequered piece of history.

Its first phase was a considerable success. This started with hard-cut imitations in shale of armlets that had been made in jet, circa 400 BC. Later in the Iron Age, and to a far greater extent in the Roman period, the bracelets of Kimmeridge shale were mass-produced by Celtic craftsmen working with wooden lathes at a large number of sites across southern Purbeck. The output of the industry was vast. An indication of its extent came at Povington when Victorian antiquary John H. Austen found flint tools, broken bracelets and more than 600

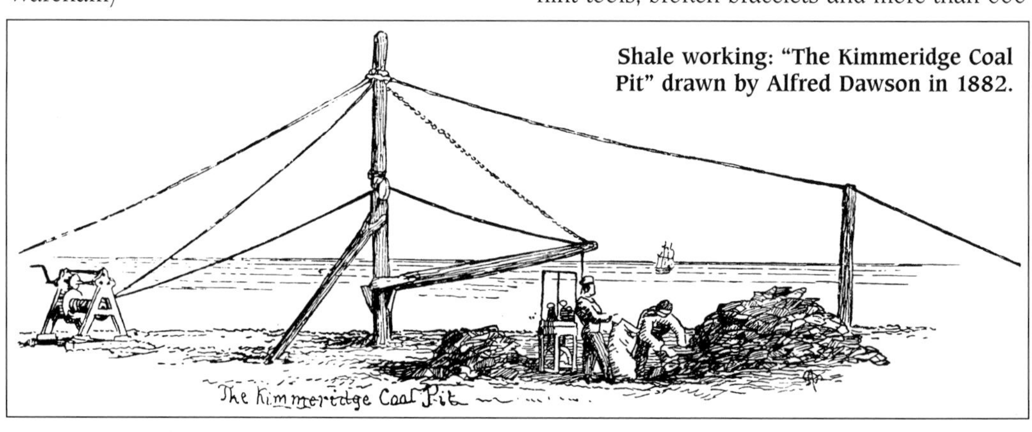

Shale working: "The Kimmeridge Coal Pit" drawn by Alfred Dawson in 1882.

shale cores from two small excavations of only about a yard in diameter [1859].

Substantial quantities have since been found at other sites but the worked shale soon disintegrates on exposure to the air and laboratory treatment is necessary if it is to be preserved.

The cores were the waste product of the process and have chuck holes, which were made to enable the rough pieces of shale to be held in the lathes. These cores are also circular and this led to the local name "coal money".

David Calkin of Langton Matravers turned a number of shale armlets by using flint tools and he cleared up many of the technical points which had puzzled archaeologists. His father, J. Bernard Calkin, fully investigated the industry, as he explained to me when I was a 14-year-old privileged to play with his personal collection in the Red House Museum at Christchurch [1961]. For the Dorset Natural History and Archaeological Society he set out the process in semi-academic terms:

"When the shale is freshly quarried, its texture and hardness closely resemble those of shale. Cleavage planes form a low angle with the bedding and often prevent satisfactory splitting. If struck sharply the shale develops a conchoidal fracture. It is light in weight, and greyish-black or brownish-black in colour. Of a dull and uninteresting appearance, it at once comes to life if smoothed and polished with beeswax, and then looks much like jet."

On the other hand, shale quarried in the distant past and later rediscovered is in a very different state. It is generally covered in cracks, which open up as it dries: "It becomes brittle, is inclined to curl and shrink, and may slowly break away in small pieces."

This decay, accompanied by a lower specific gravity, is caused by oxidation of its natural oils: "Anyone who is only familiar with shale in its weathered condition can have little idea of its original toughness and strength."

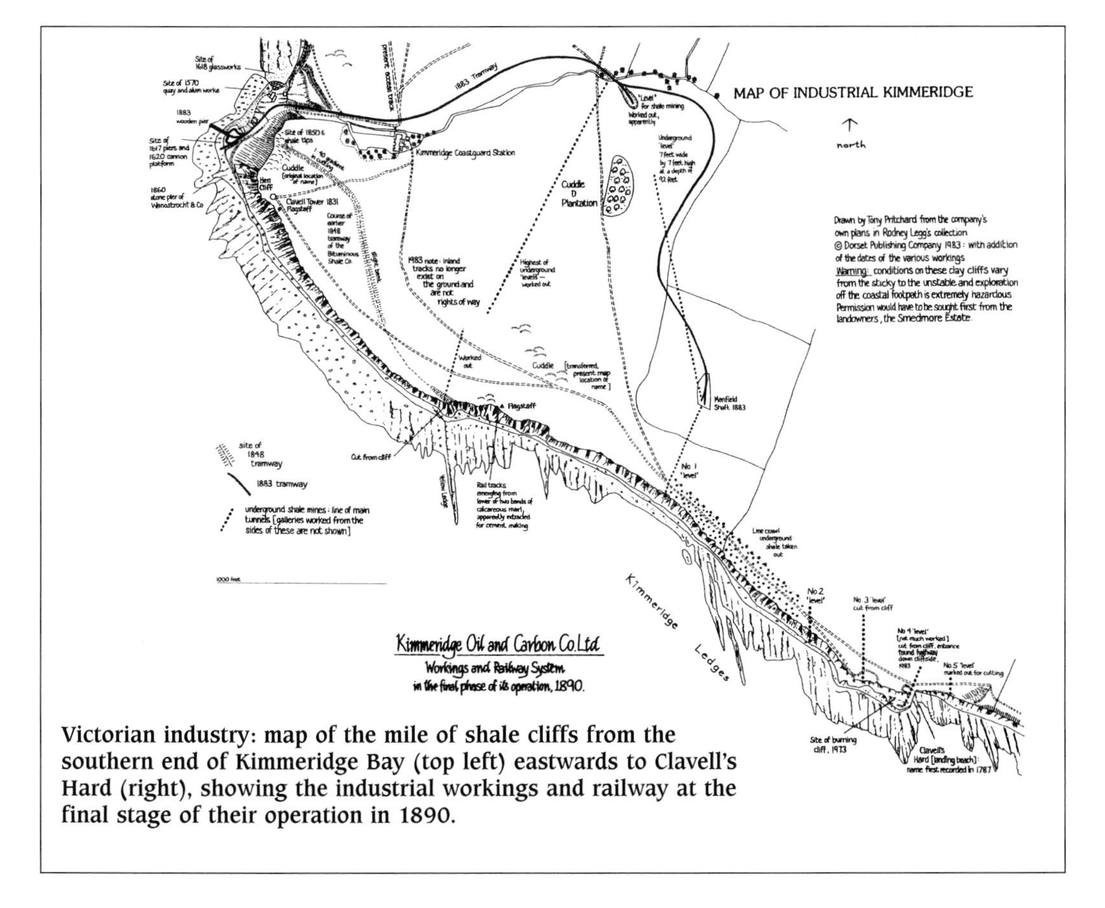

Victorian industry: map of the mile of shale cliffs from the southern end of Kimmeridge Bay (top left) eastwards to Clavell's Hard (right), showing the industrial workings and railway at the final stage of their operation in 1890.

Inside view: the underground 'level' of a Victorian shale working, driven inland from Clavell's Hard at Kimmeridge.

This remarkable material was also cut and carved into sheets for panels, flat dishes, floor tiles, spindle-whorls, small carvings, and furniture. Parts of the claw-feet and legs of a small type of three-legged table, manufactured in Dorset from Kimmeridge shale in Roman times, were found at Colliton Park, Dorchester [1937]. The remains of another table were recovered from Upper Langridge Farm, Bath [1950]. Similar pieces have come from Maiden Castle, Frampton, and Preston in Dorset, and Rothley in Leicestershire, and Foscott in Buckinghamshire, as well as a variant form excavated at Caerleon.

They were styled on metal prototypes and date from a wide period, being produced between AD 150 and 357, as a class of furniture described by J. Liversidge as "a long-lived type remaining fashionable for several centuries". He points out that "they must also have been treasured in Romano-British homes, and handed down from generation to generation as heirlooms". As with all objects of Kimmeridge shale, each would have required regular polishing, with a light oil or wax, to maintain a sheen and prevent the surface from crazing.

The patterns on this type of work were always run on strictly classical lines, which shows a surprising degree of Roman influence for what has always been looked upon as a native industry. Such a panel was copied by Lieutenant-General Augustus Pitt-Rivers for the book bindings on his famous set of archaeological works.

Because the majority of villas and town houses were owned by Romanised Celts, some traces of British culture might be expected in shale products, so its absence implies that the native workers in the trade were directed by Roman management.

It was very much a prehistoric and Roman industry; the Saxons made no effort to revive a craft that had flourished for 800 years.

Concerted industrial activity resumed with the Bituminous Shale Company which obtained an Act of Parliament for making a mineral railway beside Kimmeridge Bay [1847] to extract shale for shipment to Weymouth [1848] where it was processed for coal by-products, until liquidation after environmental protests [1854].

Tunnel entrance: "Coming out of the Shale Pit" in an 1881 sketch, courtesy Major John Mansel.

Meanwhile, at Wareham, Wanostrocht and Company established a Kimmeridge shale gas-works beside the new railway station [1848] and Ferguson and Muschamp also produced gas for lighting [1855-58] from what became the site of Wareham Pottery at Sandford.

German chemist August Wilhelm von Hofmann [1818-92] researched extensively into coal-tar products and experimented with three separate batches of Kimmeridge shale, finding that the proportion of volatile matter they contained varied from 20 to 73 per cent, publishing his findings in volume 6 of the Journal of Gas Lighting [1867].

The quantity of gas after purification also emerges very high, at 11,300 cubic feet per ton, compared with 12,000 cubic feet per ton from

Export point: the 1860-built stone pier of Wanostrocht and Company below Hen Cliff at Kimmeridge, from which shale was shipped.

Industrial area: Kimmeridge cliffs and the Clavell Tower seamark, from the stone-built jetty which survived its Victorian enterprises.

coal. Its power of illumination was also given as good; being equal to 20 sperm-whale candles.

Liquid oils could be produced at lower temperatures and yield by-products such as ammonia and an ash for use in furnaces and gas-retorts. Hofmann's data encouraged those removing shale from Kimmeridge and in Scotland, where James Young and William Young (unrelated) operated two successful ventures.

Wanostrocht and Company, using their Wareham shale plant, obtained a contract for the lighting of Paris [1858-62]. Sold to the new Wareham Oil and Candle Company [1862] who continued to operate the Wareham works until it was destroyed by fire [1872].

By this time the West of England Fireclay, Bitumen and Chemical Company was importing 10,000 tons of Kimmeridge shale to its works at Calstock, Cornwall, for the production of between 320,000 and 400,000 gallons a year of shale oil [1871]. A five-year contract for shipment of the Kimmeridge "blackstone" from Dorset to Cornwall was signed by William Camp Crane of Pentonville Road, King's Cross, London (at a rate of at least 800 tons per month, priced at 10-shillings a ton). Problems followed and the contract would be rescinded [2 July 1874]. The West of England Chemical Company went into liquidation [1876] and was formally wound-up [1892].

Yet another venture was taking its place, with the Sanitary Carbon Company being established at Wareham [1876] to convert shales into a coke-type filter for purifying sewage. This was claimed to have a 70 per cent carbon content, compared with only 10 per cent for charcoal, and said therefore to have enhanced deodorising qualities. The firm later re-named itself the Kimmeridge Oil and Carbon Company and was operating the Kimmeridge mines at the close of the Victorian period [1890s].

Scientific clergyman Rev Henry Moule [1801-80], the vicar of Fordington, Dorchester, published a letter in The Times [25 February 1874] claiming he had found a successful method of using Kimmeridge shale in gas-making. He claimed that a ton of shale, when mixed with a ton of chalk, would yield as much gas as 8 tons of coal: "London may be warmed with chalk and anthracite, and lighted with chalk and lignite; and in either case at a diminution of cost exceeding 50 per cent of that now incurred in warming and lighting."

Moule had filed a number of successful patents, including one for an earth closet which was still being sold by the Army and Navy Stores in 1908, and now on display in the Science Museum, but the practicabilities of his shale-gas proposals attracted sceptical reactions. The Times devoted a column to questioning the dubious science [2 April 1874] and no one produced a convincing defence of claims that were dismissed as "ridiculous and exaggerated".

Such advocates of the miracles of shale claimed a specified volume of gas could be extracted in half the time it would take for the same quantity to be extracted from coal. Among the proponents had been Charles Blachford Mansfield [1819-55] who pioneered the coal-tar industry and literally died on the job, being killed by burns when a naphtha still overflowed whilst he was preparing benzol specimens – now known as benzene – for the Paris Exhibition.

For him was named the Mansfield Shaft at Kimmeridge [1883], which led to two tunnels or levels 7-feet high and 7-feet wide, at a depth of 92 feet. The site of the shaft, at the centre of a 15-acre field, was a railed-off enclosure overgrown with scrub but it has long been ploughed back into the field and now shows as a lighter patch of soil.

The shaft needed constant pumping and when worked out it flooded, the mine-shaft principle being abandoned in favour of a number of workings further east that were worked instead from the cliff-face.

During the latter stage of the Kimmeridge shale industry a major expansion took its workings eastward to beyond Clavell's Hard. Its placename, however, pre-dates the 19th-century shale workings. Clavell's Hard, named for a landing beach, appears on Lieutenant Murdock Mackenzie's Survey of the South Coast of England, with this sheet from St Alban's Head to Abbotsbury being printed in 1787.

Plans of the Kimmeridge Oil and Carbon Company operations at the final phase of shale working [1890] show a total of 5,000 feet of underground tunnels, or levels as they called them. Two are charted just west of the Yellow Ledge and Cuddle "D" Plantation but both are marked "worked out". By this time the course of the 1848 tramway was no longer being shown; its rails had been lifted. All the activity was being serviced by the 1883 tramway, as far as two shafts marked as "No. 1 level".

Further east, to beyond Clavell's Hard, the levels were cut from the cliff and are not shown as having any inland shafts. "No. 2" and "No. 3 level" were west of Clavell's Hard; "No. 4 level, not much worked" ran under it; and the furthest eastwards was exploratory "No. 5 level, marked out for cutting".

Galleries branched off these tunnels on each side so they should be regarded as the main lanes of operation rather than the limits of each working. Between No. 1 and No. 2 levels these galleries were extended to a total working of the blackstone beds for the whole of the 150 feet closest to the cliff. Here the plan records: "Line crawl underground – shale taken out."

That is an area of 1,000 feet by 150 feet, which when worked to their standard height of 7 feet would call for the extraction of a million cubic feet of shale and clay.

Later in the 1890s all this frenetic activity came to an end and Kimmeridge's fortunes lapsed until the arrival of oil-drilling explorers.

In his booklet Kimmeridge and Smedmore [1967], Major J. C. Mansel documents some of the more substantial cliffside remains:

"The most obvious remains of the 19th century enterprises are to be seen in the cliff at Clavell's Hard, a mile to the south-east of the bay. Here were tunnels running into the cliff about 30 feet above the shore level. One such tunnel still remains, though its mouth is gradually being closed by falling shale. They were connected by a ledge, presumably artificial, which still remains, though in an unsafe and dilapidated condition. Along the ledge once ran a railway from tunnel to tunnel.

Below the ledge, at low tide, once can find circular cuttings in the flat rock, usually covered by seaweed or full of stones. In these are the metal bases of uprights of which the purpose was presumably to carry some sort of pier."

David Brachi considered that these cuttings were to enable a boat to go in. Donald Maxwell mentioned the workings in his Unknown Dorset [1927]:

". . . our guide made us ascend the cliff at a point where this was possible, and we came to a ledge about halfway to the summit. This, he explained, was the track of an old tramline that carried the trucks from the tunnels to the quay. At the end of this gallery was the opening to one of the workings, still accessible and not, as is the case of all the others, blocked by debris . . . It is now so irregular and so cut into by the weather and consequent landslides that it is hardly recognisable as the track of a railway."

This gallery could still be found in the 1980s. Immediately to the west of Clavell's Hard the coastal footpath crosses three small streams that flow after wet weather. The central one can then provide one of the best waterfalls in Dorset, with a drop of about 30 feet from the clifftop to a ledge about halfway down. A track skirted its west side. On the other side of the water was an extensive patch of red and yellow rock, still noticeably coloured in 1980, from the effects of the cliff having caught fire and burnt from October 1973 to the end of that year.

The coloured area was about 100 feet wide. It ran across the top of the outcrop and extended downwards to the ledge. At the east end of this level there was the shale mine that Maxwell had described. It lay in the rounded corner of the cliff at Clavell's Hard, a few feet above the level of the old terrace. The opening was still accessible, though reduced to half its height by rockfalls from the cliff above.

Running into the cliff was a long, straight gallery about 7-feet wide and 7-feet high. Off it, every 10 feet – on the west side, only, at first – are side chambers. After about 80 feet the main gallery bent and sloped to a lower level. All this is past tense, as such foolhardy exploration is not to be encouraged.

(Prehistoric archaeology / Roman archaeology / Industrial archaeology / Kimmeridge, Wareham, and Weymouth)

Kimmeridge tramways – an Act of Parliament in 1847 gave authority for the construction of "railways, inclined planes, causeways" at Kimmeridge. The earliest mineral railway beside Kimmeridge Bay, a short section of about 600 yards, ran from a short distance east of the Clavell Tower. It kept to the contours of the hill and descended in a cutting at a gradient of about one-in-40. At the south end of Hen Cliff it was set on a terrace above the boathouses.

From this terrace, which may have been abandoned after subsidence, an underground shaft ran inland for about 500 feet.

In 1883 another, longer, tramway was built to link a mine-shaft half a mile east-south-east of the Clavell Tower with a short siding that ran into a working to the north of the Cuddle "D" Plantation and then proceeded down the valley, below the old Coastguard station, on to the rocky beach and along a short length of wooden pier that disintegrated in the 20th century. Part of the line of this tramway can be seen as a scattering of stones in winter and as a crop-mark across the fields in the summer.

(Industrial archaeology / Railways / Kimmeridge)

King's Arms – public house at 27 High Street, Langton Matravers (SY 999 788). This corner building, with footpath number 25 behind and beside it on the south side of the street, is at the end of a line of 18th-century houses. First licensed as the Masons' Arms [1742], with its licensee being a member of the Ancient Order of Purbeck Marblers and Stonecutters, who had their coat of arms.

Rebuilt in the 19th century with a new porch, though incorporating older back parts, and renamed for King George III, who did so much

to popularise the coastal virtues of Weymouth and Lulworth.
(Placenames / Langton Matravers)

King's Hall – beside the Keep at Corfe Castle, being built for King John, on his regular hunting expeditions to Purbeck [1201-04].
(Placenames / Mediaeval archaeology / National Trust / Corfe Castle)

King's Tower – see entry for **North Tower**.

Kingston – the admirably neat Purbeck stone village, with a matching pump at its centre, on the hilltop south of Corfe Castle, was rebuilt in its present form by William Morton Pitt [1754-1825] of Encombe in the 1780s and 90s. He gave it an inn, originally the New Inn, built in 1787, beside the junction with the hilltop turnpike; it became the Eldon Arms and is now renamed the Scott Arms, for the family rather than their earldom. Pitt also provided a Reading Room and Poorhouse. He also started the first Sunday schools in these parts. It was all part of a programme of social works that were to dissipate the fortune he had inherited from his father.

Pitt established a manufactory on the slopes of the hill looking across to Corfe Castle, to the south of the old church at the east end of the village. It employed 200, including cottage out-workers, producing cordage, course calico, sacking, sailcloth, and spinning twine.

Richard Gough, editing the rare second edition of John Hutchins's County History of Dorset dedicated the four volumes to Pitt and welcomed his industrial initiative: "A noble example this and worthy of imitation to those who are blessed by providence with the means of providing for the wants and necessities of their fellow creatures." It failed, however, when the bottom fell out of its market with the naval victory off Cape Trafalgar [1805] and it is difficult today to visualise Kingston as a manufacturing community.

Cohesive architecture for artisans is what has survived, rather than the social scheme of philanthropic workfare. The matching stone-roofed cottages date from the time of William Morton Pitt's manufactory, circa

Nodding donkey: Dorset's first operational oilwell came on line in 1959 and is now a familiar landmark and tourist attraction, beside Kimmeridge Bay.

Village pump: matches Kingston's neat perfection.

1790, rather than from the Scott-Eldon reign of the 19th century.

Their contribution, the National School, was built as "a handsome school house with residence for the master", in memory of the late Earl and Countess of Eldon, by their children [1856]. It accommodated a maximum of 100 pupils, with the average roll in 1889 being 55 boys and girls and 26 infants, when John and Sarah Bennett were the master and mistress, and Miss Esther Blampey the infants' teacher.

Stone for the building of the village came from London Door Quarry, now known as Quarry Wood, at the head of the Golden Bowl vale at Encombe (SY 950 790).
(Placenames / Social history / Corfe Castle)

Kingston House – the former Vicarage, suitably palatine to match the cathedral proportions of the nearby church (SY 805 795). Dates from the establishment of the ecclesiastical parish of Kingston [1877]. Set in the northern edge of The Plantation.
(Placenames / Corfe Castle)

Kingston House: Victorian former Parsonage for Kingston church.

Langton coast: entirely owned by the National Trust and characterised by man-made shelves, such as at Hedbury Quarry.

L

The Lake – local name for the upper stretch of the Corfe River, at Church Knowle, from the Old English word for a watercourse. Downstream it was popularly known as the Wicken Stream.
(Placenames / Church Knowle)

Langton Manor Farm – on the north side of the summit of Steps Hill at Langton Matravers (SZ 001 789). Dating from the early 18th century it comprises a farmhouse and barn sharing the same roof. The house fronts the village street and Beech Grove Lane used to be its agricultural access, northwards, to Farm Wood and the Valley Road fields.
(Placenames / Langton Matravers)

Langton Matravers – the "Long Farm" village attaching to the Maltravers name is much as it was described by the Victorian editors of John Hutchins's County History, in that it "consists of one street, near a mile in length" [1860].

Entries for the 2,160-acre parish in this work include: Acton; Acton Quarries; AI (Air Interception) radar; Air crashes; Balloon *Gerard Heineken*; Bankes Estate; Blumlein; Brontosaurus; Chapman; Coryton; Court Pound; Court Pound Cottage; Crack Lane; Cuckoo Pound; Dancing Ledge; Dinosaur traces; Diplodocus; Durnford House; Fig Tree Cottage; Forge Cottage; Hayward; Hedbury Quarry; H2S; Ivinghoe; Jarman; Jenkins; King's Arms; Langton Manor Farm; Langton Wallis Heath; Leeson House Field Studies Centre; Mainhyde; Maltravers; Men's Clubroom; Methodist Church; Mount Misery; National School; Norman's Quarry; Old Malthouse; Priest's Way; Puck Lake; Puffins; Purbeck marble; Putlake Farm; The Rectory; Saint George's Church; Saint George's Hall; Saint George's Primary School; Saint Leonard's Chapel; Scout Hut; Serrell's Barn; Ship Inn; Steppeshill; Steps Hill; Street Well; *Sunnyodon notelyi*; Sutton; Tom Burnham's Oak; Tovey; Wilkswood Farm; Wilkswood Priory; and Windmill Knap.

Langton Wallis Heath – 41 acres of registered common land [CL88 and CL139], formerly an

Almost unchanged: Sir James Peile's sketch of the top end of the street at Langton Matravers, dated 1882, where land on both sides of the road is now in National Trust ownership.

Ship Inn: John Ball's 1878 suicide took place in the original hostelry (right) which is dwarfed by its three-storey 1884-built replacement on Steps (or Steppes) Hill at Langton Matravers.

outlying part of West Langton Manor, on mixed wet and dry lowland heath on the southern side of Hartland Moor National Nature Reserve, crossed by Benjamin Fayle's New Line which was a horse-drawn tramway from Norden claypits to Middlebere Jetty on Poole Harbour [1806-1905]. The wetter part sustained an annual right for the removal of 2,000 turves for fuel. Passed into National Trust ownership on the death of Ralph Bankes [1981].
(Placenames / Commons / National Trust / Arne and Langton Matravers)

L'Atlantique – French liner watched from the Purbeck and Portland cliffs as she blazed from stem to stern in the English Channel [5 January 1933]. Her position, as recorded by one of the onlookers on St Alban's Head who had a sextant, was about 50 degrees 34 minutes North, 2 degrees 3 minutes West.

The burnt-out luxury liner, which had cost £3 million, was recovered by Captain Schoofs, the commander, and some of his crew. They hoisted the French tricolour and the ship, with upper decks fallen in, was towed to Cherbourg.
(Shipwrecks / Worth Matravers)

Leeson House Field Studies Centre – 17th-century farmhouse, extended and gentrified into a

Winter wonderland: the road between Gallows Gore and Langton Matravers, looking east with Worth Matravers signed on the right, from the "Eight mile stone" (from Wareham) in 1924.

Victorian country house in 29 acres of parkland at Langton Matravers (SZ 005 787), laid out as Leeson Park by the Garland family [1842]. Workmen discovered a Roman vase containing a coin hoard.

The house became the property of the Earl of Eldon and was inherited by Sir Ernest Stowell Scott of Encombe. Leased to Henry Stilwell JP [1880s], followed by Miss Amy Blanche Knight [1910s] whose High School for Girls was continued, as a private boarding school, by Miss Gabbitas [1930s].

Requisitioned as an out-station of the wartime Telecommunications Research Establishment [1940-42] with a Nissen hut in the grounds being the workshop of Group 8 for the development of H2S aerial radar which enabled the blind-bombing of German cities.

Established as the principal Field Study Centre for the Isle of Purbeck [1960s].
(Placenames / Schools / Langton Matravers)

Legends – the Bronze Age burial mounds on Nine Barrow Down are said to cover the graves of nine kings killed in battle. Another Purbeck belief is that cuckoos hibernate in little woods called Cuckoo Pens or Cuckoo Pounds. The "Phantom Army" of Roman soldiers marching eastwards along the Purbeck Hill, has its entry; having caused the mobilisation of the militia to defend Wareham [December 1678]. St Edward's Fountain at Corfe has the healing waters of an "eye-well". Ghost stories surround nearby Boar Mill.
(Folklore / Purbeck parishes)

London Door Quarry – at the head of Encombe's Golden Bowl, where workings are now tree-covered and known as Quarry Wood (SY 950 791). It provided most of the stone for William Morton Pitt's late-18th century rebuilding and expansion of Kingston village.
(Folklore / Industrial archaeology / Corfe Castle)

Long barrows – communal burial mounds of the Neolithic period, circa 3700 BC to 2700 BC, with two examples in Purbeck. The earlier date is probably represented by the earliest mound on Nine Barrow Down (SY 996 815), which is otherwise a skyline cemetery of later round barrows.

Priest's Way: stony track across the plateau between Worth Matravers and Swanage, seen here on one of its few unenclosed sections, near Spyway.

Cliff climbing: above Blackers Hole on the precipitous coast south of Verney Farm.

Acton Quarries: one of a cluster of small workings on land rented from the National Trust.

A transitionary "oval" barrow, closer to the later date, lies on chalk downland at Stonehill Down in the parish of Church Knowle (SY 923 821).
(Prehistoric archaeology / Church Knowle and Corfe Castle)

Long Island – pine-clad seven acres of Corfe Castle parish, surrounded by salt-marsh, off Shipstal Point, Arne (SY 989 880). This offshore extremity of the Rempstone Estate was rented to Guy and Joan Sydenham [1955] who had been living in ex-Royal Navy Motor Torpedo Boat 453 on Mooring E12 in the Wareham Channel, off Hamworthy. Their 72-feet vessel was beached on the western side of the seven-acre island, beside its old pier, and they proceeded to collect clays for experimentation in a pioneering range of innovative slips, glazes and inlays. Graduated surfaces included a stiff glaze applied over a more liquid one. Products became as diverse as those of any craft pottery in the land, ranging from authentic-looking copies of Bellarmine mugs, named for their Dutch Protestant caricature of the grey-bearded cardinal, to erotic line-ups of terracotta mermaids with smear-glazed torsos.

Poole Harbour postman Harry Reeve not only brought the mail but milk, newspapers, and provisions. He was able to walk across the water, literally, during the big freeze in the first couple of months in 1963. Next, in December 1968, the Sydenhams and their Noah's Ark moved eastwards to another detached part of Corfe Castle parish, to Green Island between Ower and Goathorn, which was owned by Tim Hamilton-Fletcher.

Foundations can be seen of bungalow built by Wareham naturalist Charlton Xavier Hall in Edwardian times. He operated one of the first steam launches to be seen in Poole Harbour.
(Placenames / Arne and Corfe Castle)

The Long Journey – a novel by Charles Dickens, based on the dramatic shipwreck half a century earlier, of the East Indiaman *Halsewell*, between Seacombe and Winspit [1786].
(Literary / Shipwrecks / Worth Matravers)

Lynch Farm – on the lower slope of Kingston Hill (SY 960 801), this was the dairy for Corfe Castle until the mid-20th century. Fred Audley and his mare, Topsey, used to bring unpasteurised milk in an open cart daily to Corfe village, into the 1950s.

The buildings date from the 17th century, with some original ground floor windows. The remainder of the farmhouse was rebuilt and expanded over the next couple of centuries. The outbuilding on the north side dates from the 18th century and appears to have been the brewhouse and bakery.
(Placenames / Corfe Castle)

Lynch Lodge – on Kingston Hill (SY 958 799) at the northern extremity of the Kingston landscaping and woods. There is the raised line of an old road across the field to the south-west.
(Placenames / Corfe Castle)

Lynchets – see entries for **East Man** and **Winspit strip lynchets**.

Strip lynchets: the former open fields of Worth Matravers have some of the best sets of cultivation terraces in the country, these being at the head of Seacombe Bottom.

M

Machold – Luftwaffe ace **Oberleutnant Werner Machold**, Staffelkapitan of the 7th Gruppe of Jagdeschwader 2 Richthofen, who had been credited with the fighter wing's 100th victory over France and was personally congratulated by Field Marshal Hermann Göring, crash-landed at Worth Matravers [6 June 1941]. He was taken prisoner of war.
(People / Aviation / Worth Matravers)

Mackintosh – architect and water-colour artist **Charles Rennie Mackintosh** [1869-1928], from Glasgow, painted at Worth Matravers during a holiday with his London friends Randolph Schwabe and family [July 1920]. They were some of his first landscapes and are now in the collection of the Glasgow School of Art.

Its headmaster from 1885 to 1918 was Francis Newbery, who had recently retired to Corfe Castle, and encouraged Mackintosh to visit Purbeck. Schwabe was the Slade Professor of Fine Art at London University.
(People / Artists / Worth Matravers)

Mainhyde – mediaeval strip fields of the manor of Langton Matravers, later part of Langton Manor Farm and Putlake Farm, still aligned in parallel, southwards from Steps Hill (SZ 002 789) to the sea cliffs in 2,000 yards. Now mostly owned by the National Trust.
(Placenames / Mediaeval archaeology / Langton Matravers)

Mansion House – see entry for **Barnston Farm**.

Maltravers – regicide **Sir John Maltravers, 1st Baron Maltravers** [1290-1364] of Lytchett Matravers, held King Edward II prisoner in Corfe Castle [1327] and pretended he was still there, after being removed to Berkeley Castle where he was killed, in order to trap Edward's brother, Edmund, into plotting his rescue. As a result, Edmund was beheaded, for treason.

Maltravers was rewarded by a writ of summons to Parliament as a baron and appointed Constable of Corfe Castle and controller of its royal hunting grounds.

These gains were short-lived, however, as fellow conspirator Roger Mortimer was overthrown and Maltravers "fled abroad once more and in his absence was sentenced by Parliament to be hanged, drawn and beheaded as a traitor for compassing in the death of the Earl of Kent".

Eventually, in 1345, he was allowed to return to England though it was not until the age of nearly 70 that he returned to his estate at Lytchett, near Poole, where he died peacefully in his own home in 1364.

There in the church of St Mary his brass lies on the floor of the north aisle. The village was known as "Luchet Mautravers" in 1291 and, today, as Lytchett Matravers, it still preserves the family name. Likewise do Worth Matravers and Langton Matravers in the Isle of Purbeck.
(People / Politics / Corfe Castle, Langton Matravers, Lytchett Matravers and Worth Matravers)

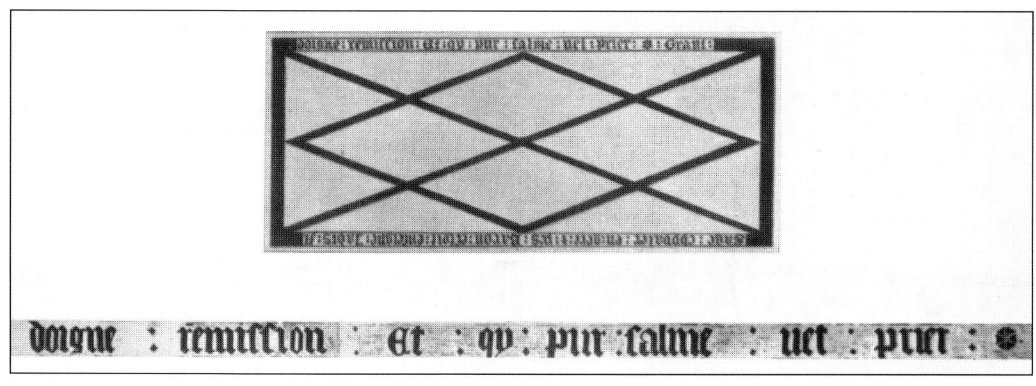

Maltravers fret: the large brass to Sir John at Lytchett Matravers.

Marble – see entry for **Corfe Castle marble industry**.

Marblers and Stonecutters – see entry for **Company of Marblers and Stonecutters of Purbeck**.

Market Cross – in the Square at Corfe Castle, on ancient steps, restored for Queen Victoria's diamond jubilee [1897]. Beside it is the Town Pump.
(Placenames / Corfe Castle)

Matcham Claypit Roman burials – found in 1882 in "stone coffins", though probably of the rougher slab-cist type, beside a buried length of ancient roadway and a "fine collection of Roman pottery" midway between the main road and the railway line at Norden (SY 957 826). Mainly comprising "urn-shaped vessels, decorated with a lozenge pattern around the neck", the pots were taken by the 3rd Earl of Eldon and since lost.
(Roman archaeology / Corfe Castle)

Mauleon – troubadour **Savaris de Mauleon** [early 12th century] was imprisoned in Corfe Castle. He had taken King John's mother, Eleanor, prisoner in the disputed province of Aquitaine. She would be rescued by John and Mauleon was fortunate in being among only ten of the 25 French prisoners at Corfe who did not starve to death.

He surreptitiously changed sides, and returned home as an English agent, becoming a famous troubadour.
(People / Politics / Corfe Castle)

Meadus's Lane – the road from Bushey (SY 975 832), north-eastwards towards the former Rempstone Heath, now Purbeck Forest, where it becomes Peppercorn Lane for the penultimate length of the mediaeval marble track from Corfe Castle to Ower Quay.
(Placenames / Roads / Corfe Castle)

Men's Clubroom – on the west side of St George's Hall on the south side of the High Street at Langton Matravers (SY 998 788). This 18th-century cottage was converted into an independent school, to rival the Church of England's National School which was then next door, by eccentric widow Mrs Francis Serrell of Durnford House [1869-74]. This initiative had been sparked by a personality clash with the rector, Rev E. F. Trotman. "Madame Serrell," as she was known, also held her own Sunday services.
(Churches / Social history / Langton Matravers)

Mesolithic midden – see entry for **Blashenwell Farm**.

Methodist Church (Corfe Castle) – built as a Wesleyan Chapel, on the west side of East Street, opposite Calcraft Road (SY 963 816).
(Churches / Corfe Castle)

Methodist Church (Langton Matravers) – on the south side of the High Street at Langton Matravers, up from footpath number 27 and Old Malthouse Lane (SY 996 787). It was built in 1875. On the west side, now the Methodist Hall, is the earlier chapel, with a datestone [1842] and original spearhead-style railings.
(Churches / Langton Matravers)

Middle Halves – known locally as "The Aves" these 17.7 acres of registered common land between West Street and East Street at Corfe Castle were mediaeval communal fields. Ownership was unclaimed at the time of registration but the ground appears to have been manorial waste of Corfe Castle, in which case title passed to the National trust with Ralph Bankes's huge bequest [1982]. This would give it rights of public access, though these are hardly necessary as footpaths already cross and converge from all directions.
(Placenames / Commons / Corfe Castle)

Middlebere canoe tragedy – took place off the southern shore of Poole Harbour [evening, 25 March 1868] when clay cutter Thomas Fry, with his son aged about six, and 16-year-old

Mary Ann Green and their three-year-old sister, Emily, attempted returning from Poole Quay to Purbeck. They had set off towards dusk, at 18.00 hours, and were heading for Middlebere, the Poole Pilot newspapers reported:

"Nothing was seen of the boat or its occupants until the following morning about nine o'clock when the canoe was found bottom upwards in the Wareham Channel, and the dead body of Emily Green floating near it. The bodies of Mary Ann Green and of Thomas Fry were picked up the following day. The little boat was evidently overladen, having on board, besides the four occupants, a sack of seed, three bundles of salt fish, and other articles."

(Shipwrecks / Corfe Castle and Poole)

Middlebere Quay – former clay export jetty on Middlebere Lake, a backwater of Poole Harbour (SY 973 866). It was the seagoing end of Fayle's Tramway [1806-1905], from Norden, taking shipments in barges to Poole Quay from where the ball clay was transferred to ocean-going vessels.

The pilot for the muddy waters at Middlebere and the voyage across the harbour lived at Ower Quay and would be summoned by a flag when barges were loaded and ready. In a favourable south-westerly wind they could be pulled by sail-power. Otherwise they were tugged by the steam tugs *Commodore* or *Telegraph*.

Middlebere Farm and Middlebere peninsula came into National Trust ownership with the estate of Ralph Bankes [1982].

(Industrial archaeology / National Trust / Railways / Arne and Corfe Castle)

Milestones – of the Wareham Turnpike Trust [1765-1876], along the main road to Corfe Castle. "IV MILES FROM WAREHAM" stands on the north side of Castle Hill (SY 959 824). The others towards Wareham are south of Catseye Cottage (SY 947 833), north of Halfway Inn (SY 936 845), and on Stoborough Green (SY 926 858).

In the other direction, towards Swanage, the milestones marked what is now the secondary main road, the B3069, being on Corfe Common (SY 964 810), showing "V MILES FROM WAREHAM," followed by Kingston Hill (SY 958 798), the Corfe side of the Worth turning (SY 971 791), the Corfe side of the Acton turn (SY 987 787), Putlake farm (SZ 002 789), and finally on the Swanage side of the Herston crossroads (SZ 018 798) with "X MILES FROM WAREHAM".

(Placenames / Roads / Purbeck parishes)

Corfe milestone: four miles from Wareham, at the foot of Castle Hill.

Milford Cottage – former habitation on the south side of Peppercorn Lane, immediately west of the stream 500 yards south-west of Ower Farm (SY 996 851).

(Placenames / Corfe Castle)

Mizmaze – field name in the vale of the Corfe River, north of Bradle Farm (SY 930 807), preserving the memory of the site of one of Shakespeare's "quaint mazes, in the wanton green, for lack of tread".

(Placenames / Mediaeval archaeology / Church Knowle)

Model Village – off the Market Square, Corfe Castle. It was designed by E. O. Holland and S. A. Walford and completed in 1966. Its centrepiece is a scaled reconstruction of Corfe Castle before its Civil War destruction, which has more meaning than is usual with these things as the actual ruin looms huge in the background for comparison.

The model demonstrates that the village is an architectural entity, with cottages merging with their neighbours. This has left the two streets much the same as they would have looked centuries before. West Street is least disturbed, the turnpiking of East Street having provided an alternative for expansion.
(Placenames / National Trust / Corfe Castle)

Montanes – steamship heading east, which rammed the rocks beside St Alban's Head and became a complete wreck [23 November 1906].
(Shipwrecks / Worth Matravers)

Morris – alleged gossip **Martha Morris** was the last person to be ducked at Corfe Castle, into Batrick's Mill Pond beside Boar Mill. The occasion was recalled for me by Lieutenant-Colonel Archie Strange-Boston who was born at West Bucknowle House, between Corfe and Church Knowle, in 1892:

"I remember seeing Martha Morris being ducked in Batrick's Mill Pond at Corfe Castle. It must have been about 1898 or 1899. Martha was the wife of Bob Morris and she lived close to Mr Mitchell who was the blacksmith. She had been gossiping about someone and I can just remember seeing her sitting on the end of a large plank and being dumped up and down in the water.

"I can also record some of those in the crowd. There was an old tough named Happy Jack. He'd fight the devil himself and was always in 'drunk' trouble with Sergeant Conquest. And there was a man named Rackham who lived in one of the cottages on the north side of the church and facing the Square.
(People / Social history / Corfe Castle)

Morton's House – symmetrical grand house, now an hotel, on the east side of East Street at the northern end of its wider section. This coherent piece of architecture, built on an E-plan dates from 1600 and was built in one operation, around a courtyard and a porch, with a layout of the country house type, rather than for one confined by a town street.

On each side of the courtyard there is a wing, with the main reception rooms and hall being placed centrally, beyond the porch. Behind the hall is a 17th-century extension.

Owned in 1635 by Edward Dackham who died that year and bequeathed it to younger son Bruen Dackham. Between 1682 and 1723 it was sold by his grandson, Henry Dackham, to John Morton, whose name has stuck. It's

Going down: an almost serene end, in the moonlight, for the steamship *Montanes*, on the rocks at St Alban's Head.

Edwardian refurbishments were carried out by Frederick Cavendish-Bentinck [1856-1948]. (Placenames / Corfe Castle)

Mount Misery – hilltop cluster of 18th and 19th-century underground stone workings on the north side of the main road at the top end of Langton Matravers village (SY 990 790). Norman's Quarry survives, though pensioned-off in National Trust care, having been bequeathed as part of the immense Bankes Estate [1982].

These days it goes under the softer name of Castle View – the outlook being Corfe Castle to the north-west – but long into the 20th century this was the hard-labour end of the village, contrasting with open-air life on pastoral Mount Pleasant above the parish church, half a mile to the east. (Placenames / Industrial archaeology / National Trust / Langton Matravers)

Mural Tower – see entry for **South Tower**.

Morton's House: among the largest in Corfe village, now an hotel.

Cotness daffodils: beside a thatched farmstead typical of those on the heathlands of Church Knowle parish.

N

National School (Church Knowle) – the Anglican day school for boys and girls was built in 1855, for 90 children, with Miss Jessie Bowden being its best remembered early mistress [circa 1890]. It became an Elementary School.
(Placenames / Schools / Church Knowle)

National School (Kimmeridge) – now the Old School, was established as a mixed facility, for 60 children [1866]. The school house was nearby, rather than adjoining, and the mistress in late Victorian times was Miss Eleanor Chamard.
(Placenames / Schools / Kimmeridge)

National School (Langton Matravers) – see entries for **Ivinghoe**, **St George's Hall**, and **St George's Primary School**.

National Trust – inherited Corfe Castle and its estate, including most of the stunning scenery and much of the village, plus outlying gems from Middlebere Farm, in Arne parish, on Poole Harbour to Seacombe Cliff, Worth Matravers, on the English Channel. Including also the Kingston Lacy Estate, making it the Trust's largest ever single bequest, it came with the death of the last private owner, Ralph Bankes [1981].

Additions have consolidated its hold on Purbeck's southern coastline, notably at Dancing Ledge and Spyway Farm [1992] and on the slopes of East Man, including a segment of Winspit strip lynchets [1999].
(National Trust / Multiple parishes)

New Inn (Church Knowle) – the 17th-century thatched building on the south side of the main street in Church Knowle, which has expanded to occupy the equally old next-door dairy (SY 938 817). It has been the New Inn since long before living memory and survived a fire in the 1990s.

New Inn: visibly exceedingly old, in the village of Church Knowle.

As for its predecessor, the name of the old inn it supplanted is lost in the hill-fog of time.
(Placenames / Church Knowle)

New Inn (Kimmeridge) – former Victorian hostelry at Kimmeridge, when Henry Hibbs was the publican.
(Placenames / Kimmeridge)

New Inn (Kingston) – its none too original first name [1787] when built by William Morton Pitt. Renamed the Eldon Arms and later the Scott Arms, for the family rather than their title.
(Placenames / Corfe Castle)

New Line – original name of claypit owner Benjamin Fayle's horse-drawn tramway from his workings at Norden to Middlebere Quay on Poole Harbour [1806-1905]. See entry for Fayle's Tramway.
(Placenames / Railways / Corfe Castle)

New Mills – early 18th-century New Mills stood at the western extremity of the Rempstone Estate, on the Corfe River near Scotland (SY 963 839). Extensive buildings seem to have had a short working life. Only a barn survives at this site but the main operation may have taken place further downstream.
(Placenames / Industrial archaeology / Corfe Castle)

Inscribed sluices: dated 1711, being all that remains of the New Mills on the Corfe River.

New Mills Sluices – 500 yards north-west of New Mills, elegant sluices with stone cutwaters now carry Corfe Castle public footpath number 80 across the Corfe River (SY 968 842).

Dated 1711, by a stone, the cutwaters also carry carved initials. Facing west, and therefore seen by those looking east, is "W. O." and the eastern side – seen as you look towards Scotland – carries "N. B." for the ownership of Nathaniel Bankes.

E. A. Roberts suggested to me that these had to be the sluices for the otherwise disappeared mills: "The bridge openings could be blocked to create a head of water backed-up to serve a leat – now much overgrown but still discernible over its considerable length – which follows the edge of the valley floor for about 400 yards before rejoining the Corfe River. There are other features in the immediate area of the bridge and its approaches; such as sunken ways, oak trees of large girth, a pond, and drainage channels."
(Placenames / Industrial archaeology / National Trust / Corfe Castle)

New Road – straight west to east length of what is now the B3351, from the Keeper's Cottage (SY 973 827) and across the drive to Brinscombe Farm, then onwards to Rempstone (SY 987 823). It dates from Victorian times and was cut to bypass the former diversion via Higher Bushey Farm and Rempstone Farm.
(Placenames / Roads / Corfe Castle)

Newbery – artist **Francis Newbery** [1858-1946] was born in Bridport and retired to Eastgate, East Street, Corfe Castle [1918], where he designed the cemetery gateway as a memorial to the village's Great War dead. He also carved a statue of the boy-king Saint

Newton claypits: at the southern end of the Goathorn peninsula, with its railway stretching westwards (left) and crossing sandy tracks, in a Luftwaffe reconnaissance photograph.

Edward for the parish church and painted the Martyr's sign for the Square.

Other of his paintings are in the Catholic Church at Swanage, and the Town Hall, Bridport. His career had been as an art master and he soon rose to the top, becoming head of Glasgow School of Art [circa 1888] and left a lasting mark on the place by choosing Charles Rennie Mackintosh as the architect for its rebuilding.

Newbery later established a substantial presence in the international art world by cataloguing and advising on purchasing to major public galleries all over Europe. For that he was created a Knight Officer of the Order of the Crown of Italy. Locally, he was remembered in Corfe Castle for his stature rather than his status. "He was a big man, with long white hair, and a walrus moustache," a former neighbour told me.
(People / Artists / Bridport and Corfe Castle)

Nine Barrow Down – prominent skyline cemetery of "bowl" shaped Bronze Age round barrows strung out from west to east along the Purbeck Hills at the eastern end of Corfe Castle parish, confusingly shown as Ailwood Down on the map (SY 995 816 to 997 815).

Just south of them, towards the eastern end, is an earlier Neolithic long barrow (SY 996 815). This mound of chalk, 112 feet long by 40 feet wide, would have been built to cover collective burials of about 3500 BC in the Late Stone Age. Aligned from west to east – the latter being the burial end.

Around it is the major prehistoric cemetery of the Purbeck Hills, with each mound covering a single burial urn accompanied with aristocratic grave goods and food for the after-life, erected by émigré Beaker Folk from the Rhine who established the rich warrior-dominated Wessex Culture of 2100 to 1500 BC in the Bronze Age. Actually there are 17 such mounds of which the largest on Ailwood Down gave their name to Nine Barrow Down (which has shifted eastwards on the map).

Only nine are more than two feet high. They are set in a line running for 800 feet along the

Skyline burials: Bronze Age barrows on the summit of the Purbeck Hills, giving name to Nine Barrow Down.

crest of the Purbeck ridge at 600 feet above sea level. The largest is 100 feet in diameter and ten feet high, surrounded by a substantial ditch that is still four feet deep. All received the attention of 18th or early-19th century barrow diggers – and should have provided above-average plunder – but no record exists of the event or their contents.

Legend has it that they are the graves of nine kings who were killed in battle. The barrows, with the exception of one on the other side of the fence at the east end, are in the care of the National Trust, having been inherited with the Bankes Estate [1982].
(Placenames / Prehistoric archaeology / National Trust / Corfe Castle)

Norden Clay Works – originally on the north-west side of Norden Plantation (SY 049 833), on the Middlebere side of the northern of the two tunnels that took Fayle's Tramway under the main road (SY 948 832).

This site was severed by the construction of the mainline branch railway from Wareham in 1885, causing Norden Clay Works to be moved to Eldon Sidings (SY 857 829), 900 yards south-east. From here a new mineral line headed towards the western claypits, across the Swanage Railway by a bridge, and over the main road at a level crossing.

Fayle's Tramway ceased operation in 1905 when a new mineral line was constructed north-eastwards from Eldon Sidings, for six miles, to a jetty of the Goathorn peninsula. That closed in 1939 and all clayfield operations at Norden were transferred to Furzebrook by 1970.

See entries for Fayle's Tramway and Goathorn Railway.
(Industrial archaeology / Railways / Corfe Castle)

Norden Claypits Roman buildings – on the opposite side of the branch railway from Norden Clay Works (SY 956 827). Roman finds have been made during the digging of pipelines and road-making. The area is highly disturbed from past digging for ball-clay and only intermittent patches of ancient ground survive.

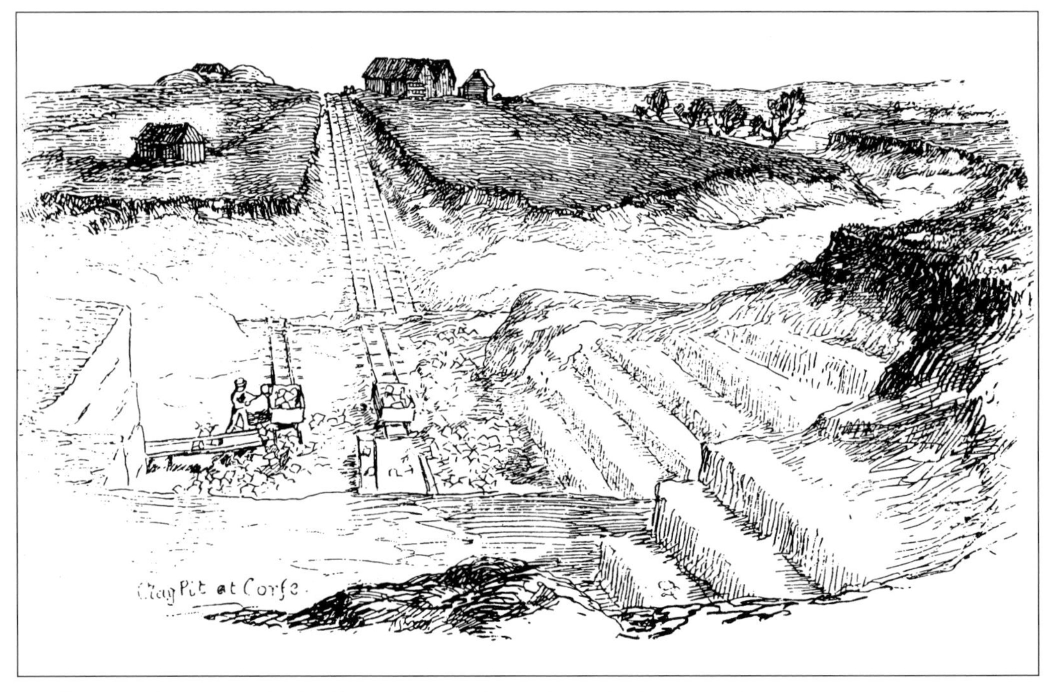

Norden claypits: the Fayle family workings, drawn by Alfred Dawson in 1882.

These are, however, rich with antiquities, including lathe-turned shale armlet cores.

A floor with stone paving and some 4th-century pottery have been found near the Wareham-Corfe road [1964] and a chalk and limestone paved floor was nearby. Another layer of stone blocks may have been part of the surface of the road. Three Kimmeridge shale plaques were found at Hill Coppices, Norden (SY 951 826) together with two carved shale table-legs and "a pair of bronze dividers" [before 1859], indicating that this was one of the major workshops for the manufacture of quality articles in the shale industry. The associated buildings are of a far higher standard than those usually found near shale workings and suggest something more important than labourers' huts.
(Roman archaeology / Corfe Castle)

Norden Station – see entry for **Railway**.

Norman's Quarry – one of the last remaining underground quarries in the Isle of Purbeck has been restored by the National Trust [1995] at Castle View, Langton Matravers, on the rise that used to be known as Mount Misery (SY 989 789). The project was declared complete by the widow of the last quarryman to work the stone mine, Ernie Norman, until the Second World War. It represents just one of hundreds of such small workings that once operated along the limestone plateau of southern Purbeck.

The hand-cut tunnels of the working are now a bat roost. Above ground, the circle around the capstan would have been trod by a donkey or pony, to winch stone up the incline.

Mechanisation and open-pit surface workings made such methods totally redundant by the 1960s and the nature of the underground work would now probably be regarded as illegal on safety grounds.
(Placenames / Industrial archaeology / National Trust / Langton Matravers)

North Castle – cottages are gone, though barns survive, in what was once a tiny hamlet below West Hill, beside heathland and what is now the A351, just north of St Edward's Bridge and Castle Hill at Corfe Castle (SY 958 824). The area

North Castle: seen from West Hill, with National Trust barn and Visitor Centre, and train approaching Norden Station.

returned to life in the 1990s with the opening of the National Trust's Castle View car-park, with an adjoining Visitor Centre, in the former quarry where a Hurricane crashed during the Battle of Britain. Along the slope behind it the Swanage Railway also experienced a revival and now steams into Norden.
(Placenames / National Trust / Corfe Castle)

North Tower – previously known as King's Tower, being part of King John's strengthening of Corfe Castle in 1201-04. In the 1750s it was the sleeping place for the rector of Corfe who set up his living accommodation in the South Tower on the opposite side of the West Bailey.
(Placenames / Mediaeval archaeology / Corfe Castle)

Departing train: 1948 Brighton-built "Battle of Britain" class Bulleid Pacific, No 34072 *207 Squadron* leaving Norden for Swanage.

Wareham next: the current end of the line, for the Swanage Railway, is at Norden.

O

Oilfield – see entries for **Kimmeridge Oil Well** and **Wytch Oilfield**.

Old Cottage – thatched 17th-century building on the east side of the Post Office in the village street at Church Knowle (SY 939 818).
(Placenames / Church Knowle)

Old Malthouse – former brewery buildings on the north side of the High Street at Langton Matravers (SY 996 788). It was operated in Victorian times by Charles Chinchen Edmunds. In the early 20th century the building was converted by Reginald Corbett into the Old Malthouse Boys' Boarding School, and is now run by the Old Malthouse School Trust.
(Placenames / Industrial archaeology / Schools / Langton Matravers)

Old Mill – see entry for **Puddle Mill Farm**.

Old Rectory – on the corner south of the parish church at Church Knowle (SY 941 819). Rebuilt in mid-Victorian mock-Tudor style by Rev Owen Luttrell Mansel, who was the rector from 1852 until 1898. An earlier Rectory on the site had six chimneys, according to the Hearth Tax Returns of 1664, but by the time of the Tithe Redemption Map of 1842 and Mansel's arrival from Smedmore House, it was a smaller building which he proceeded to more than double in size.
(Placenames / Church Knowle)

Texas rediscovered: the exploratory drilling that put Purbeck on the world oil map, from map reference SY 980 853, in the autumn of 1973.

Old School House – between Haskell's Farm and the road junction north of Grange Gate at Creech, where Alice Kerley [1872-1930] was the teacher. She was the grandmother of your present author, Rodney Legg.
(Placenames / Schools / Church Knowle)

Olive Branch – a brig, stranded on the Kimmeridge Ledges, off Clavell's Hard [20 April 1838] and later floated free.
(Shipwrecks / Kimmeridge)

Wytch Farm: mineral diversification, yet again, in a landscape which had seen in the second millennium with salt-pans rather than conventional farming.

Nodding donkeys: pumping trio on Shotover Heath, north of Rempstone.

Gathering station: hidden in the pine trees of Wytch Fir Pound.

Oliver Vye's Lane – the public path beside the Wicken Stream, to use the local name for the Corfe River, on the south-west side of Castle Hill (SY 959 822).
(Placenames / Roads / National Trust / Corfe Castle)

Orenstein and Koppel – makers of two diesel locomotives, OK 20777 and OK 21160, brought from Germany and sold at auction by the Ministry of Supply [1947], being bought by Fayle and Company for use on their mineral railway in the Purbeck claylands. The first is said to have been used on V2 rocket sites.
(Industrial archaeology / Railways / Church Knowle)

Outer Bailey – the southern projection of Corfe Castle, with surrounding defences dating from 1212-15. Previously it was inside timber palisades and crossed on the north side by a wall built in 1235, now under grass, about 50 feet south of the Great Ditch.
(Placenames / Mediaeval archaeology / National Trust / Corfe Castle)

Outer Bridge – enters Corfe Castle, across four arches on stone piers that span the dry moat. Built between 1250-85. Cobbled with stone setts. Provided with timber safety rails in 1995.
(Placenames / Mediaeval archaeology / National Trust / Corfe Castle)

Ower Farm – its notable 20th-century inhabitant, retiring to East Street in Corfe Castle, was "Granfer" Joe Wills who was born at Ower in 1860 and worked for Edwin Abbott at Ower Farm. He was still remembering the old days into the 1950s: "I can well remember the clay boats tying up at Goathorn Wharf. And the old marble road was still there when I was a boy. Soft [Shrove] Tuesday was always the day when we had a bit of excitement. For on that day the Purbeck Marblers used to come down Peppercorn Lane from Corfe to Ower Farm, and pay their rent – a pound of pepper."
(Placenames / Corfe Castle)

Ower Quay – embarkation port at high tide into the South Deep on the southern shore of Poole Harbour, for the export of Purbeck marble in the Middle Ages (SY 997 862). Also the point of importation for New Forest timber used in the building of Corfe Castle. The marble was carted from Corfe Castle, across what was Rempstone Heath, then along the approach road from the south, which is now a public bridleway.

Apart from the cottage beside the track, all that survived into recent times was a wharf of disappearing timbers and a few weathered

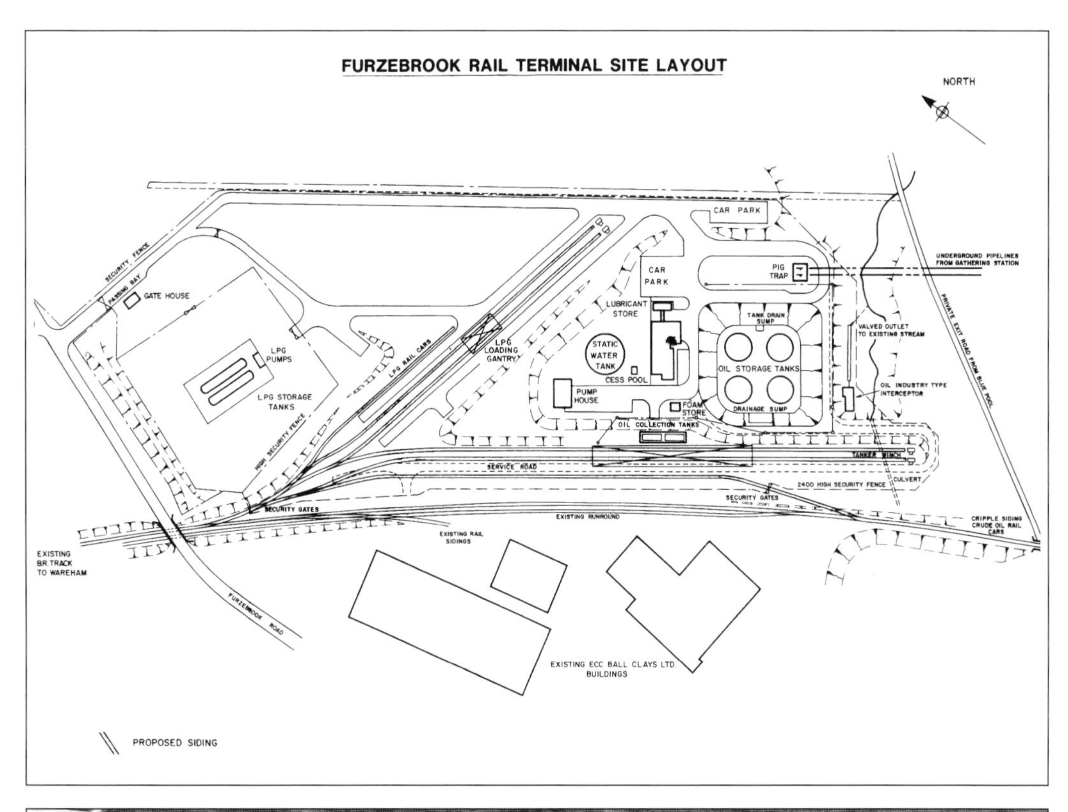

Rail terminal: tanks and an oil train on sidings at Furzebrook, constructed in 1978.

Ower Quay: mediaeval embarkation point for Purbeck marble, sinking into obscurity beside Poole Harbour.

blocks of marble from the past; now in a state of geological confusion following imports of Mendip limestone in a coastal consolidation exercise sponsored by BP. Just offshore, a line of 16 posts protruding beside the salt marsh in Ower Bay are the timbers of an old ship that was a floating cafe early in the 20th century.

Ower Quay had fallen into complete disuse by the 18th century, when John Hutchins, vicar of Wareham, was writing his county history: "Ower seems to have been formerly the chief port of the Isle of Purbeck, and it was the principal, if not the only quay, for the exportation of stone and marble. On this account the quarriers pay on Ash Wednesday yearly one pound of pepper and a football to the lord [of the manor]. The timber brought from the New Forest in Hampshire and used in the construction of Corfe Castle was landed here, and the remains of deep tracks and roads leading across the heath from Ower towards Corfe Castle show that there must anciently have been considerable traffic carried on at this place. Since 1710 the exportation of stone has been neglected here, and that branch of business removed to Swanage."

(Placenames / Mediaeval archaeology / Corfe Castle)

P

Palgrave – authoress **Mary Palgrave**, one of the five daughters of Sir Reginald Palgrave of Hillside, Peveril Road, Swanage, wrote *Brave Dame Mary*. Publishing anonymously, and then under the pseudonym Louisa Hawtrey [1873], it is a classic Victorian tale, telling the heroism of Lady Mary Bankes who defiantly held Corfe Castle against its first Civil War siege. It ran to many editions and shows how it was that several generations became conditioned virtually from birth in the righteousness of the Royalist cause.

In *Under the Blue Flag*, Mary Palgrave moved the action eastwards to Godlingston Manor, near the Ulwell Gap, and extended the conflict to the Duke of Monmouth's abortive rebellion of 1685.
(People / Literary / Corfe Castle and Swanage)

Phantom Army – the spectre of a ghostly force of "several thousand" marching men, coming from the direction of Flower's Barrow above Tyneham and heading eastwards along the Purbeck ridgeway towards Corfe Castle, was reported by four clay-cutters and authenticated by Captain John Lawrence of Creech Grange [December 1678].

Panic spread through Wareham, where boats were drawn to the north side of the River Frome, and the mediaeval humped bridge barricaded, as 300 militia were mobilised to defend the town. Captain Lawrence and his brother rode post haste to London where, according to historian John Hutchins, they "deposed the particulars on oath" to the Privy Council, "and had not he and his family been of known affection to the Government, would have been severely punished, the nation being in a ferment about the Oates Plot".

Invasion phobia must be seen in the context of turbulent 17th-century politics as well as the popular belief that a Roman legion is seen marching across western Purbeck when the nation faces war. James II was under threat from gentlemen more dangerous than Titus Oates, and in the next decade would face actual invading armies passing through Dorset, firstly flocking to the standard of the unsuccessful Duke of Monmouth [1685] and then rallying for Prince William of Orange [1688] who would take the Stuart throne.
(Folklore / Politics / Corfe Castle, Steeple, Tyneham and Wareham)

Pier Bottom – no longer with a pier, being the deep-cut valley on the coastal footpath between St Alban's Head and Chapman's Pool (SY 959 759). Offshore, two unidentified French ships, a brig and a chasse maree, were wrecked in a gale [7 April 1838].
(Placenames / Shipwrecks / Worth Matravers)

Pincher – Lord Chancellor Eldon's last dog, a German spaniel, who outlived his master by two years and died at Encombe in 1840. Lord Eldon had left him an annuity of £8 in his will. Pincher's memorial stone is beside Eldon Seat.
(Pets / Memorials / Corfe Castle)

Pitt – philanthropist **William Morton Pitt** [1754-1836], the son of Marcia and John Pitt of Encombe, was the second of the William Pitts of the late-18th century. The first was an entirely different personality – the mastermind of the "Pitt and Plunder" system of British Government, which created poverty and distress for Dorset cousin William to mitigate.

Our Pitt inherited a vast fortune from his father and dissipated it on good works. Sir Tresham Lever, in The House of Pitt, writes that because of his spending "the wealthiest branch of the family sank into the obscurity of the landless middle class". His personal programme of social works included a cordage works at Kingston, a fish-curing plant in Swanage, a spinning and bleaching school at Fordington, Dorchester, and a hat-making works in the new County Gaol.

He had been instrumental in its rebuilding [1787] and was delighted that in the improved regime many prisoners "are now behaving well and maintaining themselves and their families by their own industry".

Though hardly a Parliamentarian, by the standards of the family, he represented Poole [1780-90] and then sat as one of the county members for Dorset [1790-1826], describing it as a career which "though not brilliant has been laborious for 45 years". He seldom spoke in the House of Commons but was more influential locally. He was the first chairman of the management committee of Forston House Lunatic Asylum, Charminster.

In the process he lost his great houses at Kingston Maurward. Stinsford, and at Encombe, as well as Kingston village, and threw his final money and energy into converting the Manor House, Swanage, into the Royal Victoria Hotel. He wrote at the age of 71 that "both Mrs Pitt and I have beggared ourselves for some time past towards the accomplishment of this object".
(People / Politics / Social history / Corfe Castle, Stinsford and Swanage)

Portland Vase: bought by the Duchess of Portland in 1790, as a Roman antiquity, and copied by Josiah Wedgwood, using vitreous fine stoneware from Purbeck ball clay.

The Plantation – dense woods, partially covering mediaeval quarries (SY 804 793), separating the estate village of Kingston from its country house which lies in the Golden Bowl at Encombe.
(Placenames / Corfe Castle)

Plukenet Tower – on the north-east side of the Outer Bailey at Corfe Castle, up from the Great Ditch, built between 1250-85.
(Placenames / Mediaeval archaeology / National Trust / Corfe Castle)

Porpoises – large schools of several dozen used to be seen swimming and turning in the choppy race off St Alban's Head, with individuals frequently following paddle-steamers between Swanage and Bournemouth. They, like the paddle-steamers, are now a rarity, but the headland remains a vantage point for watching common dolphin, bull-nosed dolphin, and the occasional killer whale. A Dolphin Watch project monitors their numbers from Durlston Head.
(Natural history / Purbeck parishes)

Portland Vase – "O Attic shape! Fair attitude!" wrote John Keats on viewing the Great Vase, a 2,000-year-old Roman antiquity, which was bought by the Duchess of Portland [1785]. Ceramic copies would be made, but only after 10,000 experiments, from which Josiah Wedgwood invented Jasper, a vitreous fine stoneware, in which Purbeck ball clay was the essential ingredient [1790].
(Industrial archaeology / Purbeck parishes)

Post Office (Church Knowle) – archetypal village postal stores, in a thatched-roofed late-18th century building, between the Old Cottage and New Inn (SY 939 818) succumbed to closure [1995].
(Placenames / Church Knowle)

Priest's Way – the ancient highway between Worth Matravers and Swanage, via the stone plateau south of Langton Matravers, is for the most part a wide droveway between stone walls. Two miles of its length is owned by the National Trust (SY 979 778 to SZ 014 783).

Its name dates back to the early Middle Ages when Swanage (or Sandwich) was a chapelry of Worth parish church and the priest had to trek between the two. As a road, however, it goes back to the ridgeways of prehistoric times.
(Placenames / Roads / National Trust / Langton Matravers, Swanage, and Worth Matravers)

Primus – Purbeck's first steam locomotive, being an 0-6-0T bought by Pike Brothers of Ridge Clay Works from Bellis and Seekings [1866] to mechanise the Furzebrook Tramway. She had a low boiler and high chimney (there were no bridges). Converted to a stationary engine, for hauling wagons out of pits at Furzebrook [before 1888], and scrapped by the end of the 19th century.
(Industrial archaeology / Railways / Arne and Corfe Castle)

Puck Lake – intermittent stream on the west side of Steps Hill, Langton Matravers. Flows northwards, east of Crack Lane (SZ 002 789). Its "Puckish" behaviour is to vary in flow from total drought to flash-flood.
(Placenames / Rivers / Langton Matravers)

Puddle Mill Farm – two-storey late-18th century tiled-roofed farmhouse beside the Corfe River, south-west of Church Knowle (SY 936 800), with the ruined Old Mill being 200 yards to the west, on the other side of the lane (SY 934 800).

The road was gated near the bridge. Beyond, to the south, were the former Knowle Wastes, being a scrubby length of manorial waste that was grazed as common land.
(Placenames / Church Knowle)

Puffins – the plight of the last of the Purbeck puffins was featured by television presenter Simon Thomas as he abseiled down the limestone cliffs at Dancing Ledge for the children's Blue Peter programme [29 March 1999]. He joined a team from the Durlston Marine Project who installed a special spy-camera on National Trust land to enable ornithologists to watch and monitor the comings and goings of the last puffins in Purbeck.

At the beginning of the 20th century the puffins were described as being "as thick as grass on the Isle of Purbeck" but by the millennium their numbers had declined to the status of an endangered species. Only 16 birds were counted in what is now the most easterly colony of puffins on the South Coast.

"Nobody knows why they have declined," viewers were told. The camera is being operated remotely, from a Land Rover, so that their health, behaviour, and movements can be ascertained. "This is a very exciting project," said Julian Homer of the National Trust. We hope that the camera will give us the clues to solve the mystery of the declining puffins."
(National Trust / Natural history / Langton Matravers)

Purbeck Chase, Forest or Warren – thus was the Isle of Purbeck variously known, as the editors of John Hutchins's *History of Dorset* observed: "To the uninclosed heath which stretches away from the range of chalk hills to the northern boundary of the island, the term forest is almost as appropriate as it is to the Black Mount Forest in Scotland, where neither tree nor bush are to be seen."

King John is said to have subjected the island "to the forest laws, but it was found that it ought only to have been a hare warren. The popular idea of a forest is an uninclosed and uncultivated district thickly covered or interspersed with trees, but this could never within the reach of history have been the condition of the Isle of Purbeck."

Generally, it was called "the King's Warren" but whatever its designation, the Isle was a royal hunting ground and it provided sport and deer for the palaces from 1212 to 1615 when James I was the last King to hunt in Purbeck. As many historical documents make mention of "the King's Warren" as they do to "the King's marble" in the Isle.

The deer of Purbeck were more important than its people and no killing was allowed for sport, food, or production of crops. It was entirely a royal game preserve. No inhabitant was allowed to build a stone wall, hedge or bank "above the assay"; that is higher than a doe and fawn could leap. Any wood cutting could be done only with the consent of the King's Warrener and whatever decent timber grew in Purbeck belonged to the Constable of Corfe Castle who used it for castle repairs. All falcons nesting in the Isle were the King's property, as were all "royal fish" caught on the coast and in estuaries; porpoise, sturgeon, and grampus.

Thomas Bond described other restrictions to a meeting of Victorian antiquarians: "It was contrary to the island law for any man to take or hunt any rabbit, hare, fox or pheasant, with dogs, net, or a ferret within the warren, without licence of the Warrener; and no man was permitted to keep, carry or lead loose any dogs or curs, in the heath or elsewhere, to the disturbance of the game, or to drive them out of their pastures. Even the building of new houses in the heath or elsewhere was prohibited without a licence from the Constable."

Apparently the interference went further and probably explains the insular outlook of the old quarrymen: "No islander was allowed to marry his daughter out of the island without licence from the Constable or other officer of the Castle of Corfe ... it is quite natural therefore that in a district where the liberties of the freeholder were straightened by such despotic rules and customs, the proud mediaeval baron refused to take up his residence, and thus it is that we find the gentry of the island, though rather numerous in proportion to the extent of the territory, yet neither wealthy, nor exercising much influence beyond the limits of their own remote and secluded district. Even such influence as they possessed at home was sometimes exercised for evil rather than for good, and they seem to have entertained a low sense of the moral responsibility which attached to their social position, so far as it called upon them to set a good example to their humbler neighbours of obedience to the law."

An attempt was made in 1224 to challenge the forest laws in Purbeck but Henry III resisted it and issued orders forbidding anyone to "hunt the King's game in the warren of Corfe". He continued to use Purbeck and in the following year ordered Ralph Gernun, the Constable of Corfe, to hunt with his hounds and take 40 bucks "to be salted and retained" until the King wanted them. The only concession Henry made towards relaxing the restrictions was to exempt the inhabitants of the royal forests from having the ball cut from the fore-feet of their dogs to prevent them chasing the King's game.

By the 14th century the forest laws in Purbeck were under continuous pressure with numerous trials and disputes. The deer needed protection. In 1323 Robert Hardle was indicted for poaching deer and hitting the Sub-Constable of Corfe with a barbed arrow. Hardle took refuge in the church at Church Knowle and escaped.

Edward III complained in 1341 that much of the once abundant game in Purbeck had been destroyed. By 1401 the forest law had crumbled further and a licence was granted by Henry IV for the destruction of the "deer and all manner of wild animals except hares and rabbits in his warren of Purbeck, being so increased that they cause great annoyance to the inhabitants in eating their corn, and destroying their meadows and pasture".
(Social history / Purbeck parishes, specifically Church Knowle and Corfe Castle)

Purbeck Forest – see entry for **Purbeck Chase**.

Purbeck Island – general name for the district bounded to the north by the River Frome and Poole Harbour, eastwards by Poole Bay, southwards by the English Channel, and westwards by a land link at Lulworth with Luckford Lake stream flowing northwards. Though not correct geographically it embraces a difference that is apparent visually and historically.
(Placenames / Purbeck parishes)

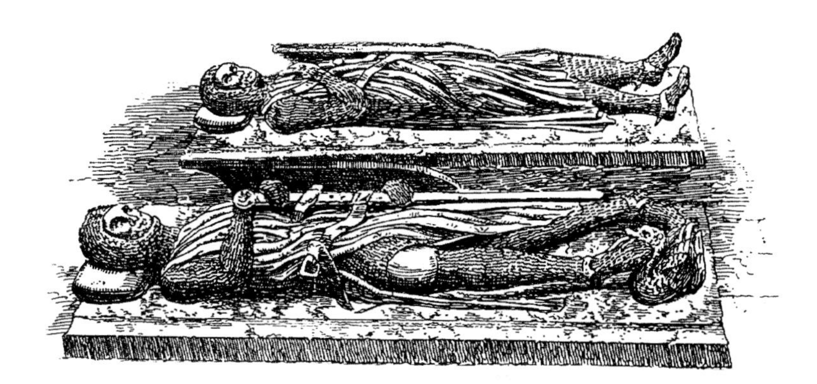

Associate Templars: mail-clad armed effigies, carved in Purbeck marble in London's Temple Church, are generally described as "Knights Templars" but were actually "Associates of the Temple" having been only partially admitted to the powerful Order.

Purbeck marble – quarried in southern Purbeck in Roman times, with a revived industry flourishing from the beginning of the 13th century. It is not a true marble but a highly fossiliferous freshwater limestone, characteristically dappled by multiple shells of a Jurassic snail, *Paludina carinifera.* Stone was hauled by sledges to Corfe Castle, where it was dressed into blocks in West Street, and carted to an export wharf at Ower Quay on Poole Harbour, from which ecclesiastical building stone, monumental effigies, fonts, and altar slabs were shipped to London and the country's principal cathedrals and abbeys.

It had been used at Canterbury in 1174 and its later acceptance as high fashion would also come about in that city, as a result of Archbishop Hubert Walter's decision in the 1190s to build himself an Archbishop's Palace with the second largest hall in England. The work spanned many years and when King John lost Normandy for a time [1204] it disrupted the import of Caen stone and led to the use of less durable Reigate stone, from Surrey.

By this time the Canterbury project had been taken over by Walter's successor, Archbishop Stephen Langton. He endorsed the use of Purbeck marble as the quality substitute for the softer, easily carved, Caen stone and his masons adapted to the challenge of the new medium by creating the splendid canopies above the dais at the east end of the Great Hall of the new Archbishop's Palace [1205].

The glossy grey sheen of Purbeck marble now made Caen stone the inferior product. Such was the general magnificence of Stephen Langton's Palace that even the Great Hall at Winchester Castle, built by Henry III, was merely a copy of the Canterbury building at a reduced scale.

Gothic churches brought marble into vogue for slender, polished shafts set in clusters, and the new phase of architecture flowered suddenly in Lincoln – which had been torn asunder by an earthquake in 1174 – where vast quantities of Purbeck marble were used in the rebuilding. The result won the acclaim of masons and patrons. Decorative shafts would arise in marble at Chichester, York, Worcester, Ely, Wells, Exeter, Winchester, Temple Church and in numerous other major ventures. Greater still was the growth of Salisbury Cathedral [1220-58] to reach the finest peak, literally, in Early English style and consume masses of Purbeck Island in the process.

The bill survives from 1291 for the supply of stone for the original Charing Cross in the Strand which was the last of a series of memorial crosses for Queen Eleanor, along her final journey from Lincoln to the capital: "To William of Corfe for marble for the Eleanor Cross, £7-19s."

The greatest tribute to Purbeck marble is that it was considered to be the finest building stone, to be used for decoration inside the grandest architectural achievements. Little exterior work was attempted in marble, and though the reddish kind was relatively resistant, other shades tended to flake when used on the outside of buildings – as at Salisbury Cathedral and Westminster Abbey – though most facing stones also weather in time. The principal reason for Purbeck marble being restricted to internal use is that it is a decorative stone, both expensive and limited in shape; a stone far too valuable and rare to be worked in quantity on the vast outsides of these colossal churches. Even internal work could put it under stress as the stone would tend to be used vertically rather than in its natural horizontal bedding plane.

Salisbury is only equal, rightly enough, to Westminster Abbey, which was reborn out of the desire of King Henry III and by 1269 had led to the establishment of an elitist colony of master Marblers firmly in the heart of London. Many of these craftsmen had come from the quarries and workshops south of Corfe Castle and their jobs in London were a mark of royal endorsement; it gave Purbeck Marblers a place inside the closed-shop of building trades. It was a bandwagon that rolled profitably along the highways of religious enthusiasm. With a footing in London, and major contracts in other cities, the Marblers could travel to work at country churches and monastic houses throughout the provinces.

Conversely, in Dorset itself, the Marblers found themselves in direct competition with another local stone, from over the Somerset border at Ham Hill. That won the day at Sherborne Abbey where one single, distinguished slab of Purbeck marble, alien amid the mellow golden Hamstone, stands nine feet high near the entrance to the Lady Chapel. Like all marble it was hewn in a length roughly horizontal, though tilting out of the ground, and then shaped and polished. When brought to the church it was upended, so that the natural grain now runs at right angles to the original plane in which it lay. In the process it became a tall stone, and yet it is only about nine inches deep; this was the only way in which the marble could be fashioned into high columns.

This renowned stone of the English cathedrals came from the northern edge of the limestone plateau of southern Purbeck, eastwards from Willwood at Kingston, where turf and scrub cover a succession of mounds that stretch along the valley slope. At Dunshay Manor the drive to the house winds through old marble workings. It was the home of Alice de Briwere, lady of the manor, who contributed marble for 12 years for the building of Salisbury Cathedral [1219-31].

Purbeck marble: used for the first British royal effigy, appropriately that of King John, carved in 1240 for his tomb in Worcester Cathedral.

Afflington has now dwindled to a farmstead but it was a busy hamlet at the height of its marble days when Henry III granted a market and fair [1270]. Other former settlements were at Lynch, Scoles, Quarr, and Wilkswood.

Their range of individual products, such as fonts, is well represented in country churches between Devon and Sussex. Much of the best of the first stone to be extracted in the 12th century would be turned into fonts. A dozen are still in use in Dorset. Purbeck altar tables and flagstones were also widely used.

The shape of the future was in monumental effigies; an expensive and immodest practice that soon became popular with the ecclesiastical hierarchy and knighted classes. A few 12th-century marble effigies have survived inside Dorset, including Philip, a priest, at Tolpuddle and Abbot Clement [died 1163] in Sherborne Abbey. Earlier was Leofric [died 1072], in Exeter Cathedral – he founded its see – though his effigy was not cut until the next century. Leofric is cut in low relief and is the best preserved of the early figures.

Two other marble effigies of this period are at Salisbury Cathedral [1186] and Abbotsbury Abbey, now in the porch of the parish church.

Each of these five examples is more than a simple incised slab, but they lack the shapely, fuller-bodied carving of the style developed in the following century. A large and perfect block was necessary for each effigy and the single vein rippling across the Purbeck hillsides was only between 18 inches and two feet in thickness. This accounts for the noticeable flatness of all Purbeck figures; it was a quality stone but with no scope for fancy adornments or big chested subjects.

Purbeck Marblers led the field and set a fashion that others would follow in the 13th century. By then the Purbeck output was being measured in dozens of effigies, and four of the finest military examples were the Knights Templar in London's Temple Church. All would be badly damaged by fire in the Blitz. These figures are show in chain mail, and as with a few other effigies, were originally covered in painted colours and gold.

More examples remain of bishops and abbots, looking frail and pious, holding the staff of a crosier in the left hand whilst blessing the onlooker with the right. There are even a few 13th-century ladies carved in marble, with the finest lying in Romsey Abbey. Folds of drapery flow across her body, and the sculpture is sublimely smooth and delicate, looking as if it has come from a mould rather than a block of stone.

Abbots tended to be unlucky in their pursuit of immortality as most of their monuments fell during the collapse of the religious estates wrought by Henry VIII. The Abbotsbury specimen, for example, was not rescued from the ground until centuries later.

Spared that humiliation was the earliest royal effigy in England, that of King John in Worcester Cathedral, which was carved in Purbeck marble [circa 1240]. It is fitting that he is carved from a piece of Purbeck – given his use of the Isle for hunting, hospitality, and hostage-keeping – but even though Purbeck marble had a part in the making of the tombs of virtually all the Plantagenet line, John is the only royal figure carved in our material.

At the lower end of the scale, the staple trade of the marble industry was in coffin lids. Business bloomed as the big churches blossomed, with their requirements of thousands of tons of carved marble, but in the lull between building projects there was always a market for coffin tops. These were flat sheets of marble, broad at the top and tapering towards the foot, often with a plain polished surface or otherwise with a cross inscribed, and with carved edges. An estimated 7,500 coffin lids passed through Corfe Castle, most of them being carried by cart over the heath to Ower Quay, for shipment out across Poole Harbour and then seawards.

Documents prove that effigies and architectural items were often sculpted at Corfe by the Purbeck Marblers. A local example is in the accounts of the Sheriff of Dorset [1254]: "For carving a certain effigy of a Queen in marble stone, carrying it to Tarrant Crawford, and placing it there over the tomb of the Queen of Scotland, 100 shillings [£5]." Destined further afield, going by sea to London, a marble altar from Purbeck was given by Henry III to the friars of Mount Carmel.

A bizarre incident happened when Poole sailors seized the *Margarete* from Wareham for use in an expedition against the French [1374]. The Keepers of the port of Poole received an order for the release of the 48-ton vessel as she was loaded with two high tombs of marble for the Earl of Arundel and his wife Eleanor, together with "one great stone" for the Bishop of Winchester.

Exploitation of Purbeck marble was one of England's first nationalised industries. Henry III himself financed the great work of enlarging Westminster Abbey and it is recorded several times that the surveyors purchased "the King's marble for the King's work at Westminster".

The royal rake-off encouraged the patronage of marble and the Westminster abbey contracts meant a lot to the trade. At the height of this work in London, 49 Marblers were employed, with 15 others to polish their work.

The Marblers from Purbeck had become some of the most sought-after craftsmen in Britain.

Purbeck marble stood above its competitors until the 15th century when it was finally replaced by alabaster, though marble continued to be produced occasionally, mainly for local use in Dorset. Decline had come over many years as the larger pieces of marble were taken from the quarries and only second-rate material remained. There was no longer the demand for thousands of tons to build towering shafts for abbeys and cathedrals. Instead there was only the old line in effigies and for this the poorer stone could not be used. Neither could the plentiful smaller pieces.

Alabaster offered a cheap, and easier carved substitute, brought from Nottingham and Derby, which took a growing proportion of the national market and caused a recession in Purbeck.

In the 16th century came the great reversal of the church building programme. A total of 186 major monasteries in England and Wales were suppressed by Henry VIII in 1539-40.

Shaftesbury, with its shrine to Edward the Martyr who was assassinated at Corfe, is a typical religious house in the category that suffered most. Today hilltop rockeries and flower beds are laid out between token piles of crumbing ground-level masonry. Here the abbey ruins became an open quarry for the town, leaving only disassembled fragments of marble shafts and capitals amid displaced greensand ashlars.

More Purbeck marble fell post-Henry in the huge capital disaster, the Great Fire of 1666, with the most significant loss being Grey Friars in the City of London. The once most magnificent of British churches is now a Post Office yard.

Other grand churches, on the whole, have survived better than the mediaeval houses and castles, where there had been a substantial domestic use of Purbeck marble and stone in their great halls and tracery windows.

Such halls and castles, including Corfe Castle itself as the greatest of all, would be brought to ruin in the 1640s for losing the Civil War. Around the ruins of Corfe the marble industry was also shattered. Later in the 17th century, it would be Portland stone that won favour with master-architect Christopher Wren in his phoenix-like London re-creations, notably St Paul's Cathedral. Alabaster had ousted marble for effigies of the dead.

It is generally supposed that the stone industry moved to Swanage because Ower Quay, its point of shipment from Poole Harbour, had silted up. That is incorrect, but had it been the case there could have been a much easier move from Ower to Cleavel Point, only 700 yards away and directly on the South Deep, or to any other peninsula jutting the harbour.

The greatest of Dorset industries had died, though marble continued to be worked in small pockets until about 1700, and the redevelopment of the building stone trade at Swanage. In the hard times the business depended on the few rich connoisseurs who wanted their luxury work in something better, or different, from common alabaster. Even after all the quarries had closed, work could always resume when there was a customer willing to

pay the price, as in 1842 when Woodyhyde was reopened to provide marble for the restoration of Temple Church in central London. On the ground in Purbeck, beside the sea, marble exposures in the Upper Purbeck beds can be seen at Worbarrow Tout, Tyneham, in the west and on Peveril Point, Swanage, in the east.
(Mediaeval archaeology / Corfe Castle, Langton Matravers and Worth Matravers)

Purbeck stone – as well as marble, vast quantities of dressed Portland-type Purbeck limestone, and random rubble, were required in the Middle Ages for ecclesiastical and military buildings. Corfe Castle itself, being the massive fortress on the doorstep, had recurring needs for several centuries.

It is difficult to over-estimate the quantities of rough stone produced by the quarries as it was enormous. Around Wilkswood, Quarr, Primrose Hill, and Downshay Farm there are extensive earthworks left by considerable extraction. The quarrying of building stone and rubble in Purbeck during the Middle Ages is often overlooked because of the attention given to Purbeck marble and its more romantic uses. Stone tended to be used locally in Purbeck whereas the marble was invariably sent outside the Isle.

Even the small settlements had their own local quarries, such as London Door Quarry a mile west of Kingston and the hilltop working beside the road above Kimmeridge. Stone for the building of Worth Matravers village came partly from the Old Quarry on the north side of West Man, a short way from the track down the chine to Winspit.
(Mediaeval archaeology / Purbeck parishes)

Purbeck Warren – see entry for **Purbeck Chase**.

Putlake Farm – originally an 18th-century cottage incorporating a barn under the same roof, south of Steps Hill at Langton Matravers (SZ 001 789). Formerly an outlying barn of the larger Langton Manor Farm. Takes its name from Puck Lake stream.
(Placenames / Langton Matravers)

Purbeck stone: being raised from a hillside quarry above Afflington Wood, in a picture looking towards Corfe Castle (faintly glimpsed between the right-hand legs of the crane).

Pincher's grave: Lord Chancellor Eldon's favourite dog was buried beside Eldon Seat amid the rolling seaward slopes of Swyre Head.

Q

Quarr – once the archetypal Purbeck quarry, with its mediaeval and dialect name meaning precisely that, but now applying only to a farmstead between the woods on the slope north of Langton Matravers (SY 989 797).

Quarry edges and ledges, following the vein of marble, are exposed in the rough grassland to the south-west, towards Primrose Hill (SY 988 795). Both Quarr and Primrose Hill lie in the parish of Worth Matravers.
(Placenames / Mediaeval archaeology / Worth Matravers)

Quarries – see entries for **Acton Quarries**, **Purbeck marble**, **Purbeck stone**, **Seacombe Quarries** and **Winspit Quarries**.

Quartus – fourth locomotive of the Furzebrook claylands railway, being an 0-4-2WT bought secondhand from a Leeds company [1889]. One of the greatest of the Purbeck pits was being dug, behind Old Bond Street, at Grange Gate.
(Industrial archaeology / Railways / Church Knowle)

Quintus – fifth locomotive of the Furzebrook railway system, being a domeless 0-4-0ST made by Manning Wardle [1914].

She remained in service until the closure of the Furzebrook sector of the clay-carrying mineral lines [1956] and then lay abandoned and derailed before eventual removal for scrap.
(Industrial archaeology / Railways / Church Knowle)

Stone working: St Aldhelm's Head Quarry, seen from the north-east with the headland forming the left-hand skyline.

Footplate view: *Quintus*, still on the rails, at Furzebrook, in 1956.

Quintus derailed: last of her line at the end of her days, at Furzebrook in the late 1950s.

R

RAF Worth Matravers – came into being [1942-70] in buildings vacated by the Telecommunications Research Establishment, as a link in the Gee Chain navigation system. Its ten national transmitting stations, operating in pairs, provided accurately timed radio pulses. Differences in arrival time between the signals enabled the aircraft's position to be determined by its navigator intersecting hyperbolic lines on a pre-printed Gee lattice sheet.

The system "revolutionised the effectiveness of RAF bombing raids" with "targets being found and bombed as never before". By the late 1960s, however, the Ministry of Defence announced that other ground-based navigation aids and airborne systems had effectively replaced Gee, leading to the standing down of the system and demolition of its tall aerials.

No. 407 Signals Unit operated the Purbeck station.

(Aviation / Worth Matravers)

Railway Bridge – over the Corfe River and the Studland road, being a virtual viaduct of the new branch line to the seaside at Swanage [1883-85]. Constructed in Purbeck stone ashlars with a matching waterworks below.

(Placenames / Bridges / Railways / Corfe Castle)

Rail relics: Drummond T9 engines, already half a century old, pulling into Corfe Castle in the 1950s.

Railway (mineral line system) – see entries from **Fayle's Tramway**, **Goathorn Railway**, **Pike's Railway**, and named locomotives.

Railway (standard gauge track) – on 12 August 1995 the central section of the Isle of Purbeck branch railway was back in steam, with passengers on board, for the first time since June 1967. It was now no longer merely the Swanage Railway, with just the far tip of this cul-de-sac lines playing "Thomas the Tank Engine" from the seaside to Harman's Cross Halt.

Extension of the line by three miles, at a cost of £350,000, has restored track through Corfe Castle – reopening the station there – and onwards into the heath where a park-and-ride car-park has been established in the former Norden clay-pits.

It is a short walk to the new Norden Station which, for the time being, is the inland end of the line. "Yes, it's not where we would have chosen for a car-park," one of the volunteer workers told me. "But the National Trust insisted that it shouldn't be visible from Corfe Castle – a cheek really, because they've already wrecked the view with their own car-park behind the Visitor Centre at the foot of the hill." The next aim in the project to resurrect the Purbeck line is to extend the relaying process from Norden Station to the hamlet itself and then link with existing Railtrack metals – currently for freight only – at the Furzebrook ball-clay and oilfield terminals.

"That's the final mile, just about precisely to the yard, and then we can make a platform for the Blue Pool," my informant continued. "From then on we'll really be in business, as the sensible person's alternative to the road, as well as Britain's best scenic and tourist line. It will also open up the prospect of through workings via Worgret Junction, into a restored Swanage spur at Wareham Station."

That was the original Victorian starting point for this offshoot of the London and South Western Railway, in 1883, for a single-track branch line that ran to Swanage via the intermediate station at Corfe Castle. They

Special train: for steam enthusiasts, being pulled over the viaduct at Corfe Castle by two engines, 41301 and 41284, on 21 February 1966.

Railway history: named locomotive *Swanage* number 34105 (built 1950, withdrawn 1964, later rescued and preserved) pushing a train towards Corfe, away from its namesake resort.

nearly failed to reach their centenary. For although the line escaped Dr Richard Beeching's axe it lingered only until 1972 and with its closure the track beyond Furzebrook to the seaside was lifted.

This stimulated a spirited campaign for its revival with the Swanage Railway Society securing a lease of the line from Dorset County Council and relaying a mile of track to Herston in the early 1980s and pushing on to Corfe and beyond a decade later.
(Railways / Purbeck parishes)

Railway Station – opened at Corfe Castle on 20 May 1885 as the midway point of the London and South Western Railway Company's branch line from Wareham to Swanage. Closed as a result of Dr Richard

Railway path: briefly busy, between removal of the track in 1972 and its relaying, through to Norden in 1995.

Restored railway: now with an extra station, at Norden, for park and ride through the Purbeck Hills.

Beeching's notorious axe [1972] but saved and resurrected by the reborn Swanage Railway.
(Placenames / Railways / Corfe Castle)

Reading Room (Church Knowle) – on the north side of the village street, having been provided under the patronage of Rev Owen Luttrell Mansel to commemorate Queen Victoria's golden jubilee [1887]. "READING ROOM" is the inscription over the door but villagers remember it as the "Men's Reading Room". Directories listed it as the Workmen's Reading Room when Ernest White was the secretary [circa 1915].

As for women, reading was for the home, rather than the club.
(Placenames / Social history / Church Knowle)

Reading Room (Corfe Castle) – in the Square, with A. C. Whittle being its secretary [1930s].
(Placenames / Social history / Corfe Castle)

The Rectory (Langton Matravers) – incorporates a stone-roofed 17th-century cottage in its south-west corner (SY 998 789). Otherwise much extended with a tall 18th-century section, also stone roofed, and 19th-

Calcraft seat: Rempstone Hall, seen from the Purbeck Hills, with conifers beyond.

Stone circle: clearly visible at Rempstone for the author to photograph in the early 1960s but since engulfed again by woodland.

century former servants' quarters under a slate roof. A consecration cross in the grounds, behind the high stone wall, has been re-set as a base for a sundial, after removal from the church porch.
(Placenames / Langton Matravers)

Redvers – rebel baron **Baldwin de Redvers, 1st Earl of Devon** [died 1155], held Corfe Castle in defiance of King Stephen [1139].
(People / Politics / Corfe Castle)

Rempstone Chapel – the Purbeck crofters' spiritual retreat was a Wesleyan chapel hidden in the outback between Foxground and Burnbake (SY 996 832). It was a small thatched cottage with the upstairs floor taken out. Destroyed by fire [circa 1920].

Most of the heath-cropping families were non-conformist. A red ridge tile from a Goathorn roof, probably dating from the early 18th century and preserved in the Town Hall museum at Corfe Castle, proclaims in scratched lettering: "Be not a Bigot against no Denamination."
(Placenames / Churches / Corfe Castle)

Rempstone Stone Circle – the Bronze Age megalithic monument at Rempstone stands in the overgrown former Withy Bed immediately south of the B3351 a third of a mile east of Rempstone Hall (SY 995 821). Its builders,

Renscombe Farm: typical Purbeck extended building, under a single stone roof.

between 2100 BC and 1500 BC, were the same as, or contemporary with, those who left the major cemetery of burial mounds along the skyline of Nine Barrow Down, just half a mile to the south.

That, however, is a very different landscape – the stone circle is set at the foot of the Purbeck Hills, on the southern extremity of the heathland, with nothing but trees as its view today.

Neither is its present state as a circle. Rather, it is semi-circular. Only the northern half survives, separated from the site of the southern half by a mediaeval field bank that runs across the full 80 feet of its diameter.

In the surviving northern half there are ten reddish-brown stones; hard iron-impregnated sandstone of the local Bagshot Beds. Four remain standing and are up to four feet high. The remainder are fallen and embedded in the ground.

The other half was destroyed by clay-digging in the Middle Ages which has left a pitted site. Close by, in the undergrowth, the displaced southern stones have been piled together.

An avenue of smaller stones, leading towards the circle, was uncovered half a mile west-north-west [1967], though nothing remains to be seen of that. A total of 23 stones, average size 2 feet 6 inches long, were uncovered in the field immediately south of the main road and to the west of the bridleway that leads from Rempstone Farm, up Brenscombe Hill (SY 986 823).

Purbeck archaeologist J. B. Calkin knew of no former boundary that might have run across the field, from east-south-east to west-north-west, and considered that the arrangement of the stones showed "a deliberate layout in two parallel lines three yards apart with stones set up at five-yard intervals". He added that they are similar in size to numerous surviving stone rows in undisturbed parts of Exmoor and Dartmoor.

Their visual alignment is now blocked by trees, but eastwards it was pointing directly at Rempstone Stone Circle, and beyond that to what is now the Isle of Purbeck Golf Course and the obelisk on a skyline Bronze Age barrow above Ulwell Gap.

They may well have performed as a ceremonial way towards the stones, combining that function with solar or astronomical bearings. One fanciful suggestion is that the rocks for the circle itself were hauled along the avenue from Rollington Hill; a name which might preserve a memory of the event. This theory can be immediately discounted as Rollington is part of the Purbeck chalk ridge that runs southward of Rempstone, whereas the stones of both the circle and the avenue are a hard gritstone russet-brown in colour – the iron-impregnated sandstone of the Bagshot Beds which outcrop on the great heath to the north.

The main circle is a scheduled ancient monument.

(Placenames / Prehistoric archaeology / Corfe Castle)

Renaud – fully-laden French brig wrecked on Egmont Point, at the west side of Chapman's Pool [27 January 1841].

(Shipwrecks / Corfe Castle)

Renscombe Farm – west of Worth Matravers, the long, low dormered and stone-roofed 17th-century building (SY 964 776) has at its core the remains of a mediaeval religious house which was an outlying cell of Cerne Abbey.

Alan Ivimey, in *Pilgrim's Pleasure* [1959], records the evidence of a monastic scandal walled-up there: "One day, early in this century, someone decided to cut a new window through the thick farmhouse wall on the west side. As the first stone was pulled away the workmen saw that the wall was hollow and that there was something inside – the golden hair and the face and black-clad body of a girl. The body, preserved in the limestone, fell to dust as the air reached it. But a crucifix taken from the hollow was long kept, I am told, by the vicar [rector, actually] of Langton Matravers – though Renscombe is nearer to Worth. Why was this girl walled-up in secret – 'left alone to God' as the men who hid her

might have put it. What was going on at this cell of Cerne Abbey, 25 miles away? Presumably she would lose consciousness fairly soon from gradual suffocation . . ."
(Placenames / Mediaeval archaeology / Worth Matravers)

Repton – architect **George Stanley Repton** [died 1858] was the fourth son of landscape-gardener Humphry Repton [1752-1818]. Pupil of Augustus Charles Pugin and associate of John Nash, he worked on the enlargement of the Haymarket opera house, London, and designed St Philip's Church, Regent Street. He fell in love with Lady Elizabeth Scott [1785-1862], the eldest daughter of the first Earl of Eldon, who strongly disapproved of the match.

She escaped from Encombe, the family's country mansion, on the morning of 27 November 1817, and eloped with Repton. They were married later in the day, at St George's, Hanover Square. Lord Eldon eventually submitted to a full reconciliation [1820] and henceforth his estate had its own Gothic architect.
(People / Architects / Corfe Castle)

Riddle – baker **Jack Riddle** supplied Corfe Castle for the entire first half of the 20th century, using a faggot-fire in a traditional brick and stone oven behind an old iron door. This remained hot for hours. "It would take the best part of a week to cool down completely," he said in 1952. "Came here for a month's trial when I was fourteen. Been here 55 years now."
(People / Corfe Castle)

The Rings – earthen ring-and-bailey siege work, National Trust owned, on the south side of the road 300 yards south-west of Corfe Castle (SY 957 820). Constructed in 1139 by King Stephen, the last of the Norman line. His reign had disintegrated into anarchy with the particular problem in Dorset being his inability to oust Baldwin de Redvers, the first Earl of Devon, from Corfe Castle.

"When traitors perceived that he was a mild man, and soft and good," a chronicler wrote of King Stephen, "every powerful man made his castles, and held them against him." Hence there never being a royal second Stephen, for reasons opposite to the problems with John.

The Rings lie on the first hillock from Corfe Castle, beside the Church Knowle road, and were placed on the side of a slope that tilts away from the Castle Hill – so that the activities of the besiegers were less obvious to watchers on the battlements.

Cromwell's Battery was the name of The Rings from the mid-17th to the late 19th century, as a result of it being purpose-built for reoccupation by Parliamentary forces for their camp and artillery emplacement in the Civil War sieges of the 1640s. A gun ramp was cut into the north-east side, facing the castle.

Bequeathed to the National Trust with the Bankes Estate [1982].
(Placenames / Mediaeval archaeology / National Trust / Corfe Castle)

Robert S. Shaw – flaming wreck of an American sailing ship, which appeared in a south-west gale off St Alban's Head [10 December 1847]. She had been struck by lightning off Ushant and abandoned by the crew. St Alban's Head marked the turning point of her passage up the Channel as the tide had ebbed and the current then carried her back against the gale, to beach on the shore beneath the Clavell Tower at Kimmeridge.
(Shipwrecks / Kimmeridge and Worth Matravers)

Roman marble workings – principally around Wilkswood and westwards to Blashenwell, where the greyish-white vein of crystalline limestone was preferred and used to form a smart speckled background to vermilion lettering in cinnabar. This style was widely used in monumental inscriptions from shortly after the Roman invasion of 43 AD to around 200, with tablets from Dorset being unearthed at Fordington, Dorchester and across the province to Chichester, Cirencester, London, St. Albans, Colchester, and Chester.

Columns, bathing basins, mouldings and mortar bowls were also produced. The industry

specialised in luxury items and had a second burst of activity in the country's economic revival between 350 and 400 AD.
(Roman and industrial archaeology / Corfe Castle, Langton Matravers and Worth Matravers)

Roman pottery industry – clays were collected on the Purbeck heaths and taken to a string of workshops and pottery kilns along the southern shoreline of Poole Harbour, from which the wares were shipped to London and the Roman garrisons on Hadrian's Wall.

Two kiln sites, a short distance south of Shipstal Point, lie on the very edge of the saltings and the old shore, though now more than 100 yards from the high tide mark and the mud-flats that have been reclaimed by the rampant growth of *Spartina townsendii*, the grass of the salt-marshes, since the early 1990s. Similarly, kilns at Fitzworth Heath and Cleavel Point – the western spit of Newton Bay – are beside the safe harbour beaches, so their products could be easily removed by boat. Because of the dense vegetation along almost the entire line of the old coastline, which is long and deeply indented, the area is difficult to explore and there must be many sites still awaiting discovery.

Remains of a hut, probably the home of a potter, have been found nearby on Fitzworth Point. Up the Frome, at Stoborough, on the northern side of Nutcrack Lane, towards Redcliff Farm, another group of potters had their wheels. The tell-tale signs are sherds of wasters, their misfired or misshapen work, which were rejected and smashed on a heap. A scattering of broken pottery in quantity usually betrays the existence of a kiln below the ground.

Molehills beside Nutcrack Lane, studded with pieces of black pottery, led to the discovery in 1952 of a basin-shaped tub which was a potters' pit for puddling clay. It was carefully lifted and taken to Dorset County

Rotten borough: political cartoon lampooning "the Rival Mount o'Bankes" in the hustings at Corfe Castle.

Museum, Dorchester, but would disintegrate whilst being moved to a new position inside the museum, in 1970.

Mineral analysis has proved Poole Harbour to be the origin of several consignments of pots delivered to Hadrian's Wall – a 500-mile voyage – and the industry flourished during the 1st and 2nd centuries AD. They were native Celtic potters, specialising in basic-shape black burnished ware, whose descendants moved in the 3rd century to the New Forest uplands where a much more decorative and sophisticated pottery industry was developing. (Archaeology / Arne and Corfe Castle)

Roman shale industry – see entry for **Kimmeridge shale industry**.

Roman villas – see entries for **Brenscombe Roman Villa**, **Copper Bridge Roman Villa**, and **East Creech Roman Villa**.

Rotten borough – negatively speaking, Corfe Castle was the catalyst for bringing us modern Parliamentary democracy. For it had decayed from a fortress town, at the heart of the industrial area manufacturing marble effigies and columns for mediaeval cathedrals, into ruination and an archetypal rotten borough.

It continued to return two members to the House of Commons. Their intellectual calibre tended to be about zero, or less. Corruption was total and contests were unknown: "The patrons divided the honours by each returning a member, and this way got over an infinitude of trouble."

The powerful Bankes and Bond families farcically abused even the accepted system of those times by parodying the motions of holding elections. Hustings were erected; speeches made; beer drunk; and the two candidates declared to be duly elected.

Tradition demanded that they then responded by solemnly affirming their loyalty to Corfe and expressing determination "to stick to the place as long as one stone held firm to another in the old castle".

Corfe Castle was disfranchised, along with 55 other boroughs of dubious status, under "Schedule A" of the Reform Act of 1832. (Politics / Corfe Castle)

Round barrows – Bronze Age burial mounds occur in quantity across Purbeck, covering single cremations or interments initially, though often with later secondary burials as well. The following are scheduled Ancient Monuments:

Church Knowle parish: Round barrows on Creech Heath (SY 926 840); Round barrow 300 yards south of East Creech Farm (SY 929 822); Icen Barrow (SY 922 839); Three round barrows on Knowle Hill; Round barrow on Creech Barrow Hill (SY 921 823).

Corfe Castle parish: Group of round barrows on Nine Barrow Down, National Trust owned (SY 997 816); Round barrow 400 yards south of Afflington Farm (SY 968 788); Round barrow 500 yards north of Afflington Farm (SY 972 806); Round barrow on Brenscombe Heath (SY 986 836); Group of round barrows on Corfe Common, National Trust owned (SY 962 809); Round barrow on West Hill, also National Trust (SY 954 824).
(Prehistoric archaeology / Church Knowle and Corfe Castle)

Round Island – about 20 acres of "winding tracks, patches of woodland and billowing rhododendrons suggesting a spaciousness greater than the real area," to quote Richard Blomfield on the private paradise off Fitzworth Farm in the north-west extremity of Corfe Castle parish (SY 989 873).

It is by far the highest of the collection of harbour islands in Corfe Castle parish with a "western peak", as Richard Blomfield calls it, that reaches the dizzy height of 69 feet. The island abstracts its own water from an artesian well, 120 feet deep, though this free-flowing supply is brackish and has to be soda-treated.

Orchestral conductor Sir Thomas Beecham [1879-1961] lived on Round Island in the early 1950s and used the uninterrupted seclusion for writing his biography of the composer Frederick Delius [1862-1934].

Alan Bromby [born 1923] wardened the island for S. L. Fowler [1958-62] before he was appointed by the National Trust as chief warden on their newly acquired Brownsea Island, which Alan and Joan Bromby were set

to run for the next three decades. Round Island was then the home of Ted Foster, before its purchase by Jo Davies of Dorset Wildlife Trust who formed the Green Island Trust [1996].
(Placenames / Corfe Castle)

Royal hunting warren – the status of Purbeck, variously given as Purbeck Chase, Purbeck Forest and Purbeck Warren, when it was a preserve for the sport of mediaeval Kings [until 1615].
(Social history / Purbeck parishes)

Royal Marines Memorial – commemorative stone and carved seat set in a little garden [1990] beside the cliff path on Emmetts Hill (SY 959 768). The stunning view, westwards from 400 feet above Chapman's Pool, is across the Kimmeridge Ledges.
(Placenames / Memorials / Worth Matravers)

Russell – preserved 2-6-2T steam locomotive of the Norden claylands mineral railway. She was built by the Hunslet Engine Company [1906], worked the pre-war Welsh Highland Railway until its closure [1937], and was requisitioned by the Ministry of Supply, being placed with the Brymbo Steel Company at Hook Norton iron-ore quarries, Oxfordshire. These closed after the war and she was bought by Fayle and Company from the Ministry of Supply, at an auction in Surrey [1947], and brought to Dorset [1948]. Meanwhile the two Purbeck clay firms merged into Pike Brothers, Fayle and Company Limited [1949] and *Russell* was withdrawn for scrap in the rationalisation that followed [1953].

Instead she was saved by Birmingham Locomotive Club, stored at Towyn Wharf station, and then transferred to the revived Welsh Highland Railway [1965]. Once, it was recalled, she ventured on to the adjoining Ffestiniog Railway [1925], though a repeat performance would be out of question as she had stuck fast in Moelgwyn Tunnel. *Russell*'s eventual restoration and re-boilering began in 1983 and she took her first passenger train on Easter Saturday in 1987, being re-commissioned in a ceremony at Porthmadog and driven by Garonwy Roberts, a driver with the pre-war Welsh Highland Railway who had last put her in steam in 1935.
(Industrial archaeology / Railways / Church Knowle)

Preserved locomotive: *Russell* at work in the Purbeck clayfields, near Furzebrook.

Viewpoint garden: forming the clifftop setting for the Royal Marines Memorial on Emmetts Hill, with a fossilsed ammonite in the foreground.

S

Saint Alban's Head (its local and maritime pronunciation), or **St Aldhelm's Head** – the southern extremity of the Isle of Purbeck, being a rocky promontory a mile and a half south-west of Worth Matravers (SY 961 753). Isolated 350-feet clifftop plateau with steep scree slopes and a turbulent offshore tide-race.

Cliffside quarry ledge, with a stone pillar left as a sea-mark. Topped by a Norman chapel, Victorian Coastguard cottages and operational lookout, and footings of a Second World War radar station. The gem is the 12th-century St Aldhelm's Chapel which is an all-stone square, except for a slit window and oak door, rising like a pyramid.

The direct approach is through Worth Matravers to a car-park at Renscombe Farm, then along a mile of stony track across featureless flat fields known as The Plain.

When you get to the chapel the view is nothing much other than the sea as the headland juts out further into the English Channel than anywhere else in Purbeck. Much more interesting is to plan your approach as two sides of a triangle, along the coastal footpath, via either Winspit to the east or Chapman's Pool on the west.

I have never heard any native of Purbeck or any Dorset-born countryman refer to the headland as St Aldhelm's (the Saxon saint who was Bishop of Sherborne from 705 to his death in 709). Whilst realising that the chapel is called "capella Sancti Aldelmi" in mediaeval documents, I regard its use today as affectation. It may only be a Saxon gloss applied to a dedication to Saint Alban who was as the first British martyr would have been a logical choice from Romano-Celtic times. I have therefore kept to the colloquial spelling because that, at least, is understood as a spelling, and has added value in annoying incomers and pseudo-academics. John Smeaton, who built the Eddystone Lighthouse in the 1750s, called it St Alban's Head, as does the first Ordnance Survey maps. All the navigation charts followed their example.
(Placenames / Worth Matravers)

Navigation hazard: not that you would think it, from the number of boats inshore below St Alban's Head in this 1856 print

Twin headlands: Rope Lake Head (middle distance) and St Alban's Head (above and beyond), seen from Kimmeridge.

Saint Aldhelm's Chapel – on the coastal headland south-west of Worth Matravers (SY 961 756), being a square all-stone buttressed Norman structure [circa 1170] with walls ten metres square and a pyramidal roof supported by a massive central column. This has 12 chamfered corners and eight arches springing outwards, four to the centre of the walls and the other into the corners. The roof circling the column is mortared stone to a thickness of eight feet.

Southern summit: St Alban's Head, topped by a seamark sculpted by quarrying.

Sited at 345 feet above the sea with the cross said to be at 379 feet altitude. The cross, topping a symmetrical building that is 30 feet high, is reputedly a Victorian addition from 1873; but a cross is shown on Julia M. Colson's published drawing of the 1850s and that by John Clavell Mansel who illustrated the manuscript Brief Notes of Purbeck for Frederick Leigh Colvile in 1855. However, the column originally supported something much heavier, such as a bell cupola, that would have made for a distinctive sea-mark.

It would be attractive to think of this as a sea-warning beacon but there are no stairs to support the fancy.

Architecturally, it seems unusual to us, though not so rare in terms of contemporary monastic outbuildings, in having only a single slit-window. This is in the northern end of the east side, where it illuminated

Stone pillar: left in situ on the edge of St Alban's Quarry, as a seamark rather than a landmark.

Headland chapel: so ancient that its original dedication may be to Celtic Saint Alban rather than Saxon Saint Aldhelm.

"traces of an altar, or rather the platform on which it stood", which was just discernible in Thomas Bond's time [1857]. Outside, the building is encircled by a low earthwork, roughly circular and about 30 metres in diameter, which is possibly of Saxon or prehistoric origin.

By the reign of Henry II the chapel was served by a Crown-paid chaplain. He earned the customary 50 shilling annual stipend of royal chaplains.

As with the Coastguard lookout of historic and modern times, this was a place – spiritual and temporal – for the safety of "seafaring subjects of the realm", to again quote the antiquary Thomas Bond. It had an unusual status, as a royal chapel

Ruin restored: with the addition of its cross, drawn from the north by Julia M. Colson in the 1850s.

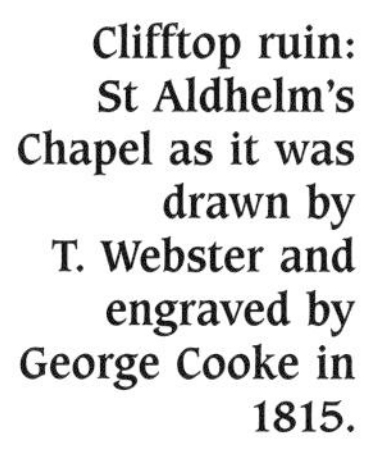

Clifftop ruin: St Aldhelm's Chapel as it was drawn by T. Webster and engraved by George Cooke in 1815.

Central shaft: Julia M. Colson's drawing of the interior of St Aldhelm's Chapel shows the clustered pier (left) and the western segment of the roof vaulting.

Western side: with the door facing the prevailing weather, drawn by Alfred Dawson in 1882.

that was not attached to any parish church, nor a monastic house.
(Placenames / Churches / Mediaeval archaeology / Worth Matravers)

Saint Edward the Martyr – see entry for **Edward**.

Saint Edward the Martyr parish church (Corfe Castle) – something of a disappointment, in the centre of Corfe Castle, as so much more of age and character might reasonably be expected to have survived where the mediaeval Purbeck Marblers worshipped (SY 961 820). Instead there is only a 14th-century tower and the rest of the building, including the original nave and north porch of the 12th century and aisles added in the 13th century, was demolished and levelled [May 1859].

The "out-walls" had bowed, to project "nearly one foot beyond the perpendicular", and the "restoration was to be of the most drastic kind, in which much more work was carried out than originally proposed", writes architectural historian Fred Pitfield in Purbeck Parish Churches.

In fact it was total rebuilding [1860] of all except the tower. The architect was Thomas Henry Wyatt [1807-88] whose principal creations were courts, asylums, and theatres.

The scale of Corfe's losses can be judged from Sir Stephen Glynne's description [1825]

Old church: at Kingston hamlet, on the hill south of Corfe Castle.

Parish church: Corfe Castle is deficient in Purbeck marble.

of its "very fine" east window which was of "rather an early period". Lesser features incorporated into the rebuilding include a few random bits of the 13th-century church, such as a reused lancet window, a foliate capital, arch springing, and a carved piscina bowl.

Items preserved, or salvaged, from "Corfe Castle, Old Church" include ten roof bosses [circa 1500] from "the Chancel roof" and the octagonal stem and bowl of a Purbeck marble font. Each face of the bowl is inset with cinquefoil panels. Also of 15th-century date are two Purbeck marble standards, now free-standing, which seem to be all that is left of an exceedingly fine reredos which was smashed by Wyatt's men – builders T. Farwell of Swanage and Meadus of Poole.

The replacement alabaster and marble reredos was added by architect George Edmund Street [1876]. Fittings that survive from the real church include a chest, by Henry

New church: in splendid Victoriana, arising behind Kingston's prim stone-roofed cottages.

Purbeck cathedral: the closest thing in the heart of stone country, being the Victorian creation of George Edmund Street, at Kingston.

Single cell: the mid-Victorian rebuilding of Kimmeridge parish church merged the former nave and chancel.

Paulet [1672] and the royal arms of Charles II [1660] plus one displaced capital, ornamented with a chevron-carved top and some foliage, which is all that is known to have survived of the original arches in the north arcade.

There may possibly be something of the old church entombed underground, such as the crypt or "Bone House" beneath the corner of the north aisle, between the porch and the tower.

The Purbeck stone statuette of St Edward, outside on the top of the east gable, was carved by Corfe artist Francis Newbery [1931].
(Placenames / Churches / Corfe Castle)

Saint Edward's Bridge – over the Corfe River, carrying the main road at North Castle, opposite the Visitor Centre at Corfe Castle (SY 859 824). The previous bridge was dated 1564 and the present one, built in Purbeck stone ashlars, was constructed in the late 18th century. It has a single semi-circular arch and rusticated voussoirs.
(Placenames / Bridges / Corfe Castle)

Saint Edward's Fountain – an "eye well" healing spring above the Byle Brook, on the east side of Castle Hill at Corfe Castle. It takes its name from the death near this spot of saint and martyr King Edward [18 March 978].
(Placenames / Folklore / Corfe Castle)

Saint George's parish church (Langton Matravers) – only a squat tower of 14th-century design remains from the original mediaeval building, on the north side of the village street (SY 998 789), and is now dwarfed by a wide nave from its second 19th-century reconstruction [1875-76].

The earlier attempt [1828-29] failed to reach its half-century before described as suffering "general decay" and being in "an unsafe condition". It was roundly denounced by the rector, Rev E. F. Trotman: "Erected not more than 45 years ago at a cost of £800, in the most debased style of the period, it is simply a disgrace to the Isle of Purbeck. The wide-spanning roof, unsupported by its single pillar, is most fortunately pushing the walls out of the perpendicular, so that the yawning crack in walls and ceiling warn the congregation of the yearly increasing danger of a seat beneath the one and within the other."

Bell cote: at Kimmeridge, in a mid-Victorian drawing by J. H. Austen.

Local smugglers, led by Charles Hayward who operated Dancing Ledge Quarry and lived opposite, had been storing kegs above the domed ceiling, having taken out stones from the newel staircase into the tower bell chamber.

Plans by late-Victorian diocesan architect George Crickmay to put a spire on the tower, after it had been duly buttressed, were never carried out. He tore down the battlements in preparation but these were eventually replaced [1950s]. Crickmay's chancel marbles, of Purbeck stone in pseudo 13th-century style, are un-oiled grey rather than polished black. St Aldhelm of Sherborne is depicted in stained glass (though, arguably, St Alban's Head was in fact named for the first Romano-British martyr). St Leonard, locally carved in stone, preserves a memory of an earlier dedication for this parish church.

Between them the 19th-century restorers threw most of its history away. Only the font, memorials to the Serrell family of Durnford House, and a single broken brass to a couple of the Havellands from Wilkswood were saved.

Distinctive tower: of the 14th century, rising from the knoll that gives Church Knowle its name.

More recent memorials commemorate boys from the local preparatory schools, particularly at Durnford House and the Old Malthouse. In 1930 there were no less than nine schools in the village.
(Placenames / Churches / Langton Matravers)

Saint George's Hall – built as National School at Langton Matravers [1845], on the south side of the High Street, opposite the churchyard (SY 998 788).

The junior pupils transferred to a converted cottage, creating the Elementary School further up the street, on the opposite side of the road [1870], and the original building was converted into a parish hall, though the Sunday School continued to meet there. It was extended in the 20th century.
(Placenames / Schools / Langton Matravers)

Saint George's Primary School – the descendant of the Church of England's National School at Langton Matravers, on the north side of the High Street (SY 996 788). It began with a cottage conversion for the juniors [1870], with the infant accommodation to the east, which was later refurbished as purpose-

Original tower: the 12th-century lines of Worth Matravers parish church, drawn here by A. Tracey, survived until 1869 when the parapet was removed and a pyramidal roof added.

Double galleries: all churches should have kept them, as Colin Graham's evocative study of Church Knowle proves.

built classrooms [1909]. The hall and the canteen were the added later [1960s].
(Placenames / Schools / Langton Matravers)

Saint James's Church (New) – church building became a family preoccupation of the Scotts of Encombe House and the 3rd Earl of Eldon decided to build a replacement church of St James in the tiny hamlet of Kingston (SY 956 796).

"The new Kingston Church" [1874-80] was the last great flourish of Purbeck marble, virtually on a cathedral scale, and the final major creation by architect George Edmund Street [1824-81] who was a skilful mediaeval restorer as well as a Gothic revivalist. He was delighted with the results, which cost £60,000, and called it his "jolliest" job.

Criticism was made at the time and included this comment by the City Press: "Lord Eldon is now spending an immense sum of money in erecting a church in a neighbourhood which, although it may be hereafter, is not at the present time actually overrun by human beings. If his lordship were to devote his attention to a railway for Corfe and Swanage he would vastly benefit the neighbourhood, and, it is needless to add, materially increase the value of his own property."

Whatever the reason for his whim, the Earl did the job properly and hired George Street, a notable architect, as the designer. Street carried out his brief magnificently and gave Kingston a fine piece of revival architecture which successfully copied the style of the 13th century in many ways.

Stone and marble were used throughout and the building of Kingston's third church of St James gave Purbeck quarrymen an easy job for seven years. Other work was dropped and most of the materials came from the old quarries at Blashenwell. Street's church was built during a recession in the stone trade but on balance it did not help the quarrymen because when the work was finished in 1880 they found it impossible to renew normal business. While Kingston gives the appearance

Corfe Church: from the castle gate.

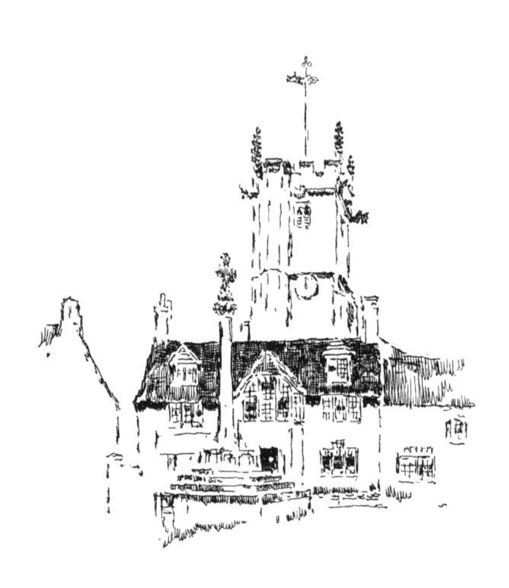

Corfe Castle: the Cross, the Town House, and the Church.

of being another quarrying village, it never was and missed out on the trade in the Middle Ages; there is still a lot of stone under the land around its neat houses.

Kingston may only have been a scapegoat for the difficulties of the stone trade in the 1880s. But just, or otherwise, the quarrymen's damning attitude towards it persisted. On the other hard, the Purbeck workers who visited Kingston left it with the greatest of the latter day examples of their craft.

Street had enjoyed using Purbeck stone and his son described the new Kingston church as "probably one of the most complete things my father ever did". During the progress of the work, the architect wrote in his diary that "the church is looking well. I hope the interior may be beautiful. It ought to be for they have already spent a large sum of money on it. It will be difficult to find, even among old buildings, anything more thoroughly elaborated, I believe. It is a real pleasure to work for such a man as Lord Eldon."

Subsequently, Street added: "It is a pleasure to be allowed to make work so much after one's heart as this will be; I think it is quite the jolliest church I have built."

Contemporary praise followed: "A model-like perfection and neatness which age will probably improve." Church architectural historian Fred Pitfield has commended its authentic 13th-century details and the lavish use of Purbeck marble for the shafting of the arcade piers.

(Placenames / Churches / Corfe Castle)

Norman arches: notably those framing the chancel, at Worth Matravers.

Oldest house: in the parish of Corfe Castle, is Scoles Farm which dates from about 1300 and is drawn here by Alfred Dawson, in 1882.

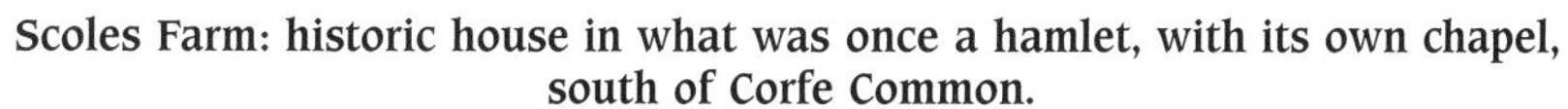

Scoles Farm: historic house in what was once a hamlet, with its own chapel, south of Corfe Common.

Saint James's Church (Old) – all that remains of the 12th-century chapel that stood at the east end of Kingston hamlet (SY 958 797) is the semi-circular arch from a Norman doorway, carved with segmented diaper ornamentation and reset solidly into the west gable of the replacement building designed by George Stanley Repton [1833].

It is a plain, uninspired, impoverished specimen of early Gothic revival architecture, now converted into a private house. Repton also re-hung a bell but otherwise it is only the position of the old chapel that was perpetuated. The work was commissioned by the 1st Earl of Eldon, of Encombe House, and carried out by builder John Tulloch from Wimborne.
(Placenames / Churches / Corfe Castle)

Saint Leonard's Chapel – mediaeval church at Wilkswood Priory, on the site of Wilkswood Farm at Langton Matravers (SY 995 795). Entirely demolished.
(Placenames / Churches / Langton Matravers)

Saint Nicholas's parish church (Kimmeridge) – a simple Norman building, from the 12th century, with a bell-cote added or rebuilt at the western end in the 15th century (SY 918 800). It was one of 16 mediaeval Dorset churches without any known dedication, but St Nicholas was chosen for it in the late 20th century. The nave and chancel form a single-cell building, 56 feet long by 15 feet wide, with the vestry at the north-west corner having been added in Victorian times.
(Placenames / Churches / Kimmeridge)

Saint Nicholas's parish church (Worth Matravers) – a gem of a Norman church, dating from the early 12th century (SY 973 774), with original chancel and tower arches, doorways, windows and a re-set corbel table that have survived the relatively modest rebuildings and extensions of the remainder of the millennium. The last flourishes, including repairs to the tower and its buttressing, were apparently among the last works of Dorchester architect John Hicks [died February 1869].

Architectural historian Fred Pitfield points out in *Purbeck Parish Churches* [1985] that the brief and undated specification carried no name but that the rebuilding was accomplished with commendable skill, blending new work with old, to the extent that "it is now difficult to distinguish the work then carried out".
(Placenames / Churches / Worth Matravers)

Saint Peter's parish church (Church Knowle) – on the knoll that provides the other element of the village name at Church Knowle (SY 941 819). Its list of rectors, going back to 1237, is claimed to be the longest in the Isle of Purbeck. The parish is also exceptional in having a complete register of births, marriages, and deaths, from 1549 onwards.

The church is of particular antiquity, beginning with its location, as it stands on a rounded knoll that was probably a Bronze Age burial mound.

St Peter's retains much of its 13th-century cruciform plan. The chancel arch is original. Windows, piscinae, and fragments of moulded stone add further contemporary flourishes.

Deer poacher Robert Hardle, indicted for unlawfully killing the King's deer and winging the Sub-Constable of Corfe Castle with an arrow, took sanctuary here [1323]. Our local Robin Hood then escaped "over the hill" as the villagers still call the other side of the Purbeck ridge.

The tower was added to the west wing of the church in the 14th century, and rebuilt in 1741, though re-using the same foundations and stone, in a style that retains the chunkiness of a castle, topped with a pyramidal spire.

Inside the notable memorial is the Clavell monument, its intricately-carved canopied altar tomb being complete with 1572-dated brasses, bringing a touch of class and quality. The general look, however, is homely – as you look down from the wooden gallery that stretches along two sides of the nave and doubles as a picture gallery with photographs of village life.
(Placenames / Churches / Church Knowle)

Saltpans or salterns – the latter word on the map, as with Wytch which derives from Wich, is evidence of Roman, Saxon and mediaeval salt-making across the harbour-side shores of Arne, Corfe Castle, and Studland, as well as from the sea at Kimmeridge Bay.

Until the mining of halite (rock-salt), saline production was a major Purbeck industry, with the Domesday survey [1086] recording that the Count of Mortain, King William's half-brother, owned 32 saltpans at Studland valued at 40 shillings and 25 per cent of the value of a manor worth £8. Similarly, at Wytch, 25 workers were employed in the salterns. Late in the 12th century a Shaftesbury Abbey survey showed that a hide of land – between 50 and 100 acres – at Arne was devoted entirely to the production of salt. This was extracted from sea-water (rather than in brine-pits) by use of leaden vessels (plumba) in which the water was collected and then boiled dry.

Sun drying was the earlier and commendably sustainable method. On the heath west of the sand dunes on the South Haven peninsula, concentrated in an area at 30 feet above sea level to the west of the ferry road between Redhorn Quay (SZ 025 855) and Jerry's Point (SZ 029 860), are at least 71 circles with single banks about a foot high and enclosing a slightly-dished horizontal floor around 20 feet across. Overall the outer diameters of these circles vary between 45 feet and 150 feet.

Interestingly, the Royal Commission on Historical Monuments noted that they lie "above an iron-pan, and clays" and that "many held rain-water for short periods". Their function "is quite unknown" and their date could be anywhere between the Iron Age and circa 1700 AD. he northern cluster are associated with 13 low sandy mounds which "have also defied explanation". Running south-east to north-west along the centre of the peninsula were a straight line of six regularly placed standing stones; now five, and fallen.

The determining evidence for the origin of circles, I have argued, is that they were built on the closest land to the harbour shore that is capable of holding water long enough for it to evaporate in the summer heat. I suggest a prehistoric or Romano-British origin both for the circles and the stones. The latter, by alignment and shadows, would have been a simple natural calendar for ascertaining the optimum midsummer months when temperature and daylight hours would have rendered the system operable.

Debris from Roman salt extraction has been discovered north of Bank Gate Cottages, east of The Moors at Arne (SY 957 869), 300 yards from the present shoreline of Wareham Channel. The area was being ploughed for conifer planting and the ground was found to be strewn with briquetage fragments of brick-like clay containers used in the manufacture of salt. More extensive remains have been found across a wide shelf of land on the edge of the scarp bordering mudflats to the south of Shipstal Point. Similar evidence has come from Fitzworth and Ower, on the eastern side of Corfe River, and just across the road from Bank Gate Cottages is Salterns Copse (SY 965 871), between Arne and Slepe.

As its dialect name records, it was perfectly sited for the process of natural evaporation as it had 400 yards of south-facing shore at the end of a backwater from Middlebere Lake. Offshore was an inland in the saltings (SY 968 868) that has been linked to the heathland by two embankments. These may have been built to regulate the water supply to the salterns but their effect now is to do the reverse and keep the sea 500 yards from the site of the saltpans.

There is also debris from Roman salt-making at Kimmeridge, beyond the pier at the south end of the bay, below Hen Cliff and the Clavell Tower, where briquetage lies in a deposit four feet thick, just above the high water mark (SY 908 786). In times of high pressure it becomes a sheltered location where the adjacent shale cliff soaks up summer warmth like a storage heater.

Manufacture of salt was later to be revived near this point. It is recorded from the 1620s that salt was being extracted from the sea by

Sir William Clavell. He obtained white common salt "in great abundance, by boiling it out of the sea water".

The site of this operation was probably at an area known as Cuddle, which was originally attached to the north-west side of Hen Cliff, though the name has now been transferred to an area of clifftop without any distinguishing features, 500 yards to the south-east, above the western end of the Kimmeridge Ledges. Cuddle, to give the literal evidence, is a Cornish mining word for "thick, muddy fluid". Cornwall usually provided the mining and engineering expertise for projects in Dorset and Somerset.
(Industrial archaeology / Arne, Corfe Castle, Kimmeridge and Studland)

Salvin – architect **Anthony Salvin** designed refinements to Encombe House for the third Earl of Eldon [1870s], notably moving the entrance from the scenic south side to the more functional north.
(People / Architects / Corfe Castle)

Samuel – schooner wrecked on the rocks off St Alban's Head, with three of her crew being drowned in the tide-race [14 November 1836].
(Shipwrecks / Worth Matravers)

Sandy Hill Lane – the road eastwards from Corfe Castle to Knitson and Ulwell, below the southern slope of the Purbeck Hills.
(Placenames / Roads / Corfe Castle)

Sandyhills – large area of Iron Age and, or, Romano-British Celtic fields across more than 70 acres on the eastern side of Corfe Common (SY 970 810).

They are on the Wealden sands and have been subsequently denuded by centuries of ploughing. All the fields are reduced to incomplete traces though there are still some low lynchets a foot or two in height.
(Placenames / Prehistoric archaeology / National Trust / Corfe Castle)

Sanitary Carbon Company – established at Wareham [1876] to convert Kimmeridge shale into deodorising sewage filters, claimed to have a carbon content of 70 per cent. Became the Kimmeridge Oil and Carbon Company.
(Industrial archaeology / Kimmeridge and Wareham)

Sarah Park – American barque, outward-bound carrying 300 emigrants from Dieppe, which grounded on the eastern end of the Kimmeridge Ledges, 300 yards west of Freshwater Steps where the Encombe stream cascades into the sea [morning, 3 October 1854]. She was a similar distance offshore.

Having hit the rocks in fog, and being driven inshore by a southerly wind, her fortunes changed as the tide rose. The wind turned to the north and she floated free. The vessel, however, was no longer in any fit state to cross the Atlantic, and had to put into Southampton for major repairs.
(Shipwrecks / Corfe Castle)

Sauropods – a family of dinosaurs living in the warm-water swamps of the Isle of Purbeck some 140 million years ago. An outstanding spread of well over a hundred prints, the largest 44 inches in diameter, was discovered on National Trust land at Keates Quarry, Worth Matravers [1997].
(Natural history / National Trust / Worth Matravers)

Scoles Farm – the oldest inhabited house in Corfe Castle parish, at a meeting place of old roads in the valley south of Corfe Common (SY 964 800). It is a fine piece of 17th-century building, with large open fireplaces and a stone staircase, that also incorporates parts of a small hall-house of about 1300. These include a mullioned window.

One original wall was rebuilt and has a series of bee-boles under stone arches. Beehives were not introduced into Britain until 1862 and before that a straw skep was used instead. Recesses were built into walls to protect them from the weather; and these are called bee-boles. They are mainly found in the wetter parts of the country and appear to have been constructed from the 15th century onwards.
(Placenames / Mediaeval archaeology / Corfe Castle)

Scotland Farm: recycled ashlar from the recent ruins of Corfe Castle, in 1665, and now also sharing its National Trust ownership.

Scotland – see next entries and also those for **Calcraft Boundary Stones** and **New Mills**.

Scotland Farm – low ceiling stone-roofed farmhouse with attic rooms, on the edge of New Mills Heath, midway between the Purbeck Hills and the backwaters of Poole Harbour (SY 962 840). The walls are particularly fine, but secondhand, being squared Purbeck ashlars recycled from the ruins of Corfe Castle in 1665, nineteen years after the fortress was demolished after the Civil War. The builder's initials, above the porch doorway, are "W. W." for William Whefer.

The porch is particularly attractive, being in proportion and scale with the low-slung lines of the building. There are chimney stacks at each end and some superb stone mullioned windows. The barn and geese complete an olde worlde setting that has the distinction of having been painted by Gordon Beningfield [died 1998]. It came into National Trust ownership with the Bankes Estate [1982].
(Placenames / National Trust / Corfe Castle)

Scotland Farm Barn – immediately north-east of the farmhouse at Scotland, north of Corfe Castle, and also National Trust owned (SY 962 841). Stone walled with a thatched roof. Its renovation in 1990 was marked with a commemorative stone featuring the Trust's oak-sprig logo.

Around the corner on the south wall, above the public path, is a larger than life head carved in relief. Set just below the eaves, it is a creditable revival of Celtic traditions, though very much a living head with a known owner. The features are those of master mason Derek Cartridge, who led the Trust's restoration team, and it was carved by Jonathan Sells of Corfe Castle.
(Placenames / National Trust / Corfe Castle)

Scott – **Lieutenant-Colonel Harold Scott** inherited the Encombe Estate in 1953.
(People / Corfe Castle)

Scott – Newcastle coal-trader **John Scott, 1st Earl of Eldon** [1751-1838] became Lord High Chancellor of England [1801-27, virtually continuously], bought the idyllic Encombe Estate on the Purbeck coast, south of Corfe Castle [1807] and was created Baron Eldon [1799] and later the Earl of Eldon [1821].

Oak leaves: the National Trust's 1990 datestone on its restoration of Scotland Farm barn, in the middle of Dorset's Purbeck heathland.

Master mason: Derek Cartridge, who led the team restoring Scotland Farm barn for the National Trust in 1990-91, sculpted on its east wall by Jonathan Sells of Corfe Castle.

A supporter of William Pitt, and the subject of ridicule from fellow Parliamentarian Richard Brinsley Sheridan, his favourite saying was that "a lawyer should live like a hermit and work like a horse". He progressed through the upper echelons of power to Solicitor General [1788], Attorney General [1793], and Chief Justice of Common Pleas [1799].

His notable legal cases included the prosecution of Horne Tooke and deprived atheist poet Percy Bysshe Shelley [1792-1838] of custody of his children, after the suicide of his wife, Harriet Shelley [1816]. Shelley's negative religious views were cited by Scott as the ground for his decision.

As a dominant member of the Cabinet he was resolute against the threat from Napoleon but rejected calls for Roman Catholic emancipation and opposed the growing clamour for reform of the voting system. He resisted the gathering momentum for extending voting rights and changing Parliamentary boundaries. Admirers thought him "almost the ideal of manly beauty". He was a prodigious port drinker and a lousy shot: "With a gun he can kill nothing but time." Critics linked his office with financial corruption. In the words of Cyrus Redding, one of his contemporaries: "He had a sterile soul for all things earthly except money, doubts and the art of drawing briefs."

When Eldon died, he left £700,000. From Love Lane, Newcastle, he had moved on to become the last major recipient of the plunder system in British politics, which subsidised the hospitalities of Encombe and his Hamilton Place town-house with £40,000 legally seized from bankruptcies, lunacies and wardships. "If we, by our industry, have acquired a degree of opulence and distinction which we could not reasonably have looked for, let us be thankful to that Government to whose favour we are, in a great measure, indebted for success," Eldon said in the smoothness of self-justification. "And do not let us, by any rash attempt upon our constitution, put it out of the power of our children to rise to similar situations."

This chance in life he presented to his own, but Eldon kept some other children in their

Creeper covered: the Scott Arms carries the family name of the Earls of Eldon.

Seacombe scenery: westwards to Winspit, projecting between the strip lynchets of East Man (top right) and West Man.

place. He had the will of a Mr Troutback, who left £100,000 for a charity school at Wapping, set aside and the money given to George IV to help liquidate the royal debts. The money bequeathed to clothe, educate and maintain poor children was applied to meet the furniture bills, tailoring, haberdashery, and riotous living of the Prince Regent.
(People / Politics / Corfe Castle)

Scott – grandson **John Scott, 2nd Earl of Eldon** [1805-54] was heir to the first Earl of Eldon, being created Viscount Encombe [1821] and inheriting the main title on his grandfather's death [1838].
(People / Corfe Castle)

Scott – landowner **John Scott, 3rd Earl of Eldon** [1845-1926, inherited 1854] of Encombe House played a pivotal part in local affairs and enriched the Isle of Purbeck with one of the best Victorian churches in the land, built to cathedral-like specifications at Kingston [1874-80] by George Edmund Street. Purbeck needed a railway more than another church, the City Press growled, and Eldon duly co-operated with its building across his land [1883-85].
(People / Corfe Castle)

Scott Arms – see entry for **Eldon Arms**.

Scout Hut – on the west side of Durnford Drove at Langton Matravers, proclaiming itself to be the "1st Langton B. P. Scout and Guide H. Q. 1953" (SY 997 788). It also has a foundation stone, in the wall beside the pavement: "Erected by voluntary service of the Scout and Guide packs and friends of the Scouts. Opened by Ralph Reader, May 1954." He was the national "Gang-Show" compere.
(Placenames / Scouting / Langton Matravers)

Seacombe gun-nest – on the side of the eastern slopes overlooking Seacombe Bottom, is a rounded metal turret which is often mistaken for the cockpit of a crashed aircraft (SY 986 768). It was is in fact put there in 1940, for a single machine-gunner who had the unenviable task of keeping watch on Seacombe in the months when invasion was a real threat. The gun would have been fired from the shuttered front which was the only opening into the canopy – the gunner had no back door from the war. This rare war relic came into National Trust ownership with the Bankes Estate [1982].
(Placenames / National Trust / Worth Matravers)

Seacombe Quarries – the most fulsome veins of workable stone on the Purbeck coast have been fully exploited, leaving gaping galleries sliced into the western cliff at Seacombe Bottom and running under the hill and along the valley side (SY 984 766). Its stone is "Portland", rather than "Purbeck", from the uppermost stratum of the Jurassic system. Portland stone is marine in origin, whereas Purbeck is a freshwater limestone. Here the former was taken out in blocks 15 tons apiece, and the roofs of the workings are up to 12 feet high. The basebed and the whitbed, seven feet thick, were worked.

One of the special jobs accomplished at A. Bower's quarry in 1871 was a 3.5 ton trough for North Woolwich Galvanising Works. Its dimensions were 8 feet long, 4 feet wide, and 4 feet deep.

These great quarries were in use from about 1700 to 1930, followed by Second World War clearances of spoil for runway hard-core, to build a series of military aerodromes across the heathlands of the New Forest.

The galleries are supported by a few huge pillars but inevitably there are rockfalls. Their makers never intended the galleries to stand for centuries, so it is unsafe to wander underground; even with a hard-hat as that would only give cosmetic protection. The disused workings came into National Trust ownership with the Bankes Estate [1982].
(Placenames / Industrial archaeology / National Trust / Worth Matravers)

Second Tower – between the First Tower and the Third Tower on the eastern side of the

Seacombe Quarry: crumbling cliffside galleries, now reserved for the bats.

Seacombe Bottom: looking northwards into limestone grassland, across level ground (centre) where *Halsewell* shipwreck victims were buried.

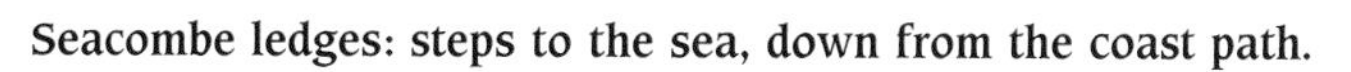

Seacombe ledges: steps to the sea, down from the coast path.

Seacombe Cliff: looking eastwards, towards Dancing Ledge.

Outer Bailey at Corfe Castle, built in 1212-15. (Placenames / Mediaeval archaeology / National Trust / Corfe Castle)

Secondus – preserved 0-6-0T second locomotive of the Furzebrook claylands mineral railway. Bought from manufacturers Bellis and Seekings [1874], for £650, she had a long working life, becoming a spare engine in semi-retirement, and was then rescued for the transport collection in the city of her birth, the Birmingham Museum for Science and Technology [1955].
(Industrial archaeology / Railways / Church Knowle)

Sells – sculptor **Jonathan Sells** of Corfe Castle has produced some of its best late 20th-century stonework. A specimen very much in the public domain, adorning a National Trust building, is the carving of Derek Cartridge set in Scotland Farm Barn [1990].
(People / Artists / National Trust / Corfe Castle)

Septimus – seventh and final steam locomotive of the Furzebrook claylands mineral railway, being an 0-4-2ST built by Peckett [1930].
(Industrial archaeology / Railways / Church Knowle)

Serrell's Barn – converted to three cottages, on the north side of Steps Hill, Langton Matravers, opposite the north-west corner of Leeson Park plantation (SZ 004 789). It was used as non-conformist chapel prior to the building of the Methodist Church [1842].
(Placenames / Churches / Langton Matravers)

Sextus – sixth steam locomotive of Furzebrook mineral railway, being an 0-4-2ST built by Peckett [1925].
(Industrial archaeology / Railways / Church Knowle)

Sharford Bridge – Purbeck's picturesque packhorse bridge across the Corfe River in the meadows between Scotland and Wytch (SY 967 847). Its presence, still at a crossroads of public paths, is the clue to a lost road. It is the remotest bridge in Dorset and also among the most unusual, being only six feet wide, on two rough arches. To Thomas Gerard, in the 1660s, "river" seemed an exaggerated description for Corfe's stream – "the brooke or river, choose you which".

The present bridge was built, probably, around 1700 but there was a predecessor as it is named as "Sherford Bridge" on John Speed's county map of 1610. Indeed it is marked "emphatically" on many maps, including military surveys, as Professor Ronald Good was first to point out. For instance it appears on Henry VIII's coastal defence map, at a time before roads were even being shown.

The name is obviously much earlier and indicates that originally it was simply a ford. "Shard" was a dialect word in Purbeck for a "gap" and was pronounced as "shar". There is a curious duplication of virtually identical placenames in east Dorset; three miles north of Wareham is a "Sherford Bridge" and less than a mile away a farmstead called Slepe. The only other occurrence of Slepe in Dorset is the farmstead north of Corfe's Sharford Bridge.

Early maps indicate that this packhorse bridge was built to carry an old road from Stoborough to the mediaeval harbour port at Ower Quay with a south fork to Ulwell Gap and the sea coast at Swanage. Perhaps it was a deliberate avoidance of Corfe Castle which in the Middle Ages acted as Purbeck's police station.

Interestingly and usefully, it remains a focal point of the rights of way network with three bridleways and a footpath converging on it from Wytch, Middlebere Heath, and Scotland Farm.

It is well restored but things were not always thus. In January 1972 I brought its rapidly deteriorating condition to the attention of the highway authority, Dorset County Council: "Since my previous visit a tree that was growing out of the structure of the bridge has died. it has now fallen over and badly damaged the parapet and east end of the bridge where it had its roots. The bridge is badly in need of repairs."

The council responded promptly to say there had been an inspection and repair work was arranged for the coming summer, as winter water levels prevented anything being done sooner.
(Placenames / Bridges / Corfe Castle)

Sharford Cottage – south-west of Wytch Heath (SY 969 843), destroyed by the mid-20th century.
(Placenames / Corfe Castle)

Ship Inn – two buildings sharing a party wall on the south side of the summit of Steps Hill at Langton Matravers (SZ 003 789). The two-storey early 18th-century cottage nestling on the west side of the present hostelry, opposite the hilltop pond, was the original licensed premises [1765].

Its Christmas tragedy would be the suicide of landlord John Ball, who shot himself after a failed attempt at reconciliation with his wife, Mary Holmes Ball. Closing-time came and they had their last row. She ran back to her mother's home and John followed with a shotgun. She was barely behind the cottage door when it was blasted with shot.

John then went back to the Ship Inn and turned the gun on himself in the stone-flagged public room [18 December 1878]. His body "was buried like a dog" [21.30 hours, 22 December], to protests by Langton rector Rev

Sharford Bridge: once the hub of the road system in northern Purbeck, now a backwater of the paths network.

Lester Lester: "It is time for even Purbeck juries to know that the sentiment of our times is dead against such verdicts as felo-de-se [felon of himself]. He wanted his wife to come and live with him. She felt that she could not. Life then appeared so black to him that he shot himself. If he was sane, why be so cruel to survivors, so uncourteous to a poor dead man; seeing that to him prayers could mean nothing, and even a suicide's burial nothing, while to them the touching service might have been of vital importance. We do hope this verdict will be the last of its kind in our neighbourhood."

This was the crime of suicide. It was society and religion's retribution on the body of the deceased. In earlier times this would have been violated with a stake through the heart in order to pin the ghost to the ground. The rector's letters supported a winning cause and the law would be repealed in Acts of Parliament [1880-82]. Subsequent suicides could be buried with dignity, in a churchyard, as if they had died normally.

The other ghost was the scene of John Ball's tragedy. The replacement Steps Inn, almost Portland-style in its austere three-storey lines, was built on the east side, on the brow of the hill [1884]. Its first publican was Henry Davis.
(Placenames / Social history / Langton Matravers)

Shipwrecks – see entries for ***Aeolian Sky***, ***Arklow***, ***Avanti***, ***British Inventor***, ***Caernarvon Castle***, Chapman's Pool Lifeboat Station, ***Commodore***, ***Don Pedro***, ***Edouard***, ***Elinor***, Ferry tragedy, ***Fortitude***, ***Georgiana***, ***Hildegarde***, ***John Richard***, ***Joseph Desiri***, Kimmeridge Ledges, Kimmeridge Lifeboat Station, ***L'Atlantique***, Middlebere canoe tragedy, ***Montanes***, ***Olive Branch***, ***Renaud***, ***Samuel***, ***Sarah Park***, ***Start***, HMS ***Skylark***, ***Treveal***, ***Tyne***, and ***Welfare***.

Shotts – the former lane south from the corner beside the Old Rectory in Church Knowle village, now public footpath number 20.
(Placenames / Roads / Church Knowle)

Six Ways – path junction on Knowle Hill, on the Purbeck Hills east of Cocknowle (SY 936 823) marked by a hexagonal stone, surmounted by a sarsen boulder, erected in memory of Ramblers' Association activist Mary Baxter, from Rempstone [died 1988].
(Placenames / Memorials / Church Knowle)

HMS Skylark – a naval brig, which struck the Cuttle Ledge, east of Kimmeridge, with 102 persons on board [April 1845]. She was a total loss but all were rescued, through the efforts of Lieutenant Smith, RN, and his Coastguards. His team nearly made their own sacrifices, finding themselves in danger of being swept away when the brig's four-oared galley was swamped.
(Shipwrecks / Kimmeridge)

Smedmore House – nearly a mile south-east of Kimmeridge village, at the foot of the steep slope of Smedmore Hill (SY 924 788). Built for Sir William Clavell, early in the 17th century, it was remodelled in the 18th century by George Clavell into a fine country house, with the symmetrical semi-circular tower-like corners to the north-west frontage dating from 1761. The Clavell crest embosses the rainwater-heads.

Set in wooded grounds, landscaped originally as 50-acre parkland, Grange Plantation and The Rookery face Kimmeridge village, and Harry's Wood stands seaward of Kimmeridge Dairy, midway to Clavell's Hard. Smedmore has been the 20th-century home of Major Rhys Clavell Mansel, followed by Major John Mansel.
(Placenames / Country houses / Kimmeridge)

Smith – farmworker **Hubert Smith** [born 1872] had a thatched cottage at North Castle, north of the Castle Hill, as his first home near Corfe Castle. It has since burned down. He remembered his mother's rent being ninepence per week that was paid half-yearly at Rempstone Hall. There, on those two red-lettered days of the year, the tenants would gather for a hot meal in winter and a cold one in summer. Hubert was an elder child and he paid the rent as his parents could not spare the time to visit Rempstone.

Smedmore House: the Clavell family seat, in the coastal hinterland between Kimmeridge and Swyre Head.

A member of the staff would inquire of each tenant how many children were living at home – and for each a chunk of bread pudding was cut and wrapped, being the traditional treat for the poor.

Young Hubert was brought up to show his respect when the third Lord Eldon's carriage passed through Corfe on its way to Encombe House. Hearing the blare of the postilion's horn, the inhabitants would run to their doors or gates to curtsy or bow. The vicar and three curates at Corfe also expected similar respect from the working class.

Hubert Smith's daughter, Mrs A. F. Riches, described the family's later life in a cottage at East Street, Corfe Castle:

"My grandmother had a fire on the hearth and a long iron rod came from the back wall. On this, a gypsy-pot hung and all the food was put in nets and cooked together in one pot. If my grandmother needed to make a cake she used to get the hearth fire red hot, spread the cinders, and made a well. The cake was put in a tin, with another tin on top, and then sunk in the cinders.

"My great-grandfather built a back-oven in which he used to roast Sunday meat and potatoes for sale in the village at a penny a tin. There were also jam or fruit tarts for a ha'penny. My father [Hubert Smith] was sent out on Saturdays to gather faggots from the woods to heat the oven.

"It was from these pennies that my ancestor earned sufficient to buy his first cow. My great-grandfather worked in the claypits and the social status of the working class in those days depended not on whether you owned your own house, but whether you had a cow. The cow was turned out on Corfe Common during the day, and to be milked it had to be brought home and walked through the passage of the house to a shed at the back."

(People / Social history / Corfe Castle)

Snug's Farm – 19th-century heathland farmstead beside Church Knowle bridleway number 35 at Creech (SY 917 839). Its small fields are surrounded by pine plantations.

(Placenames / Church Knowle)

South Tower – of the West Bailey at Corfe Castle, dates from 1201-04 and is also known as the Mural Tower. Inset are a fireplace, cupboard recess, and window [1750s], the purpose for which was recorded by visiting preacher John Wesley: "Some time since the proprietor fitted out some rooms in the Mural Tower on the south-west [side of Castle Hill] and laid out a little garden, commanding a large prospect, pleasant beyond description. The rooms were fitted up and occupied for many years by the rector of Corfe." He apparently slept in the North Tower, on the opposite side of the North Bailey.
(Placenames / Mediaeval archaeology / National Trust / Corfe Castle)

South-West Gatehouse – the inner gatehouse at Corfe Castle, previously known as Edward's Gate. Its current architecture dates from 1250-85; displaced by explosives in 1646.
(Placenames / Mediaeval archaeology / National Trust / Corfe Castle)

Spencer Watson – painter **George Spencer Watson** [1869-1932] progressed from St Johns Wood Art School and the Royal Academy School to become an established painter of formal portraits. He became increasingly involved in the club for that section of London's art scene and was appointed treasurer of the Royal Society of Portrait Painters.

For relaxation he painted Purbeck landscapes, with the family for animation, with the notable example being "The Donkey Ride" depicting daughter Mary on Studland sands; it won the Picture of the Year award at the Royal Academy [1919].

He then bought Downshay Manor, Worth Matravers [1922], from where he could indulge his principal recreations: "Four loves I found – a woman, a child, a horse, and a hound." Artistic subjects ranged from nudes, which are still a local speciality, to the chalk stacks at Old Harry Rocks, to illustrate his philosophy that "the artist sees beauty, and he tries to express his joy, by showing people what it is he sees".
(People / Artists / Studland and Worth Matravers)

Masonic name: the Square and Compass at Worth Matravers, as much a museum as a public house.

Spencer Watson – sculptor **Mary Spencer Watson** [born 1913] inherited Downshay Manor and renamed it in its mediaeval spelling, Dunshay. She learnt to work stone in the Purbeck quarries, at the age of 12, and was soon producing quantities of sad-faced figures that would be set in the walls and paving around Dunshay Manor.

She studied her masonic craft under John Skeaping at Bournemouth College and wood carving with Ossip Zadkine in Paris. Her work has strong and graceful flowing forms but faces tend to droop with a powerful Celtic edge that allows no concession to prettiness. Her mastery of disturbing undertones has been nationally acclaimed, having won local appreciation with first major exhibition at Dorset County Museum in Dorchester [1981].
(People / Artists / Worth Matravers)

Square and Compass – Masonic-named 18th-century stone-roofed public house at Worth Matravers (SY 975 776), in a picturesque setting overlooking National Trust land, across both sets of Winspit strip lynchets, in a view southwards to the sea.

Unusual in still having a bar served from a hatch, its collection outside of fun sculpture, and inside a veritable museum of locally-caught dinosaurs and their footprints. Associations, revolving around memories of publican Charlie Newman [1871-1953] and his family, include visits from Bohemian artist Augustus John, and home-based quarryman and fiddler Billy Winspit.
(Placenames / Worth Matravers)

Start – Norwegian steamship, torpedoed and sunk by a German U-boat off St Alban's Head [22 December 1917].
(Shipwrecks / Worth Matravers)

Stephen – English monarch **King Stephen** [1097-1154, reigned from 1135] built The Rings siegework in a failed attempt to oust Baldwin de Redvers, the first Earl of Devon, from Corfe Castle [1139].
(People / Politics / Corfe Castle)

Steppeshill – former Steppeshill Boarding House, for girls, on the north-west side of Leeson Park, Langton Matravers (SZ 004 789). It was briefly used as domestic science classrooms and then became a guest house.
(Placenames / Schools / Langton Matravers)

Steps Hill – or Steppeshill in its alternative mediaeval spelling, being a footpath of stone steps down from the eastern summit of the High Street at Langton Matravers, which became transformed into the turnpike road to Swanage [1761]. The prominent building, on the south side, is the Ship Inn.
(Placenames / Langton Matravers)

Stone circles – see entries for **Bushey Stone Circle** and **Rempstone Stone Circle**.

Stonehill Down Oval Barrow – a mound on the Purbeck Hills south-west of East Creech (SY 923 821). It is a transitional oval-shaped mound of circa 2500 to 2300 BC, being neither a long barrow nor a later round barrow. It stands nine feet high on open downland and is rounded in profile, though the flanking ditches at the side are characteristic of a Neolithic long barrow.
(Prehistoric archaeology / Church Knowle)

Strange – pioneer aviator **Lieutenant-Colonel / Wing Commander Louis Arbon Strange** [1891-1966] was born at Keynston Mill, Tarrant Keynston; moved to East Almer, Sturminster Marshall; farmed at Worth Matravers; had a caravan at Warmwell; a derelict cottage near Wincanton; retired to Winterborne Kingston; and is buried in Worth Matravers churchyard.

Visited the Bournemouth Aviation Meeting and mounted guard with the Dorsetshire Yeomanry on the body of crashed aviator Honourable Charles Rolls [July 1910]. Went up for his first flight with Lewis Turner of Sturminster Newton, from Race Down, Blandford [1911], and learned to fly at Hendon [1913]. Predicted the use of aeroplanes for military reconnaissance and became one of the first Britons to copy Frenchman Adolphe Pegoud's "upside-down loop". Specialised in unconventional "ragtime flying" and won the first leg of the London-Manchester-London Air Race, 35 minutes ahead of the next of the seven other flyers, but was then immobilised at Trafford Park as the heavyweight Lord Mayor, leading 100,000 spectators, clambered aboard and snapped a bracing wire that then smashed the propeller [20 June 1914]. He also won dummy bombing contests, dropping bags of flour to within 25 feet of the target, from 300 feet. By now Lieutenant Strange was seconded by the Dorsetshire Yeomanry to the Royal Flying Corps [May 1914], training at Upavon on Salisbury Plain. Landed on his Yeomanry chums in Crichel Park, terrifying their horses, to collect bets. Ordered to report to 5 Squadron, at Gosport, on the declaration of war [4 August 1914].

He was the last of 37 RFC pilots to fly four squadrons from rendezvous at Dover to the war in France, and the only one to do so with a Lewis machine-gun, in Henry Farman F-20 No. 341 [06.00 hours, 14 August 1914]. Only seven of these first flyers would survive the Great War; Strange doing so still in squadron service, decorated with the Distinguished Service Order, Distinguished Flying Cross, and Military Cross.

A "very good recce" proved the value of aerial reconnaissance, showing the German First Army was no longer heading for Paris, and Strange became the first flyer to fire a machine-gun at the enemy, and among the first to attack ground troops, with petrol bombs. Likewise he was one of the first to shoot down a German aircraft, a two-seater Aviatik, with the Lewis gun from his new Avro-504, above Armentieres [22 November 1914]. The war was not over by Christmas, but it was supposed to be a day off from hostilities. Strange broke off from the hampers and chocolates, courtesy Queen Mary, and flew alone across the silent lines to deliver a present to the Germans at Fives Aerodrome, Lille – they ran for cover as a football bounced across the grass [25 December 1914].

Promoted Captain Strange and transferred to a BE-2c of 6 Squadron, he bombed two trains at Courtrai station, from 50 feet, in the first tactical bombing in history. Witnessed the first poison gas attack of the war, in the Ypres salient [22 April 1915].

Provided with a single-seater Martinsyde Scout, armed with a Lewis gun, but hit by a German Albatross on its first flight, rupturing the oil tank. Strange reverted to Hendon-style aerobatics and flew upside-down in a roll to land on a track in hop-fields.

Later, at 8,000 feet above Menin, his gun jammed as he attacked an Aviatik. Wedging the stick between his knees and trying to change the drum, he found the Martinsyde going into a spin and hurling him from the cockpit. He literally hung on for his life from the inverted machine, clinging to the troublesome drum of the gun he had been trying to free, and kicked his way back into the cockpit, where he "jammed on full aileron and elevator" and fell "into my seat with a bump. Despite jammed controls he managed to pull out of the dive at the last possible moment and return to his aerodrome.

Acted as a decoy for Major Lanoe Hawker, luring two German aircraft to their doom under the gunfire from Hawker's new Bristol Scout [15 July 1915]. Two kills in one day was just about unprecedented and Hawker was awarded the first Victoria Cross for aerial combat.

Captain Strange was by now the longest serving pilot on the Western Front; he was ordered to depart for Dorset on home leave [2 August 1915]. From here he progressed to the new 12 Squadron, forming at Netheravon, as Flight Commander, and took it from Hawkinge to France. His presence at St-Omer was unauthorised, however, and Major-General H. M. Trenchard caught him attaching a Lewis gun to a BE-2c. "Go home at once, Strange," Trenchard boomed, "in that machine, now." He pointed to a dilapidated Maurice Farman [September 1915].

His next task, at Gosport, was to form and command 23 Squadron, in Avro No. 4741 [21 September 1915] with orders to have it trained and operational by 1 January 1916. In fact they did not receive their full quota of FE-2b fighters for another couple of weeks [18 January 1916] and illness prevented him taking them to the Western Front. Acute appendicitis led to emergency surgery at Cosham Military Hospital during which he was sewn-up with a swab mislaid in his stomach. It would keep him in the Home Establishment for two years, convincing the RFC that gunnery training was an imperative, and that flying at low level also had to be practised. He commanded the Machine Gun School at Hythe and turned it into No. 1 School of Air Gunnery, increasing its output from 20 trainees a month to 120. In the process he rebelled against tented accommodation and requisitioned the Imperial Hotel, part of the Town Hall, Tilling and Stevens Omnibus Company, Lympne Aerodrome, and the Golf Links ("for a rifle range"). It also gave him the excuse to slip across to France, visiting the French School of Aerial Gunnery at Cazeaux and his best friend Lanoe Hawker with his aggressive 24 Squadron; whose DH-2s had the reputation amongst Germans and Allies alike as being the only flyers who were a fair match for the feared Fokker Eindekker and its cowling-mounted Parabellum machine-gun. It would be the last time Major Hawker would meet his old friend; Manfred von Richthofen in his personalised Albatross D-2 prevented Hawker's escape at treetop height and shot him through the back of the head with a fatal burst from twin Spandau guns firing through the arc of his propeller.

Back in Britain, promoted Lieutenant-Colonel, Louis Strange was appointed Assistant Commander of the Central Flying School at Upavon, Wiltshire [April 1917]. He not only unbanned aerobatics but taught them, and returned yet again to France to see the rapidly developing tactics in front-line fighting and fly combat patrols with 60 Squadron, in a Nieuport Scout [June 1917]. Home again, he then appointed himself as the test pilot at Upavon of new and adapted machines.

Younger brother Ben Strange joined him as an instructor at Upavon, from where they both flew back to Dorset, before leaving for France and a SE-5 of 40 Squadron. On the integration of the Royal Flying Corps and the Royal Naval Air Service, henceforth the Royal Air Force [1 April 1918], Louis Strange was given command of No. 23 (Training Wing) and conducted King George V and Queen Mary around his Cranwell base, having flown from Waddington and failed to find the aerodrome in mist. He landed in a field three miles away and walked from there to his royal rendezvous.

His wish to return to combat in France was eventually granted, to command 80 Wing, newly formed under General Ludlow Hewitt.

He found the reconnaissance function had extended into offensive ground support for the Army and attacks on bases behind enemy lines. For this purpose he had 2 and 4 Squadrons of the Australian Flying Corps (with the SE-5); 46 Squadron of the RAF (with the Camel); 88 Squadron of the RAF (with the Bristol Fighter); and 103 Squadron of the RAF (with the DH-9). Additionally, 54 Squadron and 92 Squadron of the RAF were promised later, when they became operational.

Strange concentrated his efforts on attacking German airfields to destroy aeroplanes on the ground – arguing that tactical strikes would be far more effective than trying to shoot them down in the air. He flew to his squadrons almost every day and joined them on patrols and bombing raids. In one engagement he was "thoroughly sat upon by four Fokkers" and destroyed one and damaged another; but then had his Camel almost ripped apart by friendly fire when he made the basic mistake of making a victory swoop across Allied lines and was mistaken for the enemy. Some things had not changed. If in doubt, open fire; that was the rule of survival on the ground.

His greatest "show" came with organising and leading, with Australian ace Captain Harry Cobby, the entire 65 aircraft of 80 Wing in a devastating ground attack that delivered 150 bombs and 20,000 rounds of gunfire into

Bruno von Leutzer's aerodrome at Haubourdin [15 August 1918]. All 65 returned safely.

The following day he repeated the performance, with no one aware of the target until Louis Strange appeared on the airfield with a reconnaissance photograph of the German aerodrome at Lomme. "All yours," he told Cobby, and again followed his left wing-tip. It was a ditto situation of complete destruction with "all the six hangars enveloped in black smoke clouds, edged with reddish-yellow flames". The Germans had moved in anti-aircraft guns but it was still a ditto situation, of the previous day's result, with both Haubourdin and Lomme being abandoned for the duration of the war. Cobby wrote of Strange: "He was one of those persons with more than the average issue of guts. All he wanted was to be let loose in any old sort of trouble . . . I used to devote a lot of time to studying where one met with most 'hate' so that Strange would get a bellyful next time he wanted to get out!"

He also had reunions with Ben Strange by flying a couple of times into Bryas where his brother was an over-enthusiastic newly promoted Flight Commander for hard-pressed 40 Squadron. As he sensed, Ben would be lost on a dawn patrol, shot down after destroying a Hun in a dogfight over Cambrai [24 September 1918]: "Ben had gone to join all those other good friends of his and mine."

The citation for Louis Strange's DFC credits him with organising the low-flying raids by 80 Wing and examples an occasion [30 October 1918] when "he accompanied one of these raids against an aerodrome; watching the work of his machines, he waited until they had finished then dropped him bombs from 100 feet altitude on hangars that were undamaged, then attacked troops an transport in the vicinity of the aerodrome. Whilst thus engaged he saw eight Fokkers flying above him; at once he climbed and attacked them single-handed; having driven one down out of control he was fiercely engaged by the other seven, but he maintained the combat until rescued by a patrol of our Scouts."

The last days of the war saw a German rout and as well as airfields the Wing attacked retreating columns, with "many lorries burnt and destroyed by direct hits, many casualties caused amongst massed troops on the roads".

An orderly woke Strange with an "Urgent" message [02.00 hours, 11 November 1918]: "HOSTILITIES will cease at 11.00 today and no operations should be undertaken which cannot be completed by that hour" . . . "Then I turned over and went to sleep again, dimly wondering what on earth we were going to do with ourselves in the morning without a war."

The following day he flew his battered Camel to a reunion with wife Marjorie at Sutton Scotney on the Hampshire Downs and introduced himself to son Brian, aged two months.

His final endurance in the backlash of war, after 1,000 hours of wartime flying, was the influenza pandemic that carried off so many of the young and the fit who had considered themselves survivors.

In peacetime he took command of the Flying Wing of the Royal Air Force Cadet College, Cranwell, under Air Marshal Charles Longcroft, retiring as Lieutenant-Colonel Strange of the Dorsetshire Regiment [1922] to the family farm, now 1,300 acres at Worth Matravers. Inevitably, selling milk through drought and depression was pedestrian compared with the life that was still in his blood. The age of long-distance flight was all over the newspapers and newsreels. He was determined to play his part and became a director of Spartan Aircraft until, as Spartan Airlines Limited, it merged with Hillman's Airways and United Airways [1935].

Establishing the Swanage and Isle of Purbeck Light Aeroplane Club [1926] was followed by London-Berlin non-stop flights in his Simmonds Spartan with two up [24 October 1928]. The return flight was also non-stop and two up [27 October 1928]. These exploits are documented in his memoirs, *Recollections of an Airman* [1933], and expanded in *Flying Rebel: The Story of Louis Strange*, by parachutist and novelist Group Captain Peter Hearn [1994].

Veteran flyer: Louis Arbon Strange of Worth Matravers, drawn by Eric Kennington in 1942, was unique in surviving aerial combat from start to finish in the Great War, and then fought through the next.

That gives both halves in what soon becomes an amazing biography. Louis Strange returned to the sky for the Second World War, as Acting Pilot Officer Strange with 24 Squadron at Hendon [April 1940], flew to France and repaired abandoned Hurricanes at Merville, one of which he took back to Manston, chased by Messerschmitt Me.109s, on being ordered to return to England "as best he could". That added a bar to his Great War DFC. He then flew back to Paris and brought the last of 24 Squadron's Rapides out of France. Air Minister Harold Balfour took his hat off to him, with congratulations for showing "that the old men when put to it can do as well as the youngsters".

Sir Peter Masefield, a fellow pilot of the 1930s, wrote: "Strange revelled in action, flew with gusto, cheerfully rebelled against the rigid order of things, and endeared himself to a host of friends and colleagues, though not always to higher authorities." Richard Townshend bickers: "Louis Strange was one of the most electrifying personalities I ever met."

His next posting was to the new Parachute Training School at RAF Ringway, Manchester [24 June 1940]. He found himself Squadron Leader Strange, en route to the Parachute Development Unit at RAF Henlow. Pioneer aviator Lord Egerton loaned him Tatton Park, Cheshire, as the drop-zone, and Louis Strange at age 49 made the first jump of his life, from one of his four Whitleys [13 July 1940]. Others followed, in the call of wartime duty rather than for the thrill of the thing, from the removed rear gun-turret of the bomber. They soon decided it made more sense to jump through the bombing hole in the fuselage. Troop-carrying gliders followed, delivered by road from the Airspeed factory at Christchurch.

Strange flew operations for the secret war, over occupied Europe, and dropped a Dutch naval operative near Leiden [August 1940]. A "large-scale" parachute exercise was provided for General Bernard Montgomery at Shrewton on Salisbury Plain [3 December 1940]. Winston Churchill visited the airborne forces at Ringway [26 April 1941] and was told by Strange that "we could have trained ten times the number". He went on to an indiscretion, criticising delays and indecision between the Air Ministry and War Office, in the fall-out from which he was relieved of his post.

His next job, at RAF Speke, Liverpool, was training pilots for Hurricats – seaborne catapult-launched Hurricanes – in the new Merchant Ships Fighter Unit [12 May 1941]. Characteristically, Strange would be the first to fly rocket-launched Sea Hurricane 7253 from a ramped platform at Speke, demolishing "all top secrecy . . . also the protecting screen, which the blast of the rockets blew almost out of the aerodrome". He calculated 0 to 75 mph in 80 feet "with G-force distorting one's face, flash, and 200 feet over the Mersey". Rockets were much more fun than the other end of the procedure, which was preparing for "ditching and dinghy". They trained pilots for 804 Royal Naval Air Squadron of the Fleet Air Arm, at RNAS Sydenham, Belfast, and the Battle of the Atlantic.

Strange's next command was RAF Valley, Anglesey, and he then joined No. 11 Group Fighter Command Headquarters at RAF Uxbridge. Wing Commander Strange's following station command was RAF Hawkinge [18 December 1942] and from there to No. 12 Group Fighter Command Headquarters at RAF Watnall, Nottingham. Next it was the new No. 46 Group Transport Command Headquarters, a London-based offshoot of No. 38 Group at Netheravon, Wiltshire, and the return to Airborne Training [27 December 1943]. That gave him a Dakota and a 150-aircraft mass drop of paras, once more at Shrewton [14 April 1943].

He appointed himself Group observer for D-Day, aboard the first Dakota of the leading squadron of the 6th Airborne Division, with Squadron Leader "Dusty" Miller [6 June 1944]. They crossed the Channel between Arundel Castle and Littlehampton and on the other side saw 100 Lancasters bombing the German coastal defences at Merville, with the drop-zone 15 minutes away, where the red warning light came on "for the longest four seconds in a man's life". The hand goes down on Number One's shoulder as it turns to green, with all 16 dropping in eight seconds, as two more sticks of 16 descended from Dakotas two and three: "For a moment the great aircraft felt very lonely and empty. The urge to follow those splendid troops was almost irresistible."

So he did, landing with 20 Dakotas on a hastily bulldozed strip, in sight of the enemy, henceforth No. 46 Group Advanced Headquarters [15 June 1944]. Inward came personnel and supplies; outwards in the next three months went 50,000 wounded from the Battle of Normandy. He based himself in a rectory at Magny, near Bayeux, and established six airstrips. From there they made the leaps to Evreux, Bernay, and Orly, in Paris. They were told it had been allocated to the Americans and were given Le Bourget instead, still technically in German hands, but in fact abandoned and mined. "The RAF Ensign was run up over the control tower" [10.00 hours, 30 August 1944], and opened for flights thanks to the efforts of German prisoners and the French, a week before the promised arrival of an Airfield Construction Company.

A grass strip was next, at Amiens, where they became 111 Wing and the priority for the Dakotas was fuel, in jerrycans, for tanks of 30th Armoured Corps and the fighters of the 2nd Tactical Air Force. From here he landed in arable stubble beside Nivelles Airfield, Belgium, and found himself in the care of the Belgian Resistance who took him into Brussels for one of the greatest parties in history, "like the densest football crowd ever seen, swaying, singing and cheering continuously . . . hugging and kissing the troops". He hung the sign "111 Wing RAF" on the door of the Astoria Hotel and then took over the Chateau Lillois, to the popping of more champagne corks.

His early criticism of what became the Arnhem debacle led this time to a part in planning the final airborne operations of the war – across the Rhine and to protect prisoner of war camps – as Assistant Deputy Chief of Staff at the Headquarters 1st Allied Airborne Army, linking the four American and two British Airborne Divisions (now effectively reduced to one). He was the only officer from the Royal Flying Corps at the start of the Great War who also ended the Second World War with combat responsibilities.

Demobilisation was followed by what could have been a lifetime of squadron reunions. When he could, he attended by air, such as at the age of 68 when he flew himself from Thruxton to RAF Coltishall [1960]. He had flown 115 different aircraft types, from a Caudron and the Claude Grahame-White Box Kite [1913] to an Auster Taylorcraft [1949] and the Venom jet fighter [1955].

Amid all this he suffered a clinical depression verging on hypomania and was certified insane at his wife's instigation, on which he discharged himself, and left Marjorie for dilapidated Campson Cottage near Wincanton.

The place at Worth where he used to land became known as Aerodrome Field – indeed he called it "Swanage Aerodrome" – and was subsequently the village football pitch.

(People / Aviation / Bournemouth, Sturminster Marshall, Tarrant Keynston, Warmwell, Winterborne Kingston and Worth Matravers)

Strange-Boston – oil engineer and Intelligence officer **Lieutenant-Colonel Archibald Strange-Boston** [born 1892] of West Bucknowle House, Church Knowle, retired to Shreveport. Louisiana. He returned to the old country for a nostalgic visit with his wife, Em, and I drove them along the bumpy track of the ancient ridgeway across the western Purbeck Hills [1972]. Ramblers scowled as they were forced to step aside.

After telling me the story of Martha Morris (see her entry), and how he progressed to meet Lawrence of Arabia in his military days, he recalled seeing the first cars coming through Corfe Castle: "They had to have a man or a boy walk in front at four miles per hour slowly waving a red flag. The object was to save the horses from shying.

"A few years after the Martha Morris incident we had a great time in the Square and the castle. Colonel Nicholson ran as MP for east Dorset and gave a wonderful display of fireworks to illustrate the Relief of Mafeking. We were gallant fighters in them thar days, safe at home with the enemy millions of miles away – and could we shout defiance! Only American boasting exceeded the mighty efforts of our ten and 12-year-old 'fighting men'.

"I was a bad boy then; just give me a dare. That was all the incentive I needed. In those days the 'Law' generally had an easy time and just mounted his bike and rode away from trouble. But Sergeant Conquest did once shove me in the lone cell which was in his house, between Wiseman's shop and the Smithy. He kept me there for three hours.

"The Station Master, Mr Greenstock, once hauled me out from under the engine of the Swanage to Wareham train in 1900 just because I was beneath the engine wondering how the hell the damned thing operated. He boxed my ears to a fare-u-well. I also recall the fire-crackers or detonators being laid on the rails in the cutting close to Corfe Station, when the 'Boys' returned from South Africa [the Boer War]. One I knew well did not return. His name was Freddy Fripp.

"I saw a man, name forgotten, branded in the Square at Corfe Castle for desertion. Officials came from Dorchester Barracks and he was branded on the back of the left-hand, I believe.

"Wicken House, in the Square, was the home of Dr Toft Barker at the turn of the century, though it is his wife who I remember. She denied any knowledge of household tasks and would come out the front door for advice. 'Tell me, good people,' she asked the villagers, 'do you boil a wabbit in its skin?' That had them laughing."
(People / Social history / Church Knowle and Corfe Castle)

Street – architect **George Edmund Street** [1824-81] spent both ends of his career in Dorset. At the beginning he built what is now Old St John's Building, beside Wimborne Road, Moordown [1853], for Bournemouth vicar Rev Alexander Morden Bennett. He then worked with him on the town centre church – St Peter's in Hinton Road [1853-78].

There followed mediaeval restorations, including Salisbury Cathedral and Carlisle Cathedral, Christ Church in Dublin, and the nave of Bristol Cathedral. He designed the Crimean Memorial Church in Constantinople and won the competition for the Law Courts in the Strand [1866].

What he regarded as his "jolliest" Gothic creation would be St James's Church, Kingston, as a private chapel of cathedral proportions for the 3rd Earl of Eldon [1845-1926] which he built in 1874-80.
(People / Architects / Bournemouth and Corfe Castle)

Street Well – 50-feet deep public water supply for villagers of Langton Matravers, on the south side of the High Street (SY 999 788). Though somewhat fickle, when quarrymen climbed down to tap the trickle, it provided Langton's drinking water until the early 20th century.
(Placenames / Social history / Langton Matravers)

Sunnyodon notelyi – miniature shrew-sized dinosaur of 150 million years ago, the teeth of which were discovered on Mary and Richard Notley's Sunnydown Farm, Langton Matravers, and named for them by palaeontologist Paul Ensom [1991].
(Geology / Natural history / Langton Matravers)

Sutton – electronics engineer **Robert Sutton** [1905-98] developed the "Sutton Tube", a practical and turnable low-noise oscillator, in the wartime Telecommunications Research Establishment, at Worth Matravers and Langton Matravers [September 1940]. A modification, containing a low pressure gas, was nicknamed the "Soft Sutton" and came into use as a switching device. His team included Frank Skinner who developed a silicon-crystal mixer [early 1941].

Sutton continued to make electronic gadgets, at the post-war Services Electronics Research Laboratory, Baldock, and maintained a lifelong interest in aviation, which culminated in learning to fly a helicopter, at the age of 90.
(People / Aviation / Langton Matravers and Worth Matravers)

Swyre Head – majestic inland headland overlooking the Kimmeridge coast, St Alan's Head, and Encombe's Golden Bowl (SY 934 785). The long ridge eastwards from Smedmore Hill rises into a stony plateau with steeply rounded sides, at 660 feet above the sea, which is a kilometre to the south.

The summit is crowned by a single Bronze Age bowl barrow, with the top of the mound flattened as a platform for a stone slab that serves as a viewpoint seat. The round barrow still has a height of 8 feet and is about 80 feet in diameter.

"Swyer" as a name dates back to before 1590 and has its origin in a late West Saxon word for a promontory.
(Placenames / Archaeology / Corfe Castle)

Western view: Swyre Head overlooks Smedmore and Kimmeridge.

Flat topped: Swyre Head itself and the burial mound, also at St Alban's Head which is glimpsed in the distance (left).

T

Tank targets – zig-zag layout of two miles of earthworks at Kimmeridge, with a frying-pan shaped turning circle at the end of each section, constructed for training Sherman tank crews [1944] with rail-operated moving targets between Clavell's Hard and Swalland Farm (SY 925 780). They were levelled after the war [1961].
(Placenames / Kimmeridge)

Telecommunications Research Establishment – moved from Dundee to a new hutted base between Worth Matravers village and Renscombe Farm (SY 966 776), with young radio research scientists Alan Hodgkin and Bernard Lovell being among the advance party [26 February 1940]. They would be joined by Dr Robert Cockburn and the establishment would be fully evacuation to Worth by the spring [5 May 1940].

Later in the year it requisitioned Leeson House and Durnford School in the neighbouring village of Langton Matravers. The scientists at Worth and Langton were soon to be deeply involved in the "Battle of the Beams" as the Luftwaffe targeted inland English objectives by an intersection of radio pulses – one of synchronised dots and the other of dashes – transmitted from Kleve, in Germany, near the Dutch border south-east of Arnhem, and from Stolberg near the Danish border.

Dr Cockburn developed a Radio Counter Measure codenamed "Aspirin" which duplicated the continuous Morse dashes, transmitted on a frequency of 30 to 31.5 megacycles per second, which disorientated the German pilots by widening their direction beam [September 1940]. As these asynchronous signals were having their desired effect, the more sophisticated forms of interference – such as an attempt to "bend" the beam – were not necessary.

They would be the recipients of revelations from priceless prizes beached at West Bay, Bridport, in the form of radio equipment on a pathfinding Heinkel He.111 bomber [6 November 1940].

Scientists at the Royal Aircraft Establishment, Farnborough, reassembled its apparatus which comprised three vertical aerials and an intact X-Gerat radio receiver – also known as Wotan I – which enabled the aircraft, from Kampfgruppe 100, to follow a radio direction beam. What surprised the Air Ministry boffins was that the apparatus was tuned to 2000 cycles per second (approximating to the "C" which is two octaves above standard-pitch middle "C") whereas British jamming countermeasures had assumed a note of 1500 cycles (approximating to the "G" below this upper "C").

The discovery came too late to prevent the Coventry raid but it would ensure that radio countermeasures were perfected in time to save the vital Rolls-Royce aero engine plant at Derby. In moonlit conditions similar to those of the Coventry raid, Derby's bombs fell on Nottingham – and those intended for Nottingham fell into open fields [8 May 1941].

As part of the Battle of the Beams, Dr Robert Cockburn commandeered the BBC's pre-war television transmitter at Alexandra Palace, Muswell Hill, on what turned out to be the very night that the Luftwaffe changed to a frequency of 42.5 megacycles per second. This was jammed by Cockburn in countermeasure "Domino" – in which the German signal was re-radiated back to the attacking aircraft, from Alexandra Palace, at 46.9 megacycles per second.

A second transmitting station, constructed on Beacon Hill, near Salisbury, extended Cockburn's jamming across the whole of southern England.

Other suspicious signals were seeping out of France.

Derek Garrard, an Air Ministry scientist seconded to the Telecommunications Research Establishment, drove to St Alban's Head with a VHF radio set and found himself picking up transmissions from the Cherbourg peninsula on the 2.5 metre wavelength [24 February

1941]. The bearings suggested a source in the area of Ayderville, where Flight Officer W. K. Manifould had coincidentally photographed a "Freya" square-mesh turntable aerial only two days before.

Intercepted German radio traffic had credited this device with the sinking, off Portland, of the destroyer HMS *Delight*. As a result of Garrard's discovery, Air Marshal Sir Philip Joubert called a meeting with just one item on the agenda: "To discuss the existence of German radar."

The Purbeck scientists also developed British radar innovations, devising the Type 15 ground-to-air antenna which would be built by the Air Defence Experimental Establishment at Somerford, Christchurch, and put into the field at Sopley where it enabled combat guidance, given to 604 Squadron at RAF Middle Wallop, to achieve their first radar-controlled kill [4 March 1941].

The Special Duty Flight, attached to the Telecommunications Research Establishment and based at Christchurch Aerodrome, became the first user of the newly opened RAF Hurn [1 August 1941].

Wellington T2565, being used by the Telecommunications Research Establishment on a signals probe, was lost over France after engine failure [6 November 1941]. Six of the seven crew were taken prisoner of war but the seventh, Sergeant N. W. MacKenzie, was able to avoid capture and escaped to eventually return to Britain.

Meanwhile, the Special Duty Flight had been renamed the Research Section of the Telecommunications Flying Unit, and continued to be based at RAF Hurn [10 November 1941].

It would now make its most remarkable series of flights, which would enable Air Marshal Sir Arthur Harris, Commander-in-Chief Bomber Command, to mount the massive night raids against German cities. Using an AI (Airborne Interception) Mark VII radar set, installed in a Blenheim bomber but with its centimetric beam tilted towards the ground, scientists found themselves mapping Bournemouth and could distinguish streets and houses from the surrounding landscape of heather and pines.

Professor Philip Dee and his assistant Bernard Lovell presented the results of the initial BN (Blind Navigation) tests to the Secretary of State for Air, Sir Archibald Sinclair, who ordered six more test flights to "determine whether the signals obtained . . . could be definitely associated with ground objects" [23 December 1941].

Scientists at Worth were to receive their greatest prize courtesy "C" Company of the Second Battalion, the Parachute Regiment, who mounted a commando raid at Bruneval, on the French coast between Le Havre and Fecamp, to capture a German Wurzburg radar apparatus [27 February 1942]. This comprised a parabolic aerial, receiver, and cathode-ray tube.

On this side of the Channel, TRE's Telecommunications Flying Unit received one of the first Halifax bombers, V9977, fitted with a perspex cupola in the space which would normally have housed the nose gun-turret [22 March 1942]. Here the Purbeck scientists would install the magnetron section of a Mark VII AI (Airborne Interception) radar, adapted into the first prototype of a version codenamed H2S which was being developed for ground-mapping.

These signals would enable the team to spot Bournemouth, from a distance of six miles at a height of 8,000 feet, and to distinguish it from the outlines and land-forms of the adjoining towns of Poole and Christchurch [17 April 1942]. A repeat performance that night would have proved the system in operational conditions – in the dark and through the clouds – except that the operator failed to find a concealed switch and the radar was not turned on.

Tested by Air Commander Donald "Pathfinder" Bennett, it was put into production, at a factory in West Howe, Bournemouth. H2S was coined after Professor Frederick Lindemann had exclaimed on being given some excuses: "It stinks that it wasn't

Only a couple of the northern huts survive and the rest of the extensive site has been returned to farmland. Aerials remained for an RAF Gee station, to direct Cold War bombers, until the 1970s.
(Placenames / Aviation / Worth Matravers)

thought of before." Used operationally to find Hamburg [30-31 January 1943] and henceforth enabled night-bombing of the correct cities for the rest of the war.

The Telecommunications Research Establishment would be evacuated from Worth Matravers and Langton Matravers to Malvern College, Worcestershire [25 May 1942], because of fears that the Germans might attempt their own Bruneval-style raid.

Many ideas and projects from Dorset days would be brought into service later in the war, such as the radar-reflective "Window" which created a smoke-screen effect upon enemy radar sets, when dropped in the form of millions of thin strips of aluminium-backed paper. This made its operational debut before a big raid on Hamburg [24-25 July 1943]. That night it reduced losses among the 791 participating bombers from an estimated 48, based on normal casualty rates, to only 12.

Tertius – third locomotive of the Furzebrook claylands mineral railway, being an 0-6-0WT built by Manning Wardle [1886], and arriving in Purbeck at the time when the system was extended westwards to new pits around the prehistoric Icen Barrow and John's Plantation in the rough country towards Grange Road.

Following the merger of the Pike and Fayle clay companies, she was re-fitted with the boiler from the Norden engine Tiny [1951], with the result that the new look *Tertius* had a tall profile, with the boiler perched above its main frame. The firebox was too wide to fit inside this. She was withdrawn and scrapped in 1956.
(Industrial archaeology / Railways / Church Knowle)

Make over: clay locomotive *Tertius* before (above) and after rebuilding of her boiler and the addition of a covered cab.

Thames – outside cylinder 0-4-0ST narrow gauge steam locomotive built by Manning Wardle [1902] and used for a short time by London County Council on the Barking Outfall Sewer. Hence her name. Bought by Fayle and Company for their new Goathorn Railway [1905].
(Industrial archaeology / Railways / Corfe Castle)

Third Tower – between the Second Tower and the Fourth Tower on the eastern side of the Outer Bailey at Corfe Castle, built in 1212-15.
(Placenames / Mediaeval archaeology / National Trust / Corfe Castle)

Thrasher's Cottage – habitation on the east side of Thrasher's Lane (SY 969 835), north-west of Lower Bushey Farm. Formerly an endangered cob and thatch cottage, immediately south of the white slopes of clay waste that marked Thatcher's Pit, which was dilapidated in the 1960s. By the end of the decade its roof had fallen through.

Unlike so many others, however, it was renovated and converted from a derelict cottage to a country retreat [1971].
(Placenames / Corfe Castle)

Thrasher's Heath – scrubby through to full woodland now, mainly through self-sown pines, on the south-western edge of Rempstone Forest (SY 972 840).
(Placenames / Corfe Castle)

Thrasher's Lane – public road northwards from the B3351 towards Wytch (SY 967 830).
(Placenames / Roads / Corfe Castle)

Thrasher's Pit – Victorian clay-workings across the south-west side of Thrasher's Heath, later crossed on the south side by the mineral railway from Norden to Goathorn which crossed Thrasher's Lane at a level crossing (SY 971 836).
(Placenames / Industrial archaeology / Corfe Castle)

Three Lords' Barrow – this Bronze Age burial place is just a low mound placed on a heathland knoll in western Purbeck but it serves as the meeting point of four parishes (SY 915 847). Clockwise, from the north-west, they are East Holme, Arne, Church Knowle, and Steeple.

A piece of old church window has been planted in the top of the three feet high mound as a boundary stone. It probably came from the old priory church at East Holme which was an outlying cell of Cluniac monks from Montacute Abbey, Somerset. The building at East Holme was pulled down in 1746.
(Prehistoric archaeology / Arne, Church Knowle, East Holme, and Steeple)

Tiny – outside cylinder 0-4-0T steam locomotive, made by Stephen Lewin [1848] at the Dorset Iron Foundry, Poole, and bought by Fayle and Company to mechanise their horse-drawn clay tramway across the Purbeck heaths. Originally named Corfe but the clay workers thought Tiny was more apt.

In order to pass through tunnels, beneath the Corfe road at Norden, she was squat and box-like, appearing as a cross between a modern tractor and a child's toy. The driver had an open cab. With the closure of Fayle's Tramway the engine was transferred to its replacement Goathorn Railway and survived in regular use for 80 years.

The engine would be cannibalised after the merger of the Pike and Fayle companies with its boiler being fitted to the Furzebrook locomotive Tertius [1951].
(Industrial archaeology / Railways / Corfe Castle and Poole)

Tom Burnham's Oak – the tree on which a suicide hanged himself, some 50 yards from the site of his burial, with a stake through his heart to lay the ghost, which took place as custom dictated; beside the highway at what was then a crossroads, on the no-man's-land of the parish boundary north-east of Langton Matravers (SZ 010 800).

He was from Langton. Despite the unmarked grave, his name has persisted in local folklore, attached to the tree standing beside

***Treveal* shipwreck: showing the steam freighter split in two, but still floating, off Houns-tout Cliff.**

Burnham's Lane on the boundary between Langton Matravers and Swanage.

There are two junctions in Burnham's Lane, west of Godlingston, and George Clark of 34 Steer Road, Swanage, clarified the position of Tom Burnham's Oak as being that on the parish boundary, which was the traditional location for suicide burials. He wrote to Olive Knott on 9 August 1961:

"I attended Herston School 50 years ago and the lanes and fields close by were our playgrounds. The particular oak is quite 50 yards from the crossroads. The tree bore the deeply cut initials T. B. for Tom Burnham. The limb on which he had tied the rope had long since be swan off as was the usual custom.

"A story rife at that time was that Tom was buried under the green mound at the crossroads, but some said it was the burial place of a witch, a wooden stake having been driven through her body. Whilst on the subject of burials outside consecrated ground, a few years ago a skeleton was dug up in a quarry at Langton. It was only four feet below the surface. At an inquiry it was held to be the remains of a coloured man, no doubt washed ashore nearby. Presumably a colour bar operated in those days and he was not deemed to be a fit subject to be buried in the local church."

(Folklore / Roads / Langton Matravers and Swanage)

Tovey – "Sink the *Bismarck*" overlord **Admiral Sir John Cronyn Tovey** [1885-1971], Commander-in-Chief of the Home Fleet, retired to Purbeck after the war. He was created Baron Tovey of Langton Matravers in 1946.

He is buried beneath a large, flat slab in Swanage Cemetery, Washpond Lane, Godlingston: "JOHN CRONYN / TOVEY / ADMIRAL OF / THE FLEET / FIRST BARON OF / LANGTON MATRAVERS / 12 JANUARY 1971."

(People / Naval / Langton Matravers and Swanage)

Town Hall – appropriately, for the nation's classic rotten borough, a sign at Corfe Castle proclaims: "THE SMALLEST TOWN HALL BUILDING IN ENGLAND." It stands beside West Street, in the north-west corner of St Edward's churchyard, and was rebuilt in stone and brick circa 1770.

The top floor is the Council Chamber and the former lock-up below is now the Parish Museum. This is a fascinating little collection of carved stones, cannon-balls, animal traps, farmhouse antiquities, and other rustic bygones.

(Placenames / Politics / Corfe Castle)

Town's End – see entry for **East Street**.

Treswell – steward **Ralph Treswell** [16th century], working for Sir Christopher Hatten, mapped Purbeck in general and Corfe Castle in detail [1586].

(People / Corfe Castle)

Treveal – Purbeck's graphic and tragic shipwreck of the 20th century, from which the rescue services emerged in disarray, was the loss of the newly-built steamship *Treveal*. She was laid down at the end of the Great War in the shipyard of Caird and Company on the Clyde, Glasgow, on Government orders as a "Liberty-type" vessel which should have been named "War (Flower name)" but with the Armistice [11 November 1918] the hull was sold to the Hain Steamship Company of London and St Ives, which the previous year had become a subsidiary of P & O.

On being launched [September 1919] she was named *Treveal*; being given the "Tre" prefix of all Hain vessels (being Cornish for a settlement). The company had been formed by a Cornishman, Edward Hain, in 1838.

She was fitted out by Harland and Wolffe at Glasgow. Her tonnage was 5,200 tons unladen, and up to 8,200 tons deadweight cargo (making a total, loaded, of 13,440 tons). Cargo was intended to be "dry, bulky materials". Her colours were those of the Hain Steamship Company. Hull – medium grey. Main deck accommodation – yellow ochre. Boat deck – white. Funnel – black stack, with a large white "H" on each side.

Treveal, in the winter of 1919-20, was on the last leg of her maiden voyage, returning from Calcutta to Dundee with 8,000 tons of jute fibre and 2,000 tons of manganese. Her master, Captain Paynter, was from the Hain Steamship Company's hometown of St Ives, and she was chartered to the Liverpool-based Brocklebank Line.

Treveal put into Portland Harbour to find a North Sea pilot, but none could be found for her. This was their first British port for months; she was logged in at 18.00 hours and sailed out at 20.00 hours, on a dark Friday night [9 January 1920]. As she resumed her eastward progress, the lights of the ship were visible from Weymouth, and a Lloyd's officer placed a bet that the *Treveal* was on a course that would take her aground. She was sailing directly towards St Alban's Head and struck the south-eastern edge of the Kimmeridge Ledges at 21.00 hours.

At this stage the *Treveal* could have been saved. She had radioed for a tug and the weather was calm and clear. The tug of the Weymouth shipping agents Collins and Company was being repaired and the crew of the Portland dockyard tug were dispersed through the Weymouth pubs. It was after midnight by the time the tug was at sea but the weather had deteriorated into rain and the water was becoming choppy.

She failed to find the *Treveal* and returned to Portland Harbour. Meanwhile, the St Alban's Head Coastguard post had flashed messages to the *Treveal*.

Coastguard: "WHAT SHIP IS THAT?"

Treveal: "S.S. *TREVEAL* FROM CALCUTTA TO DUNDEE ASHORE HARD AND FAST – IS THERE A GOOD LANDING PLACE?"

Coastguard: "YES STRAIGHT INSHORE BUT YOU HAD BETTER WAIT TILL DAYLIGHT."

Treveal: "CAN YOU PHONE SENIOR NAVAL OFFICER PORTLAND?"

Coastguard: "YES."

Treveal: "PLEASE PHONE HIM TUG HAS NOT ARRIVED YET."

The tug set off from Portland on its second attempt to find the Treveal at 05.30 hours [10 January 1920] and by 07.00 had sighted her but a strengthening wind prevented her from coming close. The wind had freshened to strength seven on the Beaufort scale, from 32 to 38 miles per hour, driving intensely cold, sleeting rain, and piling up heavy seas.

The starboard lifeboats on the *Treveal* were lost as the sea smashed across the freighter and the captain was afraid she was now breaking up. His last desperate message was flashed to the Coastguards: "FOR GOD'S SAKE SEND US ASSISTANCE." Flag-signals pleaded,

to the tug: "I MUST ABANDON SHIP. I WANT ASSISTANCE. PLEASE STAND BY TO PICK UP MY CREW."

They put into their remaining two port lifeboats at 09.30 and the creaking ship cracked in two – justifying the captain's decision to abandon ship, but perhaps not taking sufficient account of the fact that the 5,500-ton iron ship, with a 10,000-ton cargo, was in his own words "stuck fast". It was a decision that had been delayed until the weather was appalling and the odds for survival could not have seemed favourable, though on a navigation chart the beach at Chapman's Pool must have looked a close and inviting refuge.

He had been told he could go straight inshore, but that was in better conditions, and into a passage through the rocks rather than the swirling current off the beach – where the outflow in a storm, the undertow or offset, is stronger than the flow on to the beach, the onset. Instead of coming between the rocks, where they still had a fighting chance, the sailors turned their boats broadside to the waves. Within seconds they were swamped and then capsized. Despite their lifebelts, some were pounded semi-conscious, and all suffered shock, hypothermia, and the "diving response" upon their metabolic rate.

Only two people in the village of Worth Matravers, just over two miles away, were outdoors to hear the boom of the maroons sent up from the stricken freighter. By the time they had struggled against the driving sleet to Egmont Point, at the west end of Chapman's Pool, the lifeboats were upturned and their crews drowning. The Weymouth lifeboat had come and gone. It was launched at 09.40 and arrived off Chapman's Pool as the tide turned – on to the flood – which with the force of the seas combined to sweep the rescue craft away from the freighter and its dying crew. It could not battle against the waters to the west and even gave up attempting to return home, fleeing to the quieter seas east of Swanage and turning into Poole Harbour. Neither did the Coastguard service contribute anything. No one came down from St Alban's Head to fire rocket lines into the water.

Horace Piercy, the young curate at Worth, and fisherman Frank Lander were the two heroes of the horror. They received later recognition, with the Royal Humane Society's bronze medal and a certificate to each signed by Edward, Prince of Wales. Frank Lander suffered nightmares from the disaster for the rest of his life; when the scenes returned to his mind he would start to cry.

Engineer Thirkell, third officer William Donald, and three more men – two completely unconscious – were dragged from the waves and shifting pebbles by Piercy and Lander before two more Worth villagers, Monty Hooper and Walter Welsh, arrived to help. They brought with them two women who played a crucial role with artificial respiration of the numbed and nearly lifeless. Seven survivors, in all, were revived. They were taken to the Anchor Hotel in Swanage.

Of the missing 36 crew members of the *Treveal*, 20 bodies were recovered by the time of the inquest, and another a fortnight later. The remaining 15 were never found. Many of the bodies were gashed and half naked. They were hauled up the shale-cliffs and brought by wagon to the Reading Room at Worth. There they were laid out on trestles, by Mrs Hooper and her daughter, Floss Welsh. One mother wrote on black-edged paper to Horace Piercy:

"Oh, how could they have been so heartless as to leave them so long without assistance? It seems too cruel. He was a devoted husband and father. It was his first and last voyage. We could but ill spare him, he was all we had. Forgive me for writing, and hoping for a reply. Would you tell me if you thought he was tossed about very much in the cruel waves? Please tell me. Yours truly, a broken-hearted mother, Mary Cogar."

Cicely Violet Wrixen came to live at Orchard Hill Farm, north of Swyre Head, in 1901 and went to school at Kingston. She told me on 6 October 1973 about "the terrible day of sorrow":

"A young sailor boy was washed up on the rocks and he was heard crying for help and saved. He was only about 15 years. A piece of ground half-way under that cliff was called Grandmother's Garden, where they could grow two crops of new potatoes a year, as it did not get any frost.

"I saw the bodies of the poor men which were taken to Worth Matravers by horse and wagon and on the Monday my neighbours and I went to Chapman's Pool and saw this man go out to the wreck. He was worried if any pet animals were on board, and a very rough sea was still running, and another body was washed in while we were there."

All but two of the victims of the *Treveal* sinking were identified and sent to their families for burial; the remaining ones being buried in the north-east corner of the older section of Worth Matravers churchyard: "Here lie the unidentified bodies of two members of the crew of the S.S. *Treveal* drowned on 10th January, 1920 when their ship was wrecked off St Alban's Head with the loss of 36 lives."

A mass grave for all the sailors had been dug by two Worth ex-serviceman, Will Corben and Herbert Hooper, but the Hain Steamship Company then decided it would pay for the bodies to be returned to their homes.

Will Corben gave his account to author Nina Warner Hooke:

"It was the worst gale that I ever saw in these parts, and I've seen plenty. More like a hurricane. Folks coming along the street had to hold on to the churchyard wall or they were knocked flat on their faces. Herbie and me went down to the Pool about midday Saturday to help fetch up the bodies. The tide was so high waves were breaking over the cliff. We tied planks together for stretchers. A hatch cover blew up the gully and precious near killed the pair of us.

"That day we fetched up over a dozen, in a wagon from Renscombe Farm. They was three feet deep in the wagon. With us and all it was a fair load. Took a team of good horses to get it up to the village.

"I was on top of the heap, unloading, when a lady come by and give me a telling off for trampling on the dead. I said, 'They'm past minding, missis, and so am I.'

"She didn't like that, didn't like it a bit. Come into the graveyard later on and she ticked off Herbie for swearing in the presence of god. Well, by that time we'd had enough. We'd shifted a mountain of earth and banked it up against the wall while the bodies was laid out in the trench. Just before the order came through to take 'em out again, the whole bloody lot fell in.

"We'd had enough. Herbie looked down and at all you could see of a good ship's company under the mud and stones, most in the prime of their lives, and he said: 'If God's listening, I don't reckon he's got much to be proud of.' She didn't get much change out of Herbie and me."

Horace Piercy, who lived to be 90 and died in Tunbridge Wells [1979] was asked at the subsequent Board of Trade inquiry whether the Coastguards could have seen the boats leave the ship. He paused before answering, and said: "Yes, if they could have kept their eyes open."

What he meant was that in the conditions, against the driving sleet, it would have been impossible. That was not how he was understood and his reply went into the official proceedings as: "Yes, if they had kept their eyes open."

Frederick Keeley, chief officer of St Alban's Head Coastguard at the time of the *Treveal* disaster, said at his court martial that if his "advice to the master had been acted on the vessel abandoned at daylight or before, the boats would have made the shore safely". He was found guilty of negligence and lost his post.

The hull of the *Treveal* was insured for £100,000 and the cargo for £250,000. Large quantities of jute were salvaged by a drifter from Turner's, the Weymouth salvage firm. The drifter was then the next victim of the *Treveal*, being swept on to the jagged break in the hold, where she stuck fast. As the stern of the Treveal settled into the water she took the drifter down with her. Jute floated from her into Chapman's Pool where it was collected into bundles by the fishermen and later redeemed by the insurers. The two halves of the *Treveal* lie in eight fathoms, a mile offshore, south-west from the rock pools at the foot of Houns-tout Cliff.

For Frank Lander's widow, at the age of 92 when she talked to Nina Warner Hooke in the early 1960s, the bitter memory was that the ship reproached them for what had happened, resting on the reef for long after her crew had been buried: "They should have stayed with her and she'd have kept them safe. They should a' known better than to trust the sea when they could stay where they was and trust their ship. The sea's no place for any but a fish. Any fisherman 'll tell you that. Takes a fisherman to know the sea. I was married to one for best part of my life. Frank couldn't swim, you know. Never went in deep enough to learn. The sea's a place that's easier to get into than out of. There's no back door to sea."

Some souvenirs were recovered, as M. F. C. Adam told me from Bedfont, Middlesex [1976]:

"I have in my possession a piece of the *Treveal*, which broke up on Kimmeridge Ledges on the morning of 10 January 1920. It is a dragon carved in black oak. Mrs Polly Andrews of Corfe Castle gave it to me some years ago. She is deceased now, but has a son living in Swanage.

"Polly was a life-long friend of my mother. They were in service together years ago. My mother's maiden name was Hounsell, and she came from Litton Cheney where she lies with my father in the churchyard."

(Shipwrecks / Corfe Castle and Worth Matravers)

Tudor Cottage – not quite that old, though it literally re-cycled mediaeval history at Corfe Castle, on the west side of the Square, being built after the Civil War with massive ashlars from the nearby ruin. The porch has a datestone for "E. B. 1677".

Reset stones in the walls and garden are much earlier. One of the latter is a chevron-ornamented voussoir of the 12th century. These must also be ex-Castle.

(Placenames / Corfe Castle)

Tumuli – the map-word for barrows; see entries for **Long barrows** and **Round barrows**.

Turner – submariner **Vice-Admiral Sir Robert Ross Turner** [1885-1977] enjoyed his final 30 years in retirement at Worth Matravers and is buried in the churchyard. In the Great War he commanded *C15*, and then *D3*, followed by *E23*. Between the wars he was in command of the First Flotilla [1924-26] and then Captain of the Submarine Depot at Fort Blockhouse [1927-29]. Later he commanded HMS *Leander* [1933-35].

His time on the retired list was only a matter of months before he resumed his career for active service, as Director-General of Shipbuilding and Repairs in India [1941-44] and Senior British Naval Officer in Greece [1945-46], when what would have been a communist take-over was thwarted.

(People / Naval / Worth Matravers)

Tyne – a Royal West Indian mail packet of some 2,000 tons, 320-feet in length, which struck the ledges off Freshwater Steps, Encombe [03.40 hours, 13 January 1857]. The crew and passengers had to be taken off, by the Encombe Estate fishing boat, the Kimmeridge Coastguard boat, and two boats from Pier Bottom and St Alban's Head Coastguard. The smaller of the latter two craft "was most unfortunately swamped, and though three or four men in her were saved by their comrades in the six-oared galley, one poor fellow was, with the boat itself, swept away".

Eventually, lightened and with leaking compartments being pumped, she was refloated on a spring tide [evening, 25 February 1857] and successfully towed into Southampton for repairs [12 March 1857].

(Shipwrecks / Corfe Castle)

U

Uvedale's House – the earliest surviving private house in Corfe Castle village is on the east side of the main street that climbs into the Square from the Wareham direction, midway between Boar Mill stream and the Bankes Arms Hotel. It is an extensive building, now sub-divided into six flats, that was built by Henry and John Uvedale [1575]. John Uvedale would become Mayor of Corfe Castle borough [1582].
(Placenames / Corfe Castle)

Castle key: a reminder that the Corfe story moved on, with defiant royalist Lady Mary Bankes, to Kingston Lacy House, where she is seen in a life-size bronze sculpted by Baron Carlo Marochetti in 1853.

Mayoral memory: from Elizabethan times, preserved in the name Uvedale's House.

Incongruous skyline: humble thatch at Vineyard Cottage, with fortress ruins rising behind, at Corfe Castle.

V

Village Hall – built in 1936, at Church Knowle (SY 941 818).
(Placenames / Church Knowle)

Village sign – Francis Newbery, an artist living at Corfe Castle, painted the village sign in the Square. It was erected in 1927 and suffered almost immediate vandalism, being hacked down the following night and thrown into the castle moat. The wooden pedestal was dumped on the policeman's doorstep.

Restored, and subsequently left in place, it features the boy-king killed at Corfe. The explanatory words credit Elfrida, directly, with the assassination: "EDWARD THE MARTYR KING OF WESSEX TREACHEROUSLY STABBED AT CORVES GATE IN A.D. 978 BY HIS STEPMOTHER ELFRIDA."
(Placenames / Memorials / Corfe Castle)

The Vineyard – rustic 17th-century cob and thatch cottage south of Castle Hill, Corfe Castle (SY 858 821). Between it and the Castle Hill the Wicken Stream used to flow through a series of mill pools. Despite the attractive label for an even nicer setting, the name "Vineyards" does not make its debut until the parish tithe map [1844].

The Vineyard and the later farm beside it came into National Trust ownership with the Bankes Estate [1982].
(Placenames / National Trust / Corfe Castle)

Vineyard Bridge – carries the Church Knowle road, with a rounded 18th century segmental arch, over the Corfe River on the west side of Castle Hill (SY 957 823).
(Placenames / Bridges / National Trust / Corfe Castle)

Vitower – see entry for **Fitzworth**.

Siege scene: a bas-relief by Baron Carlo Marochetti, in Kingston Lacy House, where the National Trust displays the Bankes family collection of Corfe relics.

Winter waterfall: at Freshwater, where the stream from Encombe tumbles into the sea.

W

Wanostrocht and Company – lit the streets of Wareham with 130 gas-lamps fuelled by Kimmeridge shale [1848]. They also provided the lighting for the town's new railway station. George Battrick was superintendent of the company's operations [1851] who prepared the way for rapid expansion. The Major of Wareham, Charles Oldfield Bartlett, laid the foundation stone for a new gas-works, south-west of the railway station at Northport [1852].

Their major coup was to win the approval of the famous strategist of the Crimean War who became French Ambassador to London. Amiable Jean Jacques Pelissier, Marshal of France and Duc de Malakoff, secured a contract to light the Paris streets [1858]. By-products of this gas production included 50 tons of shale oil and 200 tons of fertiliser; much of which was exported to America for use on the grain prairies.

The company was taken over by Wareham Oil and Candle Company [1862].
(Industrial archaeology / Kimmeridge and Wareham)

Wareham Oil and Candle Company – took over the Kimmeridge shale works of Wanostrocht and Company, on the south-west side of Wareham railway station [1862]. A heavy yellowish oil was being extracted from the shale and treated with nitric acid and water to separate out a substance smelling of nitrobenzene. The company went out of business after the works was destroyed by fire [1872].
(Industrial archaeology / Kimmeridge and Wareham)

Webber – poet of the quarrylands **John Webber** [1803-93] was a monumental mason and schoolmaster at Corfe Castle. He was the Victorian minor poet of the Isle of Purbeck, versifying for Dorset newspapers, and became Warden of the Ancient Chartered Company of Marblers.
(People / Literary / Corfe Castle)

Welfare – during the reign of Edward III, a special commission was called [1371] to try no less than a hundred persons for their part in wrecking this vessel, from Dartmouth, which had been sailing to London. She was in difficulties, off Portland, and was driven ashore at Kimmeridge. Her freight included 32 pieces of cloth-of-gold, bales of richly embroidered silk, and other merchandise to the value of £2,000 in the currency of the time.

A trial followed at Sherborne [1377] when many of the accused were found guilty of robbery. Robert Knolles, the owner of the vessel, had been "insulted, wounded, and maltreated" and the plunderers had been encouraged and assisted by no less a person than Thomas, Abbot of Cerne, who had the freight taken and stored in buildings at Kimmeridge. As the owner of the manor of Kimmeridge, the abbot had a right to the shore there but the *Welfare* – because she beached and was held by her crew – was not legally a wreck.

Among those convicted when the verdict was reached were not only the abbot and one of his monks, but members of the landed gentry of Purbeck, who included William Chaldecote, John Anderbole (of Brenscombe), William Wyatt and son (of Kimmeridge), John Russel (of Tyneham), John Swanland, and Thomas Gerard (of Corfe Castle).

The right to the wreck of the sea has continued to be attached in law to the manor of Kimmeridge. This has not yet been forgotten, as Eustace Mansel of Smedmore House recalled: "In about 1872, I saw a spar washed into Kimmeridge; it was afterwards found to measure three feet thick and 70 feet long. The Admiralty claimed it. My father produced the deed of 1554 and it was allowed that it was his right to claim it if not claimed by the rightful owner within a year and a day."
(Shipwrecks / Cerne Abbas, Kimmeridge, and Sherborne)

Well Court – evangelist John Wesley [1703-91] preached from the stone steps on the south side of Well Court, off West Street, Corfe Castle,

Strip lynchets: on West Man, captured in a 1926 reconnaissance photograph by 10 Group of the RAF, from Lee-on-Solent (taken from 4,000 feet altitude) showing Winspit Cottage to the north-east and quarries southwards and seawards.

to a gathering "quite athirst for instruction" [12 October 1744]. The Congregational Church was built beside Well Court in 1815 and registered as a "British School", making it eligible for grants until the establishment of state education in the 1880s.

The buildings at Well court were used by the Hampshire Regiment in the First World war and afterwards by a succession of artists – David Murray, Frances Hodgkins, Francis Newbery, and Edith Bowen.
(Placenames / Corfe Castle)

Wesley – founder of Methodism **John Wesley** [1703-91] preached at Well Court, Corfe Castle [12 October 1744]. See its entry.
(People / Corfe Castle)

West Bailey – the far part of Castle Hill at Corfe Castle, where herring-bone walling and windows survive from the Old Hall of the time of William the Conqueror. This building was on the site of an earlier building which excavation in 1950 showed to be Saxon.
(Placenames / Mediaeval archaeology / National Trust / Corfe Castle)

West Bucknowle House – early-Victorian home of the Strange Boston family, into the 20th century, in the hamlet of Bucknowle (SY 947 813).

The best friend of one of his sons, John Strange-Boston, was Ferdinand Cavendish-Bentinck of Morton's House, Corfe Castle, and it was a tragedy for both families that the pair would be killed on the Somme [1916]. It had been generally assumed that John would marry Ferdinand's sister, Miss Joan Cavendish-Bentinck, and his brother Archibald would write the history of the house as a novel entitled *Fallonsyde*, which was still unpublished more than half a century later

Stepping stones: across the Corfe River beside West Mills, in an intimate shot of almost Edwardian idyll.

stand the patients; mental cases – I got a job with Wax and Vitale of Genova. They were the Argenti Maritimi of the Swiss Government and I went with them for six months as interpreter."

In the event he would delay his return for five decades: "It is hard to describe the feelings I had when on the grounds of W.B.H. 58 years later. I'll send you some photographs which will offer a big contrast with what you saw. The interior was nothing like I was accustomed to as a boy. The Douglases from Smedmore House often came to our house. I recall Lord Alfred and the trouble he got into, with Oscar Wilde."

His other vivid memory concerned a less welcome visitor: "One day the door rang and I told one of the maids that I would get it. 'Is your dear Mum home, you sweet little boy,' drooled a gypsy, named Mrs Dearie Burchall. 'Oui, Madame,' I answered and let her in. Then smelled some scones from the kitchen door, and sneaked off with a few, down to the River Wicken at the bottom of the garden. Forgot all about the Gypsy Queen, having failed to mention her entry to the servants, until father called in Sergeant Conquest that evening. The house had been looted, thanks to me, though they recovered the 'valuable' articles a week later – all definitely uninteresting to any sweet little boy. I got a hell of a licking for that one."

Its late 20th-century notable occupant was the explorer, mountaineer, and author Eric Newby [born 1919]. He has been followed by Sir Jimmy James.

[1972]. He claimed that Thomas Hardy had been a regular visitor to West Bucknowle House but the author's life has only sparse documentation as a result of bonfires following his first wife's death [1912] and then before and after his own [1928].

West Bucknowle House is said to have been rebuilt on the foundations of an earlier house, of similar size, which had burnt down. The house became a private asylum at the end of the Great War, causing Intelligence officer Lieutenant-Colonel Archibald Strange-Boston to pass-up the opportunity of returning home: "When I was demobilised in 1919, instead of staying at West Bucknowle House – I couldn't

Church Knowle footpath number 18 runs along its drive.
(Placenames / Literary / Church Knowle)

West Hawes – mediaeval strip fields and boundary stones on the west side of the main village car-park in Corfe Castle, off West Street (SY 958 817). Some 20 former strips can be traced in the grass, in parallel lines running down to the Corfe River. They are each about 40 feet wide and up to 150 feet long.

Cross into the present fields by the stone stile at the side of the car-park to search out some of the ownership stones. These are known as mere-stones – mere = boundary – and look like miniature gravestones, carrying initials such as "C. C. C." [Calcraft Corfe Castle], "N. B." [Nathaniel Bankes] and "R. B." [Ralph Bankes]. Ownership is now vested in the National Trust, as the heir to the last landowning Ralph.
(Placenames / Mediaeval archaeology / National Trust / Corfe Castle)

West Hill – overlooks Corfe Castle, with the southern and eastern slopes being National Trust owned (SY 955 824). There is a Bronze Age round barrow on the 350-feet summit. This is denuded but was positioned on a superb skyline location. North of it, many sherds of Romano-British pottery have been found, and numerous 4th-century Roman bronze coins, across an exposed spot on the crest of the Purbeck Hills, leading to speculation that it may be the site of a Celtic temple.
(Placenames / Prehistoric archaeology / National Trust / Corfe Castle)

West Man – see entry for **Winspit strip lynchets**.

West Mills – one of the most picturesque settings in Corfe Castle, this was the 13th-century mill of Corfe Castle, in the trees below the western slope of Castle Hill (SY 957 823). It did not become redundant until 1790, after which it was converted to cottages, eventually falling into disrepair and being demolished [circa 1920]. Below a stone-walled channel in the surviving chunk of the south wall is a brick-arched recess in which the water-wheel turned. These and other footings have been cleared of scrub and excavated by the National Trust [1997]. The single unaltered part of the setting are steps into the river which are surmounted by a 6 feet by 4 feet flagstone.
(Placenames / National Trust / Corfe Castle)

West Orchard – historic farmhouse beside the site of a former hamlet that was Domesday Book listed [1086], in the valley south of the Corfe River, at Church Knowle (SY 941 807).

Mediaeval settlement remains to the north-east (SY 941 808) show the location of the hamlet known in Norman times as Horcerd [1086]. It belonged to Shaftesbury Abbey until the Dissolution of the monasteries [1536].

The surviving two-storey farmhouse incorporates central parts of the late-16th century, with many moulded and carved architectural features. This was extended eastwards in the 18th century, and then balanced by a western extension, in the 19th century. There is an 18th century cottage 40 yards to the west and a barn of that date on the other side of the farmhouse, 50 yards to the east of it.
(Placenames / Church Knowle)

West Street – the former main street of Corfe Castle, southwards from The Square to Corfe Common, where roads used to fan out in all directions. Along it came the marble for the Purbeck stone industry of the Middle Ages, which was stacked on "bankers", when the street thronged with people connected with the trade.

If you walk along the now quiet West Street it is obvious that it was once the key road in the market town. For West Street is aligned directly on the castle gate, market place, and village square. It contains all the major buildings – Town Hall, Lock-up, Fox Inn, historic entrance to St Edward's Church,

West Street: former main street at the heart of Corfe Castle, with the Fox Inn as its focal point.

ancient Manor House, and Chaffey's where the leading stone merchant was based.

All along West Street the old cottages huddle tightly and there are several ranges of dwellings.
(Placenames / Corfe Castle)

Westacre – see entry for **Caplestone Cottage**.

Whiteway Farm – once a manor, the present late 16th-century farmhouse a mile west of Church Knowle adjoins a suburb grouping of historic outbuildings (SY 924 812). To the south of the two-storey house are the granary, dairyhouse, and cottage. Behind these are the cowshed and barn. Several date from the time of tenant farmer William Hatchard [died 1704].

The main house has a south-facing frontage, with a blocked door to the left of the Victorian porch, and a wing extending north-east. In the far corner of this is an original spiral staircase, with stone steps. It is now the home of Richard Bond.
(Placenames / Church Knowle)

Wich – root-name of Wytch in the harbour saltings north-east of Corfe Castle, having its origins as an ancient place of salt extraction. Such placenames exist as Nantwich and Droitwich, for rock-salt mining, and Ipswich and Norwich for sea-salt trading.
(Placenames / Mediaeval archaeology / Corfe Castle)

Wicken Stream or River Wicken – the local name for the western fork of the Corfe River beside Castle Hill, Corfe Castle, upstream to Church Knowle. There it is also known as the Lake.
(Placenames / National Trust / Church Knowle and Corfe Castle)

Wilkswood Farm – two 17th-century houses, set around an earlier farmyard, are almost certainly on the site of Wilkswood Priory, on the wooded hillside north of Langton Matravers (SY 995 795). They were the home of the Havelland family.

The farm and nearby woodlands, including Langton West Wood, Talbot's Wood, and The Wilderness, are in National Trust ownership,

Winspit Quarries: lorry, buildings and derrick, viewed from the south.

having been inherited with the Bankes Estate [1982]. Marble was dug here in Roman and mediaeval times.
(Placenames / National Trust / Langton Matravers)

Wilkswood Priory – scantily-recorded minor religious house founded by Cluniac monks [circa 1154] in the vicinity of Wilkswood Farm, Langton Matravers. It may well have been connected with the adjoining, and extensive, Purbeck marble quarries.

As for its location, given that nothing has been found in the adjoining fields, and the remainder of the hillside was excavated by contemporary quarrying, it must have been on or beside the present farm buildings.
(Placenames / Churches / Langton Matravers)

Winspit Quarries: in operation, seen from the cliffside to the south-east.

Wills – glider pilot **Philip Wills** was towed by an ancient Avro 504 biplane into the middle of the English Channel, and released in a German Minimoa glider to drift back to the Purbeck cliffs at St Alban's Head, Worth Matravers [23 June 1940]. The object of the exercise, which

Winspit Quarries: in retirement, with a figure for scale (beside what is the eastern support in historic photographs).

Wytch Passage: rustic backwater on the harbour shore was once the harbour-master's house and the ferry point from Purbeck to Poole.

was successfully accomplished on behalf of the Telecommunications Research Establishment, was to ensure that current radar technology would pick-up signals from the wooden gliders of any German invasion force.
(People / Aviation / Worth Matravers)

Windmill Knap – rising ground at the 200-feet contour just west of Burnham's Lane at Godlingston, above Langton Matravers public footpath number 13 (SZ 007 801). It has two claims to fame though nothing can be seen of either on the ground today.

The ruins of a tower windmill were still visible in Victorian times. This rarity was reputed to have been built with stone from a rangers' lodge of the mediaeval Purbeck Chase. Its walls were still standing on this rounded knoll in 1618 and, as with a similar hunting lodge on Creech Barrow Hill – six miles to the west and which still has visible foundations – it is said by local legend to have been built by King John.

East of the Knap the memory of the windmill is perpetuated by Windmill Barn (SZ 009 800). Its existence shows the comparative lack of dependable water power in the Langton-Swanage valley.
(Mediaeval archaeology / Windmills / Langton Matravers)

Window – codename for radar-reflective foil, deployed from the air in the form of millions of strips of aluminium foil, developed by the Telecommunications Research Establishment at Worth Matravers. Perfected in Dorset by radar pioneer Robert Watson-Watt [winter 1941-42] it was devised to create a smoke-screen effect upon enemy radar sets at the onset of mass bombing raids.

Fighter Command blocked its operational use, however, fearing that it might give the Germans the idea at a time when they were still able to carry out major air attacks against Britain.

"Let us open the Window," Prime Minister Winston Churchill eventually decided, and was first used in a raid on Hamburg [24-25 July 1944] by 791 British bombers. Forty tons were dropped – a total of 92 million strips – and all but 12 of the aircraft returned. Normally the losses from such a raid would have been about 48, so the use of Window had saved 36 aeroplanes and their crews.
(Aviation / Worth Matravers)

Winspit – quarryman **Billy Winspit** [1886-1966], baptised William Jeremiah Bower, was universally known as the former, and both names appear on his gravestone in Worth Matravers churchyard. "Rest after weariness," it records, with the date being 9 August 1966. A fortnight earlier I found him at Winspit, chipping away at a fireplace. He told me about set-netting the mackerel shoals and how 16 cubic feet of the cliffs represented a ton of building stone:

"My father before me worked the quarries like I do, and granfer worked on the cliffs and his father. When I was a boy, father and I worked underground. In the old fashioned way you moved the stone out, cut it, and sent it to London in blocks. But all that is finished with now and I only do a carving job as a part-time. Once I had a 14-foot boat and went fishing in the summer as well. You couldn't do it in winter as we have some terrific weather here – seas 50 feet high. I have seen the waves come over the cliff into the quarry."

He stopped to sharpen some tools as he had done since the age of 16 when he became the quarry's blacksmith. He had started quarrying when he was 11-years-old and recalled the year of 1907 when pay was 25 shillings a week (£1.25) and £11 was the total weekly wage bill for Winspit Quarries. Till his death, oil lamps gave the only light in stone-roofed Winspit Cottage, which was without either gas or electricity.

He told me about playing his fiddle in the Square and Compass, named for the Masonic tools of this trade, on the hillside in Worth village. That was in the reign of publican Charlie Newman, who would die at 82 in coronation year, 1953. Their best remembered guest was the wild-living artist Augustus John from Fryern Court near Fordingbridge.
(People / Industrial archaeology / Worth Matravers)

Winspit Quarries – cliff-side gallery workings, at the seaward end of Winspit bottom, south of Worth Matravers (SY 976 761). The local names for the beds were listed in 1895 and corrected for me by Billy Winspit: burr, shrimpstone, bluestone, pond freestone, flintstone, listy bed, house cap, underpicking cap, under freestone and cliff beds (chert).

These appear to be the quarries visited by John Smeaton who surveyed workings throughout the West Country before beginning work on the new Eddystone Lighthouse [1757]:

"The strata of merchantable stone lie here in the upper part of the cliffs, as they do at Portland, but having more cover they are in some measure worked underground. This stone is of the like nature, and puts on so much the appearance of the Portland that it is often used in lieu of it. It is, however, inferior in colour, harder to work, and, according to the information I then got, not in general so durable. But what seemed to me like for ever to prohibit this field of stone from coming into competition with Portland is that, as it cannot bear the expense of land carriage down to Swanage to be shipped, the workmen are obliged to let it down with ropes from the place where it is wrought, to the surface of the sea, either into vessels lying at the foot of the cliffs, where there is deep water, or where there is a dry strand at low water, but there being but little shelter from the winds and seas, this can only be done in very moderate weathers, and particularly winds; wherefore the shipping it must necessarily be somewhat precarious."
(Placenames / Industrial archaeology / Worth Matravers)

Oilfield roads: British Petroleum map of Wytch Farm to Goathorn, and obstacles to plant, in 2000 AD.

	HAZARD	SIZE	COMMENTS
1	height	6.52m	overhead cables
2	height	5.34m	overhead cables (BT)
3	height	7.34m	overhead cables, and also road side
4	width	5.0m	gates
5	height	7.55m	overhead cables
6	width	4.2m	causeway access through gate
7	width	4.2m	causeway access over grid
8	height	8.26m	overhead cables
9	height	7.16m	overhead cables, also road side
10	width		drop either side of road length
11	height	6.08m	overhead cables
12	height		cables at track side
13	height		high overhead cables
14	height	4.90m	cables over passing place
15	height	4.86m	cables over passing place
16	width		two posts marking ditch
17	width		steep banks
18	height	3.87m	overhead cable encroaches on road
19	width	3.5-4m	banking either side to bund
20	height	6.25m	overhead cables at junction
21	width	4-5m	thro' trees, steep drop both sides
22	width	4.42m	thro' gate
23	height	6.63m	cables over passing place
24	height	8.20m	overhead cables
25	width		bollards delineate road surface
26	height	7.55m	overhead cables
27	height	6.66m	overhead cables 4300V through trees
28	height	6.84m	overhead cables
29	width	5.00m	gate
30	height	7.54m	overhead cables
31	height	7.72m	overhead cables
32	height	min. 3.23m	overhead cables overhang along length of road side
33	height	4.30m	passing place
34	height	8.81m	overhead cable road side

Goal post height barriers of 5.3m sited at points A, B & C

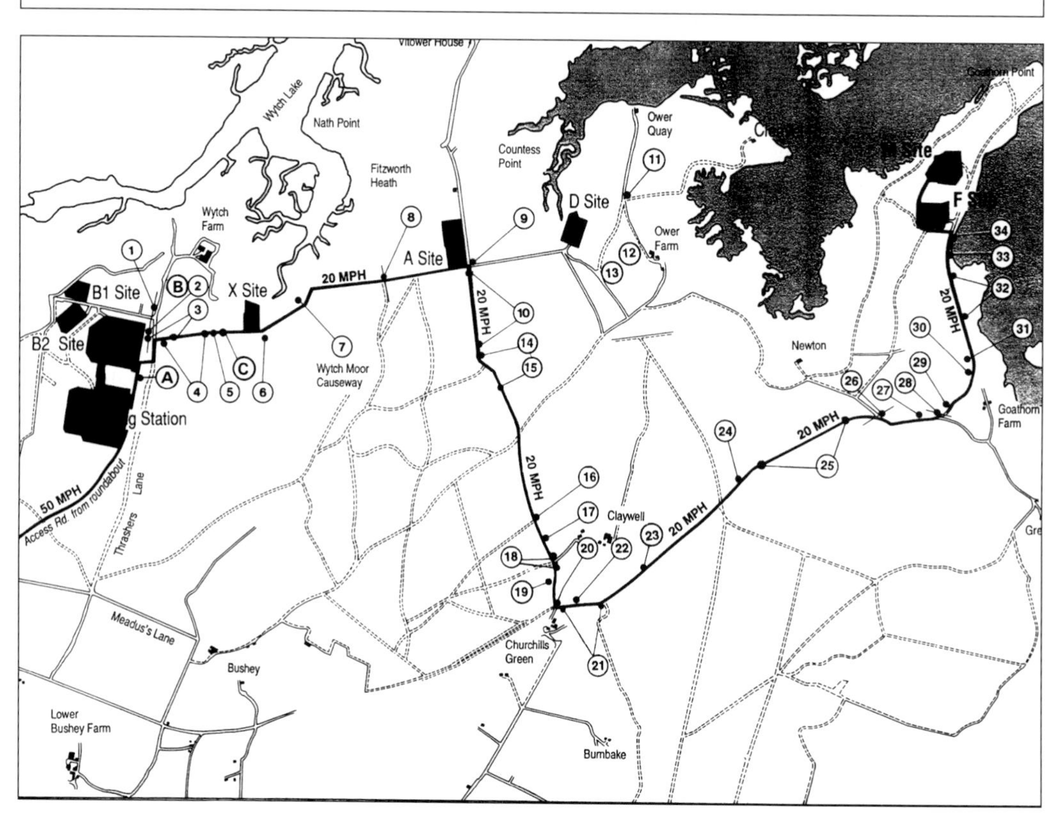

Winspit strip lynchets – well preserved contoured cultivation terraces, particularly those on the rounded slopes of East Man headland (SY 977 766) which have been partly acquired by the National Trust [1999], are among the finest mediaeval agricultural survivals in the British Isles. They also terrace the facing hillside of West Man (SY 975 760), on the other side of Winspit Bottom, and were the strips of the open field system of the manor of Worth Matravers. The whole system covers 190 acres with about half that still being clearly visible in an unusually good state of preservation.

One terrace on East Man is 450 yards long but this may have been sub-divided as the average length is less than half that; normal sizes being between 70 and 280 yards. The usable treads vary from three to 30 yards in width. The risers supporting these keep changing in height to embrace the contour, from a matter of inches to an extreme of 15 feet, at angles of slopes between five and 15 degrees.

The noticeable thing about their east-west configuration is that there is a virtual absence of anything similar across the stone walls to the west and east, from Weston south to the sea and Eastington Farm seawards through Seacombe Bottom. All the eastern terraces are now out of arable farming, and have reverted to limestone grassland, as have those on the eastern side of West Man.
(Farming / Mediaeval archaeology / National Trust / Worth Matravers)

Woodyhyde – mediaeval marble workings in the north-west corner of Worth Matravers parish (SY 973 803), extending towards Corfe Common, that were reopened [1842] to provide stone for the major Gothic revival restoration of Temple Church, London [1840-45]. Some marbling was renewed but the key parts of the ancient fabric were found to be in a much better state than was feared and "six elegant clustered columns needed but slight repair".
(Placenames / Industrial archaeology / Worth Matravers)

Worth Matravers – nuclear village of stone-roofed cottages, attractively clustered around a green and pond in the lee of the coastal plain, a mile up the valley from Winspit (SY 974 774). "Worth" means simply "the enclosure" with its specific name being added to show ownership by the Mautravers or Maltravers family, with the first recorded manorial member in residence being John Mautravers [1335].

Entries for the 2,700-acre parish in this work include: *Aeolian Sky*; Air crashes; AI (Air Interception) radar; Anchoress's Cell; *Avanti*; Bankes Estate; Baxter; Benfield; Blumlein; *British Inventor*; Brown; Chapman's Pool Lifeboat Station; Dunshay Manor; Edward VII; Firestone; *Fortitude*; Gee Chain navigation system; *Georgiana*; *Halsewell*; Harman's Cross; Hill Bottom; Jesty; Keates Quarry; *L'Atlantique*; *The Long Journey*; Machold; Maltravers; *Montanes*; Marines Memorial; Pier Bottom; Priest's Way; Quarr; RAF Worth Matravers; Renscombe Farm; *Robert S. Shaw*; St Alban's Head; St Aldhelm's Chapel; St Nicholas's parish church; *Samuel*; Sauropods; Seacombe gun-nest; Seacombe Quarries; Spencer-Watson family; Strange; Square and Compass; *Start*; Sutton; Telecommunications Research Establishment; *Treveal*; Turner; Wills; Window; Winspit; Winspit Quarries; Winspit strip lynchets; Woodyhyde.
(Placenames / Worth Matravers)

Wyatt – architect **Thomas Henry Wyatt** [1807-88] rebuilt the chancel and nave of Corfe Castle parish church [1859-60], destroying most of its mediaeval treasures in the process. His principal creations were assize courts, lunatic asylums, the Adelphi Theatre, Knightsbridge Barracks, Liverpool Exchange, and Middlesex Hospital; functional products of their age.
(People / Architects / Corfe Castle)

Wytch – see entry for Wich, for name origin. That was for salt production. By the time of the Domesday Book survey it had 25 workers in the salterns "but no plough" for the thin heathland soils on the southern shore of Poole Harbour (SY 978 856).
(Placenames / Mediaeval archaeology / Corfe Castle)

Wytch Oilfield – though the Kimmeridge nodding-donkey beam pump had been familiar as a coastal oddity since 1959, its output was trivial in international terms, so it was to everyone's surprise that an oil reservoir of immense proportions and value would be discovered on the other side of the Isle of Purbeck [1973]. Petroleum production licence PL 089, held jointly by the then publicly-owned British Gas Corporation and pre-privatisation British Petroleum, had hit the bull's eye at Wytch Farm in a heathland clearing beside the Poole Harbour (SY 980 853) after years of fruitless seismic surveys and exploration failures across the country. Cranes would now stride across the pine-covered heaths south of Poole Harbour for the rest of the century and rigs would also appear offshore.

It had the financial press talking of a £450 million price tag in the Thatcher Government's sell-off portfolio. Recoverable reserves were estimated at 9,000,000,000 tonnes of oil – nine billion, to put the figure into words. This assumes an extraction rate, achievable with current technology, of 35 per cent.

The story turned into an oilman's dream, with a remarkable year [1974] when more oil was discovered in Purbeck than the whole of Texas. Production licence 089 was issued by the old Ministry of Power in 1968. Seismic work was carried out in the winter of 1970 on the 5,123-acre Rempstone Estate owned by Major D. C. D. Ryder of Rempstone Hall. The bulk of this land was leased to the Forestry Commission and planted with blocks of conifers [1948-50]; with the estate retaining the mineral rights.

Drilling at oil site X – for "Exploration" – took place in the autumn of 1973 and lasted six weeks. The Gas Council (Exploration) Limited had issued a cautious press release: "The purpose of the well is to prove or disprove an extension of the oil deposits which are already known to exist at Kimmeridge and Wareham. It follows that the depth to which the drilling well will be carried out is fairly closely defined, being the depth of the oil-bearing measures – the Bridport Sands – and it is not expected the depth would be more than 3,500 to 4,000 feet."

These oil-impregnated sandstones of the Jurassic and Triassic ages are between 144 and 248 million years old, being the result of organic decay of liptinite, exinite, and vitrinite materials at temperatures between 95 to 105 degrees centigrade. Despite the strong sulphurous smell of the Kimmeridge coast, the oils from this deposit are sulphur free and of the finest quality. Known as "British light sulphur-free" they need minimal refining though they are mixed with heavier Arab oils for the manufacture of end products.

A larger, deeper – and for many years untapped – Sherwood reservoir was discovered in 1978.

The Bridport reservoir was soon supporting four operational wells, pumping 4,000 barrels a day from 3,000 feet below Wytch Farm, by 1980. Wytch was henceforth firmly established as Britain's largest onshore oilfield – with more than double the output of Kimmeridge and eight other oilfields, in the Midlands, added together.

Costs were a minimal 30p per barrel for oil then being sold at £32 – a profit of £127,800 a day. That was substantial but was still only 0.2 per cent of national oil consumption. As for its monetary value, that is a moving feast as the world price for oil would prove, by collapsing from £32 to £9 a barrel [1986].

The hub of the operation is Wytch Gathering Station which soon took up just about all of the former Wytch Fir Pound (SY 973 852). Historically, until the creation around it of Purbeck Forest, this six-sided enclosure was the only pine wood in central Purbeck.

Fears of a constant stream of road tankers were blunted by the laying of an underground pipeline, westwards to the surviving spur of the Swanage Railway opposite the sheds of ECC Ball Clays Limited, with its own sidings at Furzebrook Rail Terminal (SY 933 842).

British Petroleum plc is the operator of the field and the other half interest, previously held by the Gas Council, was split between five other oil companies – Tricentral, Premier, Carless, Clyde, and Goal – who formed a consortium known as the Dorset Bidding Group in 1984.

Energy Secretary Cecil Parkinson approved a 56-mile pipeline via the New Forest, linking Wytch with the oil refineries at Fawley and Hamble, on Southampton Water [1987], in a project that would cost BP £300,000,000. Sales gas also goes by pipeline, to Sopley, and rail tankers are now only used for Butane and Propane liquefied petroleum gas, with five trains a week [2000].

Production from the Purbeck oilfield rose from 6,000 to 10,000 barrels a day [1990], which was the maximum that could be carried by rail, and was then stepped up towards 60,000 barrels a day when the long distance pipeline came into use [1992]. A barrel, incidentally, is 35 gallons.

Ferry point: crossings from Wytch Passage to Poole are currently discontinued.

Purbeck now provided two percent of national consumption with forecasts of reserves lasting to beyond 2020. Coincidentally, with the rise in the oil price that followed the Iraqi invasion of Kuwait, the value of its output had in just one week increased by more than £200,000 a day, though reality would soon be restored. Reserves still have a Mickey Mouse value – £2,500,000,000, which is two and a half billion.

In fact, the flow has already peaked, having reached 101,000 barrels a day [1998], dropped to 82,000 barrels [1999], and currently at 78,000 barrels [2000]. "It's become a mature field, and is now in a gradual decline" oil analyst Lesley Brown explained. "We are still drilling but no longer exploring, with the additional effort going into pockets not yet reached, as in-filling to sidetrack off an existing well hole to a different part of the reserve." The field still has about 60 oilwells, with the more conspicuous beam pump being the less productive than the mass of pipes that comprise an electronic pump. For the mechanical nodding donkeys can only lift a maximum of 2,000 barrels a day from the

Bridport reservoir, 900 metres below, whereas an electronic pump is capable of bringing up 20,000 barrels from the deeper Sherwood reservoir, at 1,600 metres below Poole Bay.

Lesley Brown emphasises that the Sherwood reservoir is by far the largest. Of the remaining reserves, 30 million barrels are in the Bridport strata whereas the Sherwood has an estimated 370 million barrels. There is also a considerable usage of sea water "as a pressure support" to encourage the oil to rise from the wells. Some 85,000 gallons a day are extracted from Poole Harbour by a plant on Cleavel Point, opposite Green Island.

She described the demobilisation of the M-site mast on Goathorn peninsula [February 2000] as "the end of an era". It had been in operation since 1993 and had even made an appearance on Admiralty charts, though with a "mobile" legend. The Deutag T47 drilling rig was 60 metres high and had an extended reach of five kilometres, with half that distance being under Little Sea and Studland beach and the extremity in Poole Bay. Its demobilisation and dismantling was accompanied by the placing of tree trunks and other truck-calming measures to ensure that roadside verges were not damaged by departing leviathans. BP pointed to the honouring of its "'Wytch Farm Promise" that the Purbeck landscape was on loan and would be returned untarnished as withdrawal took place. By 2025, on current estimates, it is quite possible no one will know they have been, except that someone is bound to mount a campaign to have the original nodding donkey on the Kimmeridge cliffs preserved by the National Trust – to go with their obsolete mobile phone mast and a representative pylon line.
(Industrial archaeology / Corfe Castle)

Wytch Passage – on the shore of Poole Harbour, where a short length of public path extends from the public road at Wytch to the reedbeds beside Wytch Lake (SY 977 858). Wytch was the embarkation point on the weekly market-day run across the harbour, taking Corfe Castle residents to Poole.

Thirteen drowned on what should have been their return voyage when the vessel stuck in the mud and sank off Brownsea Island [9 March 1759]. Now its site is almost gone, though my notes record it as "marked by the timbers of a decaying boathouse that lie in a reedbed next to a rusting winch" [1968].

What does remain, on the low gravel ridge overlooking it, is a two-storey 18th-century stone cottage, with a thatched roof, occupied by tenants of the Rempstone Estate. Their view down Wytch Lake, across to Hamworthy, used to be that of professional eyes, when the building was the home of Poole's Harbourmaster.
(Placenames / Shipwrecks / Corfe Castle)

X, Y, Z – currently deficient, with entries being eagarly awaited from those who arise to the challenge.

A to Z format
with alphabetical
self-indexing entries